EVANSTON PUBLIC LIBRARY
3 1192 00690 5937

D0323621

Cuba

The Revolution in Peril

JANETTE HABEL

With a preface by François Maspero

Translated by Jon Barnes

VERSO

London · New York

First published as *Ruptures à Cuba: le castrisme en crise*,
by la Brèche, Paris 1989
This revised and updated edition published by Verso 1991

Verso
UK: 6 Meard Street, London W1V 3HR
USA: 29 West 35th Street, New York, NY 10001-2291

Verso is the imprint of New Left Books

British Library Cataloguing in Publication Data

Habel, Janette
Cuba: the revolution in peril
1. Cuba
I. Title
972.9106
ISBN 0–86091–308–2

US Library of Congress Cataloging-in-Publication Data

Habel, Janette
[Ruptures à Cuba. English]
Cuba : the revolution in peril / Janette Habel, with a preface by François Maspero : translated by Jon Barnes.
p. cm.
Translation of: Ruptures à Cuba.
Includes bibliographical references and index.
ISBN 0–86091–308–2
1. Cuba—Politics and government—1959– 2. Cuba—Economic conditions—1959– 3. Cuba—Social conditions—1959– 4. Political participation—Cuba—History—20th century. I. Title.
F1788.H2313 1991
972.9106'4—dc20

Typeset in Times by Ponting–Green Publishing Services, London
Printed in Great Britain by Bookcraft (Bath) Ltd

For Michèle Firk,
militant of the Guatemalan FAR,
died 7 September 1968

For Ania Francos,
author of *La Fête cubaine*,
died 24 January 1988

Contents

Preface

The Torn Out Page

According to the history books, a few days after the landing which marked the start of the second Cuban War of Independence, on the night of 5 May 1895, the three leaders of the insurgents, Máximo Gómez, Antonio Maceo and José Martí, held a final meeting in the La Mejorana sugar plant near Santiago to consolidate their plans for the campaign. History has it that this discussion was particularly stormy. What did they say to each other? Neither Gómez nor Maceo ever recorded it. Martí, for his part, noted it down in his diary – on one of the very last pages, as he was to die twelve days later, hit by a bullet during a charge in the Battle of Dos Ríos. And here history becomes an enigma, for no one can read this page. It was torn out and lost.

It is claimed, however, that the discussion was about the problem of power following the victory. The three historic leaders all had in mind nearly one hundred years of independence in Spanish America. From the start – ever since the resignation of San Martín and the eviction of Bolívar – the fundamental issue that had run through the whole century as a threat constantly reborn could be summed up in a single word: *caudillismo*. Power conquered by the people by force of arms is here embodied in a single man claiming to act solely for the good of the people, and maintaining himself in power against the people – if necessary, by the same force of arms. A word which meant a hundred names in the subcontinent: Sáenz, Rosas, Francia, Melgarejo or Porfirio Díaz. Did the Cuban leaders talk about how to exorcize this 'shadow of the *caudillo*' together, or did they remain mutually suspicious, each suspecting the other of having no other aim than to seize power for himself once victory had been won? On the eve of his death, Martí noted down his mistrust of Máximo Gómez, and in this case the page has been preserved for us: 'Do not call Martí president. He is only here in his capacity as general. ... Indeed, I do not know what happens to these presidents: once they are elected, they are done for. Except for Juárez, and even then. And Washington.' At which, added Martí, an insurgent waved his machete and said: 'Everything depends on the will of the people. ... We joined the revolution in order to be men, not for our dignity as men to be wounded.'[1]

Martí died at Dos Ríos. Maceo was killed in combat the year after. And Máximo Gómez, for his part, achieved victory in 1898 – to see the United States take over following its last-minute intervention. He turned down the offer of power and ended his days in uneasy retirement. He lies in the Havana cemetery, and history recounts that he had a mausoleum built with a deliberately low entry so that access could only be gained by stooping down: he wanted to remind Cuba's elders of their humiliation, knowing full well that they would not fail periodically to pay a ritualistic homage to him.

This island has a remarkable history, forged of extreme grandeur and extreme humiliation; always out of all proportion to its real size. The island was the first foundation of the Spanish Conquest. When Christopher Columbus spread the news in Europe of the discovery of these Indies which were still not America, it was essentially Cuba he was describing. It was on the strength of this description that Thomas More naturally thought of Cuba to map out a new world when writing his *Utopia*; a new world which also quite naturally ended up being the island of Shakespeare's *Tempest*. It was from Cuba that Cortés and the conquistadores set out for the subcontinent. It was in Cuba that the first genocide against the Indians occurred, and the first African slaves were introduced. It was from Cuba that the first riches were extracted in the pillage of America. And the first cathedral and university were built there. The island was the last as well as the first foundation of the Spanish Empire, with slavery only abolished in 1886 and independence declared in 1898. In other words, when Fidel Castro and his supporters came to power in 1959, such events still belonged to living memory: peasants would speak of their slave childhood and their slave mothers, and testimonies would also come from ex-veterans of the war against Spain who had shaken the hand of Máximo Gómez.

Having, for centuries, been the point where the riches of the Empire had been concentrated, Cuba was always the anchorage of the power of the metropolis; and, located at the crossing of the sea routes, it was simultaneously the place where ideas blown from one continent to another would ferment. This doubly rich profusion of the most precious goods and new ideas was described by Alejo Carpentier in *Explosion in a Cathedral*. Throughout the nineteenth century, the Cuban bourgeoisie managed this paradox of being a slave society in which the most progressive currents of thought in Latin America were in circulation, despite their constant repression. Having smouldered for such a long time, the first war of independence, when it broke out in 1868, gave immediate expression to a national demand that was more massive and cohesive than in the other countries of the subcontinent (except perhaps for Mexico at the time of the French intervention); but it also gave expression to a social and political project which – as can be read in the life and writings of José Martí – extended to the dimensions of the whole subcontinent.

Cuba has a remarkable history because of the proximity of the United States. With all that the USA could represent as a spur for creole aspirations – from the Boston Tea Party to abolitionism – it meant that the independence victory in fact marked the entry into another period of dependence; a dependence which from then on seemed to stem from the inevitable logic of geopolitics. The more the United States spread to the South through its successive acquisitions and conquests (Louisiana, Florida, New Mexico and Texas), the more Cuba seemed an obligatory appendage to US territory. Jefferson said so as early as 1817: 'If we seize Cuba, we will be the masters of the Caribbean.' Cuba was the link between the two Americas; it straddled two geographies, two economies, two cultures. It was bound up with the South in history and language; it was very close to the North, if only by geographical distance. It is not just apocryphal that it was in New York that José Martí held in 1894 – under the chairmanship of Rubén Darío, the great Nicaraguan poet of continental significance – the crucial meeting which preceded the start of the second war of independence; it was José Martí who was able to articulate better than anyone else the mortal dangers of US expansionism. Three components of Cuba's intercontinental status could be found at this meeting: creole aspirations and the Latin American dimension, as well as the ambivalent presence of the great neighbour which provided a haven at the time for the island's most progressive features – 'in the bowels of the monster', as Martí would say.

Such proximity was both fascinating and awesome: the history of these last two hundred years has thus been characterized by what could have been a dialogue of antagonistic and complementary cultures, but which has been inevitably turned, by the uneven balance of power, into a fight to the death between two different approaches, even to life itself. 'The American way of life' as against what the Cuban poet José Lezama Lima defined as the *angel de la jiribilla*, the luminous and fantastic spirit of the Cuban popular puppets; the land of Manhattan and the Empire State Building, as against the country where towns drowsing in tropical mugginess await the nocturnal breeze, dreaming of being the 'just measure of grace, the response to the caresses of the hand'. It is also a history that is characterized, in a much more decisive way, by economic subservience and the exploitation of the weakest by the strongest – all sanctioned by the famous Platt Amendment, introduced to the Cuban Constitution in 1906, which until 1934 gave the United States the right to intervene in the country's affairs.

The island's history in the first half of this century, then, was one of semi-annexation, both directly – there were three US military interventions – and through imposed dictatorships or governments. The annexation was also economic. All this was carried out against a people that had pushed to the extreme (and paid the price in hundreds of thousands of lives) its ideal of national independence – a term that can be taken here as a synonym for the 'dignity' of the *mambí*, the machete-wielding insurgent evoked by Martí in his diary. From then on, this ideal constituted the cement uniting the people above class differences, backgrounds and interests: the urban liberal bourgeoisie, the patricians of the plantations, the eternally marginalized and dispossessed peasants, urban workers, sugar-cane workers (who were just as subject to the corvée as the old black slaves), and even colonies of Mexican, Haitian and Chinese origin (brought in to make up for the abolition of slavery). Such subservience, involving intolerable humiliation, was thus chequered with bursts of anger, uprisings and strikes.

This state of semi-integration into the leading industrialized world power could only increase the paradoxes of the last colonial country on the continent: the takeover by US capital fuelled and further fostered such a spirit of rebellion that it did not lead to the final annexation that some had envisaged. In 1958 the big US firms on the island owned 90 per cent of mines and 50 per cent of land; they controlled 67 per cent of exports and 75 per cent of imports. Although such a grip obviously enabled a section of the bourgeoisie to benefit, and favoured a high level of European immigration, particularly in Havana, at the same time it led to deep frustration in most of this bourgeoisie. For its part, an intellectual elite, based at the crossroads between the North and South, Europe and America – and, more than ever before, this was Havana's significance in the 1920s and 1930s – could no longer tolerate the suffocating nature of the insular confinement to which it felt condemned. The methods of exploitation on the larger properties, modern in their pursuit of output and traditional in terms of the absence of agricultural mechanization, created a massive rural proletariat for whom the deed of the wars of independence still provided succour. Meanwhile, in the towns, new firms came in from the United States and set up alongside the old nineteenth-century factories. For obvious reasons of lower costs, the United States ended up building firms that were as symbolic of the lifestyle of the North as the biggest Coca-Cola factory in the world. The firms used on-the-spot raw materials, sugar and cheap labour, as well as the most powerful Spanish-language printing house, that of *Reader's Digest*, in order to exploit Cuba's privileged position in the Spanish-speaking world. And in 1927, the first regular route created by a completely new company – Pan-American – was, quite naturally, to be between Miami and Havana.

In the course of the century, then, Cuba saw the formation of the most developed labour movement in Latin America – the first to mobilize on the basis of the theses of the Third International (and, symmetrically, the most influenced, as far as its urban component was concerned, by the corporatist trade unionism of the United States) – as well as the emergence of a highly active core of intellectuals who were open to all ideas and forms of liberation. Given the period, they were inevitably open to Marxism (as was more or less the case with Pablo de la Torriente Brau, Juan Marinello, Julio Antonio Mella, Rubén Martínez Villena, Raúl Roa), as well as, it must be stressed, other movements such as surrealism. This was the case of Alejo Carpentier, Nicolás Guillén, Lydia Cabrera and, in a more long-lasting way, José Lezama Lima, Virgilio Piñera and the 1939 creators of the magazine *Orígenes*.

So it can be understood why the page torn out of Martí's diary was also at that time a forgotten page. Its potential significance remained far from more pressing concerns. Only the first part, the unhidden part of the insurrection's leaders' message has been kept: the recovery of lost dignity was, as we said, essentially the recovery of national independence. Meanwhile, here and there on the subcontinent, *caudillismo* still held sway, reactionary in Venezuela and progressive in Argentina. In Cuba the problem of power was above all that of the direct control, whatever its form, which the dominant power exercised over the country. Roles became confused. In the 1920s it was possible for a dictator like Machado, an out-and-out admirer of Mussolini and 'Latin-ness', to rule through terror and corruption and yet give an air of popular legitimacy to his hold on power (which had been gained with the assent of the Communist Party). This was precisely because he confronted US pretensions with a nationalist discourse. On the other hand, it was possible for an elected president like Grau San Martín, because he embodied all hopes for democracy (having first managed to quash the Platt Amendment), to sink into shady deals and sell-offs to the highest bidder. It was also possible for a typical *caudillo*, ex-sergeant Batista, to get himself elected on a 'sweeping' populist programme; to again obtain the support of the Communist Party and the business bourgeoisie, both anxious to assert national independence (with two Communist ministers even participating in his first government, including Carlos Rafael Rodríguez who is now a top leader of the Castro regime); and to return to power in a coup d'état and rule through clientelism and gangsterism. As was the case with the first presidency of Grau San Martín, all this came with occasional, short-lived bright spots in which was visible something precious and a little unusual, but nonetheless there: the Cuban Republic. The republic of which José Martí had dreamt; and in the name of which Eduardo Chibás, the leader of the Ortodoxo Party and Fidel Castro's first political teacher, committed suicide in 1952, crying live on the radio: 'People of Cuba, wake up!'

It was Fidel Castro who, after many others, attempted this awakening in Santiago on 26 July 1953. He failed. But when he appeared three years later at the head of the 26th of July Movement – a movement which seemed to embody the purity and intransigence of youth and break with the compromises of the past – it was this return to the idealism of José Martí which gradually cemented around him the unity of all opposition forces to the dictatorship and all the dynamic forces of the country: 'The wounding of our dignity must stop.' Over agrarian reform, the reduction of inequalities and the elimination of privileges granted to foreign companies, his programme, the Moncada Manifesto, stated that nothing should ever be as it was before. As to everything else, what form would power take after the victory, and who would hold it to represent the people? For more than sixty years, the Cuban people had clearly exhausted the possibilities of a 'democracy' that had been perversely distorted in the shadow of the star-spangled banner. They wanted another democracy. What would it consist of?

It was to be invented. Who thought at the time of the page torn out of Martí's diary? Wasn't achieving victory the crucial issue? And didn't its achievement require the unity of all forces behind the armed party that was in the process, militarily, of winning the war?

There were many differences, debates, reservations and instances of mistrust between the components that united under the hegemony of the 26th of July Movement. But events finally took their course. On 1 January 1959, Fidel Castro took power at the head of the 26th of July Rebel Army. For a short period of time, he said; and certainly not in order to become president.

Time of the *Cronopios*

'My first voyage to Cuba in 1962', wrote Julio Cortázar, 'meant doing something. I discovered there a whole people that had recovered its dignity, a people that had been humiliated throughout its history, by the Spanish, by Machado, Batista, the Yankees and all the rest of them;

suddenly, at every level – from the leaders I practically did not see to the peasant, and from the official responsible for the elimination of illiteracy to the small employee and the sugar-cane cutter – they all assumed their personality, discovering that they were individuals, each with a role to play.'

In order to read Janette Habel's book properly, it is perhaps useful to understand – and recall – what the takeover by the Cuban revolutionaries meant for the world thirty years ago. And not just in Latin America. For Janette Habel was one of a handful of young internationalist French activists who travelled to Cuba in the 1960s, forging links with a revolution that, for all its ups and downs, has left a lasting impression on them.

Between that first trip and this book, twenty-five years have gone by. Following its victory, the Cuban Revolution represented the youngest group of people in power in the world and seemed, for a time, to personify a new youth in a world that, with its world wars, cold wars and colonial wars, never stopped growing old from them. Fidel Castro's movement has now exercised total and uninterrupted power for thirty years: its leader has become, if not one of the oldest heads of state on the globe, at least one of the longest in power. Meanwhile, the revolution has moved from a phase where the future was open and everything still to be written, to one where history has been written: this and no other among all the other histories that seemed – and were – possible. From a stage of hopes, to one of balance sheets. As is known – and as is stated in this book – the latter do not necessarily match the former. Should such hopes therefore be renounced? Or should an effort be made to understand them: not to give lessons, but, on the contrary, to draw lessons from them?

It is in this sense that Janette Habel's book should be read. First, as a book of fidelity. Fidelity to a past, to a memory and to a political project. Fidelity to those with whom hope has been shared; and alongside whom – both living and dead, here as well as there – one has struggled and shared successes and defeats. It should also be read as the fulfilment of duty: a political duty; a duty towards and against everything; one of friendship which, as such, does not mean an inevitable break with the past, dumping it pell-mell into the dustbin of shattered illusions and defunct 'revolutionary myths'. It means discussing a present and a future that, for better or for worse, will in any case continue to concern us.

It is perhaps difficult today to understand what the Cuban Revolution represented for that handful of European activists – firstly, because the very word 'activist' is out of fashion. My use of the word 'handful' is deliberate. For the situation was, of course, quite different in Latin America where a huge wave of hope surged from the Río Bravo to the Southern Cone. The situation was clear and simple. This was a revolution that threw down an open challenge to US economic domination and dependence – and through measures that spoke immediately for themselves: agrarian reform, expropriations, nationalizations and the complete revision of the terms of trade – the refusal to renew sugar quotas, for example. And, for the first time, such a revolution managed to triumph, militarily and politically, over the big stick. Revenge was suddenly taken for a century of humiliations and bulldozer intervention. What had still seemed impossible only yesterday was now there – though everyone still had fresh memories of how an 'anonymous' armoured column had, in Guatemala in 1954, destroyed a government that intended to be democratic. A new era was beginning. One where people could speak loud and strong – just like the First Declaration of Havana, proclaimed before a million people: 'This great people has said: enough!' For the peoples of the subcontinent, Fidel Castro was the first person to speak the truth, and who practised what he preached. Who could accuse him of demagogy at the time? His proposal in Buenos Aires in 1959 that the United States should loan Latin America the sum of US$30,000 million was rejected as 'grotesque and demagogic'. But was it really demagogic? Or was it the lucid anticipation of a new deal that it would have been reasonable to take seriously before it was too late? Indeed, three years later, Kennedy put forward US$25,000 million for his Alliance for Progress. Today, the overall debt of Latin America is around US$400,000 million. In Bogotá in October 1989, François Mitterrand was able to deplore the 'growing poverty' of the peasant masses; but apart from pious wishes, he could not offer credible solutions to deal with it.

For what was then just beginning to be called the 'Third World', for the colonial countries that had recently achieved emancipation or were in the process of doing so (as was the case of the whole of French black Africa), and for the countries in struggle – with Algeria at the head – the Cuban Revolution meant that emancipation was possible.

Even in Europe there was a clear, if slightly amused, wave of sympathy for the revolutionaries who could dance the cha-cha: 'Long live Castro!', wrote Jacques Lanzmann in a book on the picturesque *barbudos* [bearded ones]. Beyond folklore, however, there were few people, at least in France, who thought that Cuba was opening up new prospects that could change their vision of the global balance of power and the possibility of affecting it. They were basically the same very small groups that had been formed in the search for a response, outside the Communist Party – this could be called the *Etincelle* [the spark] or the *Voie communiste* [the communist road] – to Khrushchev's revelations on the Stalinist period. These revelations had sounded the death-knell on any reasonable hope for the Soviet Union as the 'workers' fatherland'. And so it was that the very word revolution, hijacked for more than forty years by the Soviet Union, was questioned and, above all, put back on the agenda by a movement whose victory, unlike events in China and Vietnam, owed nothing to Soviet strategy, and which even turned all roles upside down. Small groups which, for a variety of reasons – ranging from 'proletarian internationalism' to making a mere moral demand – considered that the major drama faced by our generation, namely the war waged by France in Algeria, was an act of criminal madness; that it was their duty to refuse to participate in a 'pacification' that had already led to hundreds of thousands of deaths; and who were prepared, to this end, to face being ostracized by the majority, as well as prison – the Cuban Revolution seemed to give them a hint of what a free Algeria, dreamt of as at peace again, could be like. It was important to go and have a closer look.

Later, one would talk of 'Third Worldism' and Third World activists. It is worth dwelling on this point for a moment. For it has been common in the 1980s to describe this passion for new perspectives in the midst of an ocean of conformism – and it is also worth recalling that conformism was the bearer of death at the time – as the result of a 'myth' (the 'revolutionary myths of the Third World' analysed by Gérard Chaliand). Third Worldism has even been scoffed at (Pascal Bruckner's 'sob of the white man') as if it could be explained merely as an aberrant display of some sort of Judaeo-Christian guilt; a guilt leading the 'white man' to sob over the fate of his 'brothers' in the Third World, even though he would not feel ashamed of colonial achievements in comparison to the chaos of the newly independent states. (It should be noted, however, that if white men were 'sobbing' in the 1960s, they were above all those frustrated by the loss of colonial paradises and profits, and not anti-colonialist activists who were instead delighted.)

As often happens with practical terms in history, the term 'Third Worldism' was invented after the event. Indeed, the term 'Third World' had just been penned by Georges Balandier and Alfred Sauvy. And coming after the works of such respectable professors, Frantz Fanon's *Les Damnés de la terre*, a posthumous work and incomplete from any point of view, suddenly provided a vision of the world that could tear down the division between blocs and superpowers. He established as actors in their own history and that of the world, peoples that had hitherto been silent and with no power other than to revolt or be crushed. But it would be quite artificial to make of this a real movement, organized around the simple idea that the Third World was to become the new and only pole of revolutionary struggle in the world, with the peasantry of the underdeveloped countries in the twentieth century taking over from the proletariat of the nineteenth. Indeed, this idea was advanced in Jean-Paul Sartre's preface to *Les Damnés de la terre* – a preface which was much more polemical, much more 'messianic', than the book itself – to the point where it masked and deformed the book's real intention. This was as much to warn Fanon's Algerian and African comrades in arms against the dangers he perceived in the imminent arrival of independence, as an appeal to the conscience, or bad conscience, of European leaders. This preface was debated and contested by many of those who were discovering the Third World at the very time it was written.

If it is at all worth the bother, someone will perhaps one day turn their attention to a serious study of the first issues of the magazine *Partisans* which began publication in 1961 and is considered as one of the first expressions of militant Third Worldism by those who today speak *ex cathedra* about the period. They would find an extreme diversity of thought. They would find the following admonishment by Régis Debray, for example: 'The socialist camp/capitalist camp alternative cannot be avoided, especially by hiding behind the myth of an undifferentiated Third World. ... Are you unreservedly on the side of the socialist camp, headed by the Soviet Union, the main guardian of its security and the most advanced in the construction of communism? ... Are you on the side of the party representing the interests of the working class?' This admonishment was followed by a long convoluted reply from the magazine's editor – today the signatory of these words – saying yes and no at the same time: it was difficult for him to do otherwise, for, given the radical differences among editorial staff, a second issue would otherwise never appear. They would also find Robert Paris's pertinent analyses of Italian polycentrism; the first repercussions of the break of Chinese communism with Moscow; or Gérard Chaliand's exaltation at the 'national-democratic' stage as performed in Sékou Touré's Guinea – now that's where a revolutionary 'myth' really was being formed.[2] Above all, they would find, from the second number, at the end of 1961, a special issue on the Cuban Revolution. It was an issue that was full of enthusiasm. And in the dark years at the beginning of the Fifth Republic, shadowed by the crushing and discredit of all left-wing forces, it meant that somewhere, in another part of the world, there were grounds for hope; that a new way of grasping the future and, Cortázar would write, 'recovering one's dignity' was being put into action there. For the first time in France, one could read writings by Fidel Castro and Che Guevara, who were no longer merely bearded operetta characters or international gangsters. To understand the atmosphere of the time, the following detail must be added: this issue was banned and impounded, as were Frantz Fanon's books. Why? Quite simply, and without any further explanation, 'by virtue of special powers' passed by the French government in the context of the war in Algeria: they disturbed public order. Indeed, the same year the censors also banned the film of a dangerous extremist, *Cuba sí*, by Chris Marker.

For it should also be added that to be interested in the Cuban Revolution was, at the time, like breaking a taboo, joining an extreme minority fringe – at least as far as its confidential and almost underground expression was concerned. It meant challenging the 'ox-headed stupidity' of a moral-order, public-order – simply every-order – society; a society of order for order's sake. It meant disturbing public order. And thus it even meant joining a fraternity of oppositionists: the anti-authority word *contestataire* had still not been invented. Once again, it was Cortázar who expressed this well, referring to his first voyage to Cuba as a 'journey to the country of the *cronopios*'. According to the comments of Cortázar's biographer, Karine Berriot, '*cronopios* roughly represent the human category of perpetual drop-outs and peace-loving anarchists. Unlike the Famous, their vital goal is not social success and its compulsory corollaries of power-seeking, fame and wealth. Far from it.' At a time when Cortázar saw 'poetry at the end of a gun', many of us were attracted by the lights of Havana, and we amounted to quite a few *cronopios*.[3]

I am not saying that those who made the journey to Havana were all 'drop-outs' and 'peace-loving anarchists'. Janette Habel and her comrades were fighting for a political project that did not invoke pacifism at all. But they had this search for a different society – that went beyond the laws of power, fame and wealth, in other words the laws of the jungle – very much in common. Romanticism, one might say. But the political expression of the Romantic movement was, after all, the People's Spring of 1848. It was not that bad. And in the early 1960s, Cuba was hope. It was not a myth – unless hope itself is a myth. For those who then made the journey, either literally or figuratively, to Cuba – coming as they did from this narrow-minded and grey France where one could only breathe the smell of death – it was indeed the 'Cuban fiesta' described by Ania Francos in 1962.

There was a people to whom arms had been handed out on a massive scale and who had driven back the US-financed landing at Playa Girón for two days. There were the columns of children teaching literacy; and the agricultural workers organizing themselves on the expropriated latifundia. The leaders were the very antithesis of the usual image given by politicians. They would accept discussions – in which the world was cheerfully remade – into the small hours of the morning and then leave for the outpost. And those of us who had read Nizan thought of the following sentence introduced by Bukharin as an epigraph to *Les Chiens de garde*: 'Thus came about the sort of men who, while studying philosophy, go on night guard with a gun in their hands; who discuss the most important issues and are off an hour later to cut wood; who work in the libraries and also work in the factories.' But I would maintain that this fiesta was still a serious affair as far as most of this first wave of activists were concerned. For they could see quite easily that, in spite of the victory, everything was fragile and under threat, as much from within the revolution as without. They also had a tendency to trust the fraternal discourse of the revolutionaries, of course; to take it at face value. Their knowledge of twentieth-century revolutions was bad – because of Stalinism they had inherited little from the previous generation that was not falsified, twisted, distorted and hidden, and everything or almost everything remained to be rediscovered or written – and they knew nothing at all about the history of Latin America. Had not Fidel Castro movingly proclaimed at a political trial: 'The revolution must not devour its own children'? They admired that. And then there was the emergency, always emergency: the permanent aggression of a real enemy, the greatest power in the world; the vital need to produce in order to survive in spite of the blockade; and the no less vital need, in order to break the blockade, to hand over the movement's baton to the forces waiting in every country in the subcontinent, sweeping old formulae aside. It was a time when Cuba would hurl abuse and sarcasm against the Latin American communist parties wedded to Moscow, accusing them of impotence with their legalism and reformism. It was a time when new revolutionary fronts appeared each month: in Argentina, Peru, Venezuela, Guatemala.

The year of Che Guevara's death, 1967, can be seen as a watershed. For it was then that the decisive transformation (which had clearly begun earlier) of the group led by Fidel Castro took place, moving from the revolutionary stage – by definition, in a state of permanent development – to one where it formed the state government and was thus, also by definition, characterized by the need to maintain, above all else, the durability of its power. This power was now embodied by Fidel Castro alone: those who had come to embody power at his side – like Frank País in the Santiago insurrection; Camilo Cienfuegos during the victory of the guerrilla war; Che Guevara during the establishment of revolutionary power – either died or were relegated to the status of custodial shadows.

This transformation slowly became clear in the light of various, occasionally violent, adjustments and – already – crises. In 1961, when US aggression seemed unavoidable, there was Fidel Castro's shattering declaration: 'I am a Marxist-Leninist.' Following the first rapprochement with the Soviet Union, there was an attempt to create an 'integrated' organization, aimed at bringing together all groups that had supported the revolution. This was challenged in 1962 and led to the trial of leaders of the former Communist Party. Then there was Cuba's isolation in the wake of the October 1962 'missile crisis' which saw Khrushchev reach a direct agreement with Kennedy for the United Nations to be granted a controlling right over Cuban territory; a right that Fidel Castro refused to endorse. And above all, there was, in the years 1962–64, the violent polemic on the ends and means of the revolution: was priority to be given to the revolution's consolidation 'in a single country', or was one to bank on its spread throughout the subcontinent? On what foundations was the new economic system to be based? Was enterprise to be autonomous or centralized? Were workers to act out of material interest or as a result of moral emulation? This debate also contained another on the nature and functioning of a socialist democracy – in other words, how workers were to participate in, and have political control over, the economic activity of which they were the architects and driving force. And this other debate was never really dealt with in a profound way because it was constantly covered up, masked, and put off by the emergency – always the emergency – nature of the situation. The mobilization of the 'Committees for the Defence of the Revolution' seemed more urgent than workers' control. The latter could wait. Everyone to the front. It is the same old story throughout history.

It was in such circumstances that Che Guevara was brushed aside, following a long conflict in which he had insisted on his principles – appealing, within Cuba, for maximum responsibility to be devolved to workers, and abroad for a militant internationalism that challenged all the rules of power relations. (Intervening in this conflict were economists Ernest Mandel, who also defended the emphasis on measures tending to challenge the law of value, and Charles Bettelheim who, on the other side, advocated more classical planning methods derived, after criticisms and adjustments, from the Soviet model.)

Che Guevara summed up his interpretation of this debate in a long letter sent to a Uruguayan journal, drafted in 1965 and published under the title *Socialism and Man*. He recalled that the debate had take place 'in the midst of violent class struggles' and that 'the surviving elements of capitalism are clouding understanding of its true nature'. 'By pursuing the chimera of achieving socialism with the aid of the rotten arms left by capitalism (goods taken as an economic entity, profitability, individual material interest as an incentive, etc.), one runs the risk of ending up at a dead end.' With an optimism that would seem to us, twenty years later, to be an implausible, generous and formidable Utopia, he envisaged the appearance of a 'new man', while taking care to add that the latter could only emerge after a process of 'discussion at all levels'. And in order to define his conception of true internationalism, he declared, in his last public appearance in Algiers in March 1965: 'It must no longer be a question of developing mutually beneficial trade based on prices rigged at developing countries' expense through the law of value and the international relations of unequal exchange that that law entails.' He was not heeded. Could he have been? History settled the matter. Did it close the debate?

Having been politically defeated in Havana – and this should be remembered at a time when Fidel Castro is reviving, for the needs of his 'rectification' campaign, a form of economic thought that he himself had abandoned twenty years earlier and which he is now adapting in a totally different context – Che Guevara gave up his Cuban nationality at the same time as all his responsibilities, and left to lead the armed struggle 'in other lands of the world'. 'One, two, several Vietnams', he proclaimed, were needed. Was it thus a question of sharing tasks with Fidel Castro? That was the impression the latter gave when publicly reading Che's farewell letter. Che died in October 1967 in Bolivia at the end of a military campaign that is glorified in Cuba. Yet it is difficult to ascertain whether the logistical support that he might have expected was indeed granted, even when a breakdown is made of all the errors and acts of fate that may have intervened. Some have explained that Che committed strategic errors. Others have spoken of adventurism pure and simple; and others of a suicidal approach.

On the island, the rapid economic expansion promised by Fidel Castro – forged with blows of giant-size voluntarism – was a resounding failure. Seen as the major challenge, the ten-million-tonne sugar harvest planned for 1970 was not reached, despite all the sacrifices undergone to achieve it, and the country again found itself bled white. Fidel Castro declared: 'It really is a very hard blow. It is very distressing. And that affects honour and dignity. ... Criticism rests with us all.' It was then that the long-term return to the perverse but indispensable system of Soviet aid took place, and that the whole apparatus of state power was finalized once and for all with the structuring of the hierarchical and militarized Cuban Communist Party and the 1975 Constitution. The latter was democratic because it was based on an original form of 'people's power' at all levels, and was approved by a 97 per cent 'yes' vote – not a particularly encouraging sign of democractic functioning. Janette Habel's book assesses the real use – or absence of use – that has been made of such institutions, as well as their current state.

On the subcontinent, Che Guevara's death prefigured the end of specifically 'Castroite' guerrilla movements. The Cuban example had managed to raise the enthusiastic hopes we have referred to; but it had also provided a lesson to an enemy that from then on would no longer allow itself to be taken by surprise. The success of the Nicaraguan resistance would be achieved by means of a frontist strategy that was very different from the Castroite 'foco'. With its Maoist logic, Sendero Luminoso has taken the opposite course, not just from the Castroite road to the seizure of power, but from the humanist principles of Che Guevara. It has preferred another kind of 'humanism' – that of Pol Pot. Cuba would obviously continue to support particular movements, choosing some and excluding others from Havana. At the end of the day a generation of young Latin Americans lost many of its best representatives in this bloody struggle. When Cortázar wrote of the poetry at the end of a gun, he could not imagine the cruel sense that such a formidable image would take on: Javier Héraud, a Peruvian poet, René Castillo, a Guatemalan poet, Roque Dalton, a Salvadorean poet, and so many others died from wanting to live it out. Following a state policy, the Cuban government was from then on to privilege relations with governments judged to be progressive, be they Popular Unity in Chile or the military junta in Peru. Its internationalist support would become part of a global strategy in line with the interests of the Soviet Union: military aid and interventions in Ethiopia and, above all, Angola.

It could be said that 1967 was the year that many activists – who in France or elsewhere had placed so much hope in the Cuban Revolution – distanced themselves. While prepared to do a lot for the revolutionary movement, they were less willing to serve a 'reason of state' of any kind. The Cuban government's endorsement of the Warsaw Pact's intervention in Czechoslovakia the following year demonstrated the limits of a conception of independence and popular dignity that would henceforth be restrictive. That did not necessarily mean retreat or abandonment. Some felt that they could continue – without Cuba, but in no way against the Cuban Revolution – the internationalist struggle. Such was the case of Michèle Firk, a French activist who lost her life amid the ranks of the Guatemalan revolutionary movement. Others, rightly or wrongly, found the opening of huge realms of the possible in the effervescence surrounding May 1968 in France. Others (and I was one of them) rejoined the ranks of the Fourth International.

Paradoxically, it was at this very time – when it still seemed that the die was not cast and that the 'sharing of tasks' between Fidel Castro and Che Guevara, evoked above, might work – that the Cuban government (which wished to break out of its fatal isolation at any price) took the 'Tricontinental Conference' initiative. Organized by the Moroccan leader Ben Barka, the conference made the voice of the Third World in struggle – of Vietnam, Angola or hundreds of others – heard in the face of the superpowers. It was also at that time that the Cuban government, taking advantage of the wave of sympathy towards a small heroic people, alone and under attack, called a 'congress of intellectuals'. It was held amid great enthusiasm at the end of 1967, without many of the guests seeming to realize that what they were applauding was already in the process of slipping into a bygone era. If one can speak of 'Third Worldism' and of myths, it was certainly at that time they flourished. And it was in 1968 that one saw the appearance of posters in which Che became a slightly hippy apostle figure. Their use and interpretation would have made him shudder on many counts. His life and writings showed him to be a cultured man who was fond of the classics, a man of austerity and discipline who was morally and politically demanding – things that were hardly compatible with the 'non-direct' and spontaneous nature of his 1968 fans.

With the arrival of more apparent signs that the Cuban apparatus had changed course and taken the situation back in hand – the disgraceful Padilla affair, in which a poet was seen to appear before an assembly of writers and 'confess', surrounded by members of the security service, that he was an agent of imperialism – Cuban intellectuals would pay, very dearly, the price. There was a wave of rejection that was every bit as radical as previous sympathy and support had been. Many went from one extreme to another, from an excess of enthusiasm to an excess of condemnation. Few, it would seem, attempted to understand the difficult and complex reality: that in this struggle of a small people for the ideals of dignity, independence and social justice – at the cost of untold sacrifices – the worst was inevitably, and at all times, going to be mixed with the best; that nothing could ever be definitively won, but that nothing could be definitively lost either.[4]

It must also be said that the Cuban government had set the example in terms of simplistic reduction. Was not friendship synonymous with eulogy, indeed sycophancy, as far as it was concerned? K.S. Karol who, with the encouragement of Fidel Castro himself, had written a rigorous analysis of Castroite power that remains today the most honest and most complete work of reference on the period, had a taste of this. So too did René Dumont, who had talked agronomics and socialism with his usual outspokenness. Both were denounced by Fidel Castro as agents of the CIA, before a crowd of 500,000 Cubans – who had heard another story.[5]

And what of Julio Cortázar who had not stopped visiting and revisiting Cuba since his first trip? In 1971, he was one of the first to sign a public letter denouncing the 'regrettable masquerade of self-criticism' of the Padilla affair, 'reminiscent of the most sordid moments of Stalinism'. To which Fidel Castro replied, as always before a huge throng of people: 'No, bourgeois sirs. Our problems are those of underdevelopment, of catching up from the backwardness that you, the exploiters, the imperialists, the colonialists, left us.' Cortázar participated in the creation of *Libre*, a Spanish-language magazine intended by a group of intellectuals to destroy the Havana-based *Casa de las Américas* magazine. He would not give up hope, however; struggling, sometimes pathetically, not to burn bridges. In 1979, he wrote to Roberto Retamar, editor of *Casa de*

las Américas: 'I do not believe in social crystallizations, but I do believe in a revolutionary dialectic towards the freedom and happiness of man. For me the Cuban Revolution will never be a mountain, but the sea incessantly rebegun. When the time arrives, the mountains of the whole of the rest of Latin America, infinite and petrified, will witness the wave of human sea rise as I did in Cuba. It will be the day when the content of those two almost irreconcilable words – hope and reality – will be united in a single present.'

Winter of the Patriarch

Incessantly rebegun? And is it true, as we said above, that nothing is ever definitively lost?

As far as an assessment of the current Cuban regime is concerned, it would seem that everything has been said and repeated *ad nauseam* – ranging from irrevocable condemnations in the name of democracy and human rights to admiring expressions of support in the name of man's most elementary right not to die of starvation, passing through all shades of indulgence and balanced judgements on the way.[6] Let's face it – there is no point mincing one's words – democracy does not exist in Cuba. Human rights have not been and are not respected: at the worst moments, the figure of 80,000 political prisoners was reached.[7] And nor are the rights to freedom of information, expression and movement respected. But it is also true that, forty miles from Cuba's coast, people die from hunger every day – in Haiti children go naked in the dust and mud. And in the countries of the subcontinent nearby, people die from police and army bullets – at the beginning of this year, 300 people died (and, how strange, were quickly forgotten) in a day of food riots in Caracas, the capital of the richest country in the subcontinent. Whether collectively or individually, human rights are no more respected there. In Cuba people do not die from hunger, and they are decently dressed. Life is difficult, but there is no Third World poverty. And here the litany of the regime's achievements comes in: compare the level of schooling, child protection, doctors, health care and social facilities, scientific research, with Santo Domingo or even Puerto Rico. The problem is that those who write – we who write – this kind of assessment, are short of a crucial piece of information. They have never lived and we will not live in Haiti, Cuba or Puerto Rico. None of us is forced to live the life of an inhabitant of Havana or Port-au-Prince for the rest of our lives. And even if we were, it would not be a case of our sharing the lot of the worker-slaves in the Dominican *bateys* or even in Cuban institutions. That is what some would call a guarantee of objectivity. And that is also what makes many of us blandly get off the hook by repeating the following phrase that we have borrowed, for want of a better source, from Winston Churchill: that, having weighed everything up, our democracy is the least bad of possible systems. Too bad if the others are not crafty – or strong – enough to imitate us. We are intent on giving lessons.

Janette Habel's book is on a different level. It does not take part in the general distribution of good and bad marks in this competition of experts in democracy assessment. It is the first book for twenty years that gets to the bottom of the issues. Its perspective is simultaneously based on an exhaustive knowledge of economic, social and political data (both as they have developed and as permanent facts) and on the very logic of what the Cuban Revolution has been, intended to be, and still claims to be. Such a work had never been carried out, either inside the country or abroad. It had not been carried out inside Cuba because everything is seen, said and written through the prism of what the supreme leader sees, says and writes. It has been understood for thirty years that it is Fidel Castro who does the making, saying and being when it comes to history – present and past. Abroad, it is disturbing to see how important studies published in recent years take the same format, delineating the history of Cuba through that of Fidel Castro, the central and almost sole actor. Indeed, his personality provides the material to satisfy and fascinate the journalist and the most demanding historian.[8] And it is sufficiently overwhelming to polarize all the energy of opponents in exile, in a strict reversal of the personality cult.[9] Thus read, Cuba's history becomes so confused with that of its leader that it can never be seen whether there could have been one or several alternatives – and which ones? Beyond interesting monographs, on the other hand, nothing has been written on Cuba's recent history as the collective destiny of a people; and which treats this people as the true subject of its history, not as the chorus of walk-on characters in an ancient tragedy.

Almost a hundred years after José Martí's death, this history continues to be even more characterized by torn out pages than by blank ones. Janette Habel's book enables some of their traces to be rediscovered. And, just as a century ago, the same word is inevitably to be found inscribed on the principal page: *caudillismo*.

A whole series of questions seem to have been eliminated from the Cuban issue, as if they had never needed to be raised. As if they never had been raised.

One of these concerns the pretension of the current ruling group to embody the whole of the forces which supported the movement until its 1959 victory; and Fidel Castro's claim, at the head of this group, to represent the whole of the forces which seized and assumed power in the early years. For as we have said, such forces were numerous and diverse. Some, like the Communist Party (albeit a latecomer to the struggle) rallied round and participated in power. Others went into opposition, sometimes returning to Miami and even taking to armed struggle. Basically, one saw at the beginning a movement founded by a small core of young people with a bourgeois background achieve a military victory with the main and crucial support of the most dispossessed rural masses, overcoming all forms of opposition, whether traditional or otherwise, in the towns. A movement like the Revolutionary Directorate, for example, which was very strong among student youth in Havana, again found itself divided in the early years of revolutionary power. Some of its cadres are still participating today, while others have ended up in prison or exile. And this split did not spare the 26th of July Movement.

This question brings up another one: that of the island's underdevelopment. For the assertion of this is also one of the basic axioms of Castroite logic. It has repeated, ever since seizing power, that Cuba was in 1959 a typical underdeveloped country, at the same level as other Third World countries – countries which were not situated 90 miles away from the US coast, and did not possess a creole bourgeoisie that had studied for centuries in the best Spanish Jesuit colleges (like, as we know, Fidel Castro himself). Conversely, denying the reality of Cuban underdevelopment has been the classical argument of those who have always wished to prove that the revolution had meant nothing but regression and that, without it, Cuba would now be at the same level as a state of the United States. One might in any case enquire as to the degree, precise significance and nature of underdevelopment. The issue here is one of a dual economy: the coexistence, within the same geography, of two distinct systems – one of extreme underdevelopment, the other of advanced development – and thus of two distinct societies so mutually alien that they could almost have been unaware of each other. For Fidel Castro, such a view has always been an imperialist invention. If there were zones of prosperity on the island, they were isolated patches in Cuban society, able to exist merely as cancerous growths amid monolithic underdevelopment. These were due to, and further exacerbated, the latter – they were not expansion zones which would progressively overcome pockets of backwardness. In the 1960s, militant economists became fond of demonstrating that, in practice, the apparently dualistic economies of the countries of Latin America did nothing but perpetuate overall underdevelopment; and that at the end of the day they were even a factor in the 'development of underdevelopment'.[10] This was not an academic question. If it was admitted that the whole of Cuban society was governed by a single, uniform underdevelopment in which social strata were totally interdependent, then the ruling group had the right to stifle any political expression which refused to comply with such a framework. Such expressions could only represent class enemies that were committed to the perpetuation of the underdevelopment off which they lived. The ruling group would also have the right to put into concrete action its policy of systematic mistrust against the towns, 'polluted' by capitalism and living off the exploitation of the countryside. And it would have the right to present the departure into exile of thousands of possibly indispensable cadres as proof of the justice of its views: those leaving were irredeemable profiteers.

In other words, the following questions must be raised again today in the light of the situation as presented by Janette Habel. Could the disappearance of the plurality of democratic forces that had supported the revolution have been avoided? Could the mass exodus of the country's professionals have been avoided? In both cases there was a tragic loss of dynamic forces and a terrible waste.

Another question refers to the island's management. The very title of Janette Habel's book is significant in that it fits the current situation perfectly – there is indeed a Cuban crisis and Fidel Castro has proclaimed it to us himself. The same was true five, ten, or twenty years ago. Indeed, from one self-criticism, voluntaristic U-turn and rectification to another, the history of Cuba has been one of permanent crisis. It could be said that self-criticism is not a very common virtue among political leaders and even less so among heads of state. It cannot be denied that when, twenty years ago, Fidel Castro recognized before his people and the world that he had made a mistake, such an attitude was hailed as a model of revolutionary humility. But with the repetition after so many years of a self-criticism which takes the form of 'us' – implying collective guilt for mistakes when one cannot see when or how they had been collectively decided on – admiration is followed by incredulity. Could any world leader do this? No leader in the world would be able to stay in power having admitted such failures.

What is the role of the Cuban people in all of this? And what is the price they have to pay? At issue here is the whole system of power. That Fidel Castro has been vested with power by the majority of Cubans for thirty years is an undeniable fact. But who would dare to bring up the following declaration: 'When I have finished my task here, I will retire and devote myself to other affairs.'[11] This was on 8 January 1959. What has welded this majority around him and probably still provides his popularity today, despite all opposition and in spite of daily shortages and discontent, is the principle we have stressed repeatedly: the Cuban people's assertion of dignity and national independence in the face of those denying them such gains. In this sense, Cubans have never been as united round Fidel Castro as when he has expressed this principle loud and strong in the event of crises. This is the foundation of the only legitimacy of Castro's power which one cannot deny. Writing in 1968, nine years after the revolutionaries' victory, it was a Catholic poet, perhaps the greatest Latin American poet this century, José Lezama Lima, who expressed this general feeling: 'The 26 July has broken the infernal spells of evil. It has brought joy, for it has led, like a prism in the light, to the rise of the age of the image, and has enabled the cithara and flute players to light their hearths in the heart of the impenetrable night.' José Lezama Lima, who dreamt of a happy town with the colours and tenderness of his Havana, a sort of city of God 'in the reconciled light', could only have been wounded by the years of thoroughgoing cultural revolution that preceded his death: one Utopia against another, and it was not his which prevailed. It remains the case that what radically distinguishes the Cuban regime from the 'popular democratic' regimes of Eastern Europe is that it is based, not on a revolution that has been endured by the people, but on one that historically has been – and continues to be – the latter's work. On the other hand, the constant expression of unanimity against the 'imperialist' US enemy has always slipped into support for a one-party society. No one had given Fidel Castro a mandate for his sudden proclamation: 'I am a Marxist-Leninist' – he who had come from a movement of predominantly anti-communist tendencies at the time of the Cold War, the Auténtico Party of Eduardo Chibás. The institutionalization of 'popular power'[12] would have to wait until 1975. But how is people's power exercised? What role, even if consultative only, has it played in the major decisions of the latest 'rectification' campaign? What role did it play in the economic choices that had been previously made, such as the opening and subsequent closure of the free market? All the same, a large section of the Cuban people, especially among the dispossessed, has for a long time identified with Fidel's actions and speeches, even when he referred to a moral exigency and to values that were more evangelical than Marxist. (Fidel Castro's Marxism would require a long study in itself.[13]) Can people's power be recognized in the system as a whole and in the political decisions taken in its name? One can thus see confusion between popularity and political support which is so much a feature of *caudillismo*.

This is not to say that every event in Cuba can be interpreted with reference to a classical Latin American dictator. Nor is it to put its specificity down to the transplant of a belated and, it would seem, particularly tenacious brand of Stalinism. This of course exists and such a framework will probably satisfy those who conceive and classify the world according to broad categories. But it is just as reductionist as the official version which continues to magnify the power of the people.

What I mean to say is that, because it has never been evoked, because the very word is taboo, the shadow of the *caudillo* will continue to hang over Cuba's history; and that it is no longer possible to believe, as it was in the early years of the revolution, that ignoring the problem, denying its existence, is enough to reduce it to nothing.

What Janette Habel's book teaches us, first of all, is that, after thirty years and consecutive crises, a number of gains exist in Cuba that exist almost nowhere else in the Third World. Also, that such gains still seem fragile, from one crisis to another. And that in the current crisis – an economic crisis but now, above all, a crisis of *direction* as well (occurring in a world environment that is itself in crisis) – this fragility is increasing further. Fidel Castro can be just as well credited for such gains as held responsible for not having been able to consolidate them. For, today, the more the crisis increases, the more he tends to appear as the only solution: the only one who can steer the people to land safely. The personality cult, stifling and omnipresent, becomes the answer for everything. That is the very basis of *caudillismo*.

Sinister images and echoes reach us from the events of summer 1989. Some of the most senior, loyal and high-placed cadres of the party apparatus with the confidence of Fidel Castro, were suddenly accused of the worst crimes, and executed. Whether or not they had committed these crimes is one question. Whether they had been able to commit them outside all control, without any endorsement, is another. In any case, there was something rotten in the apparatus. Either the discourse of humanism or integrity, which has always been at the core of Castroite ideology, has been nothing but a cynical screen; or it has become completely detached from the daily reality of the practice of power and those wielding it. It was therefore not an affair that could be bracketed off, as if it could be resolved with the show of a summary trial. It was a brutal flash that suddenly cast light on the sordid chaotic workings of a state apparatus increasingly shut off with its secrets and struggles – a classic case of bureaucracy becoming synonymous with fiefdoms.

If there really exist gains of the revolution, they are, above all, the result of thirty years of sacrifices, suffering and heroism by a people whose watchword was *¡Siempre se puede más!* [One is always capable of more]. What is the point of priding oneself on the education and training of young school-leavers, students, teachers, doctors, engineers and technicians, or of developing the mastery of technical methods and research – all of which have reached an unparalleled level for a Third World country – if democracy is reduced to an unequal face-to-face between the people and its leader, in which dialogue is replaced by a monologue and the leader always asks the questions and gives the answers himself? What is the point when the party supposed to represent the people merely repeats the leader's lessons in that inimitable set language that Cubans call *teque*?

In one of his most famous poems José Martí wrote: 'I have two fatherlands, Cuba and the night.' As we have said, the history of this people, whose destiny was often greater than the mere boundaries of its land and which struggled for so long against the night, is a remarkable one. Those, like us, who were attracted by the Cuban Revolution, went precisely because they saw the sudden shining emergence of a great light from that night, a light stronger than that of its tropical sun. And that is why the island and its people, after so many shared hopes, can no longer be thought of as a mere dot on the map.

On reading Janette Habel's book, the question raised is not so much whether the Castro regime will once again find an inspired ploy, if not to get out of the crisis, then at least postpone it. Nor is it about knowing which group in the regime will gain the upper hand or the costs of this or that confrontation – regardless of whether or not one takes the succession to Fidel Castro as one's perspective. To my knowledge, that is not an open question. They are all real issues. But the real question is whether and in what way the people can today take their destiny in hand, escaping the 'Fidel or chaos' alternative and the oppressive prospects of the system and the apparatus being perpetuated. This would not mean renouncing what they have achieved at such dear cost, but building on it. Only then will one be able to speak of the Cuban Revolution again.

François Maspero
October 1989

Notes

1. José Martí, *Nuestra América*; an anthology compiled and edited by Roberto Fernández Retamar, translated and with a preface by André Joucla-Ruau, François Maspero, Paris 1968, p. 338.

2. The return of the pendulum: in 1967, Régis Debray was a prisoner in Bolivia, having written *Revolution in the Revolution?*, a book which sums up Castroite theory. He was seen for a time as the spokesman of 'Third Worldism'. And Gérard Chaliand wrote a critique of this book (refused at *Partisans*, but published in *Esprit*) which already foreshadowed his book, *Les Mythes révolutionnaires du tiers monde*.

3. Karine Berriot, *Julio Cortázar l'enchanteur*, Presses de la Renaissance, Paris 1988.

4. It is in Jésus Díaz's beautiful novel, *Los iniciales de la tierra*, recently published in Cuba but written more than fifteen years ago, that one finds the most perceptive record of the hopes and despairs of this period, as lived by the Cuban people.

5. K.S. Karol, *Cuba, les guérilleros au pouvoir*, Robert Laffont, Paris 1970. René Dumont, *Cuba, est-il socialiste*, Le Seuil, Paris 1970.

6. A good example of this eclecticism is provided by *Autrement* magazine in its special issue, 'Cuba, trente ans de révolution'. Maurice Lemoine's editorial highlights perfectly the unease felt by a seasoned and free-thinking journalist when faced with the complexity of such a violently contradictory record, even though long experience of the Third World has shown him the atrocious development of the poverty that does not exist in Cuba.

7. This figure, covering the whole of the prison population, was provided in 1967 by Charles Rivière on return from a mission carried out on behalf of the Cuban Ministry of Health. It is recorded by Jean-Pierre Clerc in his book *Fidel de Cuba*, Ramsay, Paris 1988, p. 358. In December 1966, Fidel Castro had stated in an interview with *Playboy* that there were 20,000 political prisoners. It was the period of the UMAPs, labour units where 'deviants', including homosexuals, were sent. It must be stressed that such camps were eradicated following the intervention of Fidel Castro himself. Such figures are unverifiable and this is one given by the Cuban regime. This explains why there may be some discrepancy here with those given by Janette Habel. Another example of unverifiable figures: it is impossible to put a figure on the number of dead in Angola. Every Cuban arrives at his or her own personal estimate by carrying out a crosscheck around them.

8. Tad Szulc, *Fidel, a Critical Portrait*. Jean-Pierre Clerc, *Fidel de Cuba*, Ramsay, Paris 1988.

9. Thus, in Carlos Franqui's hefty recent book, *Vie, aventures et désastres d'un certain Fidel Castro* (Belfond, Paris 1989), anger conceals documentation. The latter is nevertheless substantial. Carlos Franqui was responsible for Castroite propaganda and, in this capacity, was the organizer of the 'congress of intellectuals' in Havana at the end of 1967. Also in this capacity, he had been appointed by Fidel Castro to compile his biography. This explains the importance of the source material which Franqui still possesses. Jorge Valls's book, *Mon ennemi, mon frère* (L'Arpenteur, Paris 1989) is a different story altogether. The author, a Catholic, who was one of the founders of the Revolutionary Directorate, spent many years in Castro's prisons. He has managed the feat of only mentioning Fidel Castro's name once in the compilation of his book. His testimony, as well as being dignified and inspiring respect, is, among others, crucial to understanding the reality of the different components of the Cuban revolutionary movement and Fidel Castro's seizure of power within it. It is also the most damning testimony of the prison universe under Castro.

10. Among others: André Gunder Frank, *Capitalisme et sous-développement en Amérique latine*, François Maspero, Paris 1968; *Lumpen-bourgeoisie et Lumpen-développement*, François Maspero, Paris 1971; *Le Développement du sous-développement*, François Maspero, Paris 1972.

11. Fidel Castro, *Etapes de la révolution cubaine*, texts collected and edited by Michel Merlier, François Maspero, Paris 1964. Fidel Castro was in fact speaking here of the command of the Rebel Army. He would remain its 'commander-in-chief' until 1975 when he became 'president'.

12. The 'people's power' system was explained at length in the book by the Chilean – and now Cuban – economist, Marta Harnecker: *Cuba, dictature ou démocratie?* François Maspero, Paris 1976.

13. Many clarifications on Fidel Castro's ideological development can be found in his interviews with the Brazilian friar, Frei Betto, *Fidel y la religión*; as well as in *Un encuentro con Fidel* by the Italian journalist Gianni Miná. Of note is the place which the education acquired from the Jesuits occupies, in the form of Utopian socialism characterizing Fidel Castro's Marxism. In particular, he explains how he made the transition from 'religious faith' to 'political faith'.

Introduction

The Cuban Revolution used to occupy a special place at the crossroads of the Third World and the so-called 'socialist' camp. But thirty years after the seizure of power, confronted with a serious economic crisis and the collapse of the bureaucratic regimes in Eastern Europe, it has entered a new phase. At a time of major ideological reversals, Fidel Castro marked the thirtieth anniversary of the revolution by invoking a new role for the country – no longer that of an outpost in the anti-imperialist struggle, but as a vanguard in the defence of Marxism-Leninism and socialism:

> At this difficult time for socialism, when imperialism uses every means at its disposal to sow doubt and ideological confusion, it is for us a patriotic mission and sacred international duty to wave the flag and banner of socialism, the potential, possibilities and prestige of socialism. ... Our country has major international responsibilities today. Not because we are a major power, but because we are an example of revolutionary spirit, of internationalism, of heroism and courage, through our ability to confront imperialism and to build socialism boldly alongside American imperialism.[1]

By immediately affirming his total solidarity with the November 1989 offensive of the Farabundo Martí National Liberation Front, Fidel Castro matched word with deed, understanding that Cuba's survival would benefit greatly from a revolutionary victory in El Salvador. But with the Malta accords and the electoral defeat of the Sandinistas, the international situation has not developed in a way that will allow such hopes to be realized.

Cuba's economic difficulties, extensively highlighted by the international press, are mainly the result of the embargo imposed by the world's leading economic power on a small underdeveloped country of ten million people which depends for its survival on unstable revenues from sugar resources insufficient to propel the country's development. And in addition, the already haphazard and conditional aid provided by the Soviet Union has now been placed in question.

The disintegration of the bureaucratic regimes of the Eastern bloc has major implications for a country with such limited resources, strangled like other Third World countries by debt and the fall in raw material prices. This is especially so given that Soviet aid has not enabled Cuba to escape the constraints of an economy dependent on foreign trade. The problem is also one of the 'socialist' division of labour within Comecon and of the unequal exchange between the rich and poor countries.

In such a context, is not the campaign for a solution through the application of market reforms (in a word, perestroika) a myth? How can perestroika be a solution in an underdeveloped country beset by shortages? Would it not mean calling into question the important social gains still ensuring a popular base of support for the regime? Is not the real problem one of drawing up a development strategy that would involve ending the US blockade, putting a stop to protectionist measures and unequal exchange by the most developed countries, cancelling the debt, and gaining credit on favourable terms? This would presuppose a change in the international balance of forces. Such issues are now not just vital for Cuba but for the whole of the Third World.

To recognize the absence of socialist democracy in Cuba is not to minimize its significance. On the contrary, the claim of making the Cuban Revolution a pole of attraction for all oppressed peoples and for the international labour movement – the latter racked by an unprecedented crisis of outlook – is totally incompatible with restrictions on political rights and with bureaucratic repression. Castro has so far revealed not only his inability to respond to the democratic challenge presented by Gorbachev but, further, his inability to build a new society by and for the 'new man' spoken of by Che. This presupposes democracy which, while not identifiable with the parodic displays of Western electoral campaigns with their easy and rarely respected promises and in which money is king, would none the less respect freedom of opinion, expression and organization in whatever form. This would not be a formal concession to the pressure of opinion; it is a question of having indispensable devices which limit the bureaucratic arbitrariness inherent in a one-party system.

In Cuba itself, multiple 'rectifications' – the calling to order of leaders and the repeated emphasis on the virtues of setting an example – have not been enough to eliminate well-known defects: venality, corruption and cynicism have been denounced in vain for years. Marta Harnecker explains the reasons why. Recognizing that the control mechanisms intended to prevent self-interested membership have failed, she writes:

'The practice of ensuring that it was the workers who, one way or another, controlled the party by selecting members has gradually disappeared. The problem posed by the one-party system – a party, it should not be forgotten, that controls the state – is to know who controls this party.' In so far as the party facilitates social promotion in a 'one-party socialist society', one is better advised, if one wants to be a member of this party, to silence one's criticisms of administrative cadres that are members, rather than run the risk of combating errors. 'That is how opportunism and follow-my-leader attitudes have come about'; and as Harnecker again points out, it is also one of the reasons why 'the prestige enjoyed by the party in 1975 has fallen'.[2]

At least it can no longer be claimed that the Cuban leadership is erring through ignorance, lack of understanding or weakness of analysis. The appropriate solutions remain to be introduced. In principle, this is the aim of the Fourth Congress. In calling the Congress it was – rightly – stressed that it is to be held at a time when Cuba is going through the most important moment in its history, and when 'the harshest of setbacks are being inflicted on socialism', thus making it essential for 'the strategic unity of all forces and all sectors around the Party and Fidel to be reinforced'. (A sign of the times, the call was addressed to 'compatriots' and not to 'comrades', thus breaking with usual practice.) But if the Congress is confined to such an aim, it will not respond to the expectations of several sectors of Cuban society and will not solve the problems denounced by Marta Harnecker. For only the freedom of information, debate, organization and action within the revolution can curb bureaucratic arbitrariness. A democracy where only the Commander-in-Chief asks the questions and gives the answers, and in which he alone can hold power and be the opposition, is not in the end compatible with the aspirations of the new generations.

Will Fidel Castro tolerate the possibility of 'his' youth interrupting his long monologue?

Janette Habel
July 1990

Notes

My warm thanks to Anne-Marie Eche, Yiğit Bener, Armando Lodina, Michael Löwy, François Maspero and the Rotographie team for their criticisms, advice and friendly support.

1. Speech of Fidel Castro, 18 December 1988.
2. Interview with Marta Harnecker, '¿Ha llegado la hora de Cuba?', June 1990, text printed in Cuba.

1

The Economic Crisis

The Third Congress of the Cuban Communist Party (PCC) in 1986 marked an economic, political and ideological turning point. Ten years after the introduction of a new Economic Management and Planning System (SDPE) aimed at remedying the serious difficulties of the Cuban economy, Fidel Castro drew a negative assessment of its application. The second session of the Third Congress (deferred to December 1986) provided the occasion for the launch of a 'process of rectification of the errors and negative tendencies in all spheres of society'. Fidel Castro described the significance of this process as 'strategic'; it was decisive 'in order to avoid serious political problems, for we were weakening the revolution'.[1]

Waste and muddle in the management of the collectivized means of production had worsened, and social inequalities had grown. To this crisis of bureaucratic management were added the imbalances caused by the fall of raw material prices, as well as the effects of debt on an economy characterized by a structural trade deficit. The dependence of the Cuban economy on foreign trade is marked by a high level of imported goods, while Cuban products for export are limited. Sugar is the country's principal source of foreign exchange, other exports mainly being raw materials and food products.

Given the unequal terms of trade, this situation has a particularly negative effect on trade with the capitalist countries. For Cuba's economic development requires the importation of goods that cannot be produced nationally; and the country's increasing economic integration in the Council for Mutual Economic Assistance (CMEA, formerly Comecon) cannot eliminate the need for high-level technological imports from the capitalist countries. The fall in sugar prices, interest payments on the debt, the shortage of foreign exchange, increased dependence on the

Soviet Union; all create a bottleneck for the Cuban economy, which must drastically reduce its imports and raise its exports, in spite of the economic crisis. It is in this context that we must analyse what the Castro leadership saw as a historic reorientation.

Sugar, Always Sugar

In the 1960s the Cuban leadership opted for a development strategy based on agriculture: agricultural exports – mainly sugar, then citrus fruits, fish products and tobacco – were to provide the foundation for industrial development. Combined with a policy of import substitution – which was advocated by the economists of the nationalist-oriented Economic Commission for Latin America (ECLA) so as to escape sugar monoculture – such aims were to collide with a number of obstacles: the energy resources needed for industrialization were limited; and the number of export products that could produce the foreign exchange resources to finance a process of industrialization were restricted, thus leading to a high level of Western imports.

Moreover, such an option rested on several assumptions: that world sugar consumption would continue to grow (in view of the malnutrition of the underdeveloped countries); that the price of sugar was guaranteed on a global scale by the agreements reached with the Soviet Union, in spite of fluctuations in the world market; that this guarantee would lead to the relative stability of external resources (thanks to the barter agreements concluded with the East European countries); and that surpluses earmarked for the open market without fixed quotas would provide the foreign exchange needed to import Western technologies that the Soviet Union could not offer.

Today, this analysis is being partially challenged. Despite considerable technical progress in sugar production (cane-cutting has been 70 per cent mechanized and significant economies have been made in energy use), the dependence on sugar is making itself cruelly felt: sugar accounts for between 75 and 85 per cent of exports – the same proportion as before the revolution, even though its destination and financing are different.[2]

The need to transform the structure of external trade – by substituting nationally manufactured products for imported goods and thus accelerating the country's industrialization – has become increasingly crucial. The debate over economic strategy has thus been reopened. The predominant role of sugar exports to the Soviet Union and CMEA has been criticized on the grounds that economic independence is needed, and also on the grounds of the vulnerability represented by a single agricultural product occupying such a key position, subject as it is to climatic

Table 1 Structure of Cuban Exports 1957–78 (%)

Year	*Sugar*	*Tobacco*	*Minerals**	*Others***
1957	78	6	6	10
1958	78	7	3	11
1959	77	9	2	12
1960	80	10	1	9
1961	85	6	6	3
1962	83	5	7	5
1963	87	4	6	3
1964	88	4	5	3
1965	86	5	6	3
1966	85	4	7	4
1967	86	4	8	2
1968	77	6	12	5
1969	76	6	13	5
1970	77	3	17	3
1971	76	4	16	4
1972	74	5	15	6
1973	75	5	14	6
1974	87	3	6	4
1975	90	2	5	3
1976	87	2	6	5
1977	83	2	5	8
1978	87	2	5	6

*mainly nickel. **mainly fish, seafood, fruit and rum.

Sources: *Statistical Yearbook of Cuba*, 1976; *Report of the National Bank of Cuba*, 1977; *Statistical Yearbook of Cuba*, 1980.

fluctuations and – as has been dramatically illustrated in recent years – fluctuations in the prices of agricultural raw materials.

Such criticisms have come just as much from close sympathizers of the Cuban Revolution as from figures hostile to it,[3] and they find a certain echo in Cuba today, even though no abrupt change can be envisaged in the short term. In spite of everything, however, Cuban leaders have had no shortage of arguments to justify their choice: first, that the agreements reached with the Soviet Union provide an effective guarantee for the stability of resources; secondly, that the prospects for increasing the volume of sugar production – through the mechanization of cane-cutting, the modernization of existing sugar-producing centres, the construction of new refineries and the development of products derived from sugar –

should contribute to raising the productivity of sugar; and thirdly, that the sugar industry uses bagasse (a waste product of sugar, used in Brazil as an alcohol fuel to replace oil), thus enabling it to make substantial energy savings, in other economic sectors too. In other words, the sugar industry has developed and is crucial to financing imports of intermediate goods and extending the process of industrialization. The debate over the 'new economic dependency' is therefore not admissible 'in terms of national and international realities'.[4]

Defended by B. Pollitt,[5] this position is beginning to be qualified as a result of uncertainties in the sugar market. Periodic crises are not a novelty, of course, and Cuba is relatively protected from them. But the scope and speed of fluctuations in the sugar market bear witness not only to uncertainties in the short term, but also to questions over the long-term development of consumption. While surpluses on the world market reached 38 million tonnes between 1986 and 1987,[6] or around 40 per cent of world consumption, world stocks represented only 33 million tonnes in 1988.

In 1988–1989, world production was to be of the order of 107.5 million tonnes for a consumption of 108 million tonnes.[8]

Underproduction by the Soviet Union, drought, and unforeseen massive imports by India, China and Indonesia have meant that sugar stocks are at a very low level. And the slightest risk of shortage, even a momentary one, makes the price go up. As an expert commentator stressed: 'Speculation leads to a too sudden increase in prices ... and prices fall abruptly as soon as a reequilibrium between supply and demand is announced.'[9]

If one looks at price trends, the fall that began in 1982 worsened in 1984 to reach the lowest prices since 1970 (3.6 US cents per pound in December 1984 on the open market). According to the National Bank of Cuba, 'the deterioration of the nominal price is even worse in terms of purchasing power, which in 1984 was well below what it was during the Great Depression'.[10]

Such fluctuations have been confirmed in recent years: in mid-1985 the price per pound ranged between 2 and 3 US cents, the lowest nominal value price for seventeen years, which represents only a quarter of the most efficient production costs.[11] In the second half of 1985 and 1986 the price of sugar rose (around 5 US cents a pound) to reach 10 cents a pound in September 1988[12] and even 13 cents a pound in 1989.[13] This recovery was the result of a fall in production between 1985 and 1986, due to drought and other climatic factors which affected the main sugar-cane producers (Brazil, Cuba, the Dominican Republic and the Philippines). The recovery was also helped by massive purchases from China, as well as by Cuba's need, in spite of a good harvest in 1989 (8

Table 2 Evolution of the Purchasing Power of Raw Sugar on the World Market (US cents per pound weight)

Year	*Average price of sugar per pound*	*1st index*	*2nd index*	*Constant sugar prices*	
		Wholesale prices USA (%)	*Unit value tonne oil (%)*	*against 1st index (%)*	*against 2nd index (%)*
1932	0.78	100	100	0.78	0.78
1950	4.98	244	143	2.04	3.48
1960	3.14	284	156	1.11	2.01
1970	3.75	331	152	1.13	2.47
1975	20.40	523	969	3.92	2.11
1980	29.01	844	2539	3.44	1.14
1981	16.93	921	2731	1.84	0.62
1982	8.55	940	2857	0.91	0.30
1983	8.50	953	2463	0.89	0.35
1984	5.18	972	2394	0.53	0.22

Source: Report of the National Bank of Cuba, February 1985.

million tonnes), to return to operators the quantities it had removed in 1987–88 to fulfil its obligations with the Soviet Union.

But the effects of the 1988 upturn in prices and the drop in world stocks had hardly been felt when the Group of Latin American and Caribbean Sugar-Exporting Countries (GEPLACEA) considered the prospect of a good harvest in 1989 as inevitably working towards a fall. They were afraid that the 1988 price rise might provoke a strong increase in production, and thus lead to a further drop in prices. 'The Third World debtor countries producing brown sugar (amongst others the Philippines and Brazil) continue to flood the market without restraint [*sic*], thus putting extra pressure on prices,'[14] commented one journalist. It is true that the producing countries, when their revenues are falling, seek to increase their production and thus contribute to a fall in prices. Even though the most efficient producers do not cover their production costs, they attempt, despite such disadvantageous conditions, to sell more to finance crucial imports.

Far from blaming the countries of the Third World, as many do, for the uncertainties hanging over sugar production, it is important to stress the real causes of these uncertainties: the protectionist policies of the industrialized countries and the development of substitutes and synthetic sweeteners, in particular corn syrup.[15]

The Effects of Protectionism by the Capitalist Countries

The protectionist policies of the developed capitalist countries – the United States, the EEC and Japan – have had disastrous effects on Third World producers. The United States has guaranteed its producers a price of between 18 and 20 US cents a pound. This high price has encouraged the use of sugar substitutes, thus provoking a fall in natural sugar consumption and imports.

The EEC has become the world's leading sugar producer. The members of the EEC (the Ten) who imported 1 million tonnes of sugar from the world market in the 1950s are now the leading exporter on the open market, with 5 million tonnes. This has been made possible by the subsidies granted to beet growers who are guaranteed a price of 21 cents a pound, in other words double the recent rising prices.[16] And in order to export this sugar, the EEC finances the difference.

Japan, which was the second highest importer of sugar after the United States (2.5 million tonnes) in the 1970s, today imports no more than 1.9 million and subsidizes the domestic production of sugar-cane and beet. Thanks to this aid, beet production has increased from 600,000 to 900,000 tonnes.[17]

In 1981 US purchases from the main world producers rose to 5 million tonnes, while in 1987 they were of the order of 1 million tonnes![18] It is mainly the underdeveloped countries that have paid the costs of these decisions. The Philippines' export quota to the United States, for example, was reduced to three-quarters of its former size, while that of Nicaragua was eliminated altogether.[19] On 15 December 1987 the United States fixed a quota for sugar imports which was 25 per cent below that of the preceding year. This meant that the GEPLACEA member countries' foreign exchange revenues from sugar sales now reached no more than around US$190 million, while North American consumers would have to pay around $3,000 million more for the sugar they bought, due to subsidies to sugar producers under the sugar programme.[20]

In ten years, more than an extra 7 million tonnes of sugar on the open market have come from the United States, the EEC and Japan, because of artificial subsidies suffocating the less developed sugar-exporting countries which must face the unfair competition of huge volumes of subsidized sugar. Once an importer of sugar, the EEC now contributes to the overproduction of sugar with its subsidies, and has begun to compete with Third World countries by demanding additional export quotas.

How remote the so-called North–South dialogue is!

> Two hundred years after enslaving people to work on sugar plantations, rich countries are enslaving them again by ruining those same plantations and the poor countries that rely on them. ... For it and other agricultural sectors to develop efficiently, Gatt [General Agreement on Tariffs and Trade] rules against dumping of manufactured goods will have to be extended to agriculture. ... Last year the [subsidies] regime cost European taxpayers and consumers around US$ 2 billion. The EEC sugar regime is a parasite, damaging the commodity it feeds on.

Such was the irrevocable judgement of the English conservative magazine *The Economist*,[21] confirmed by the last Gatt report.[22] The authors of the latter noted a 4 per cent growth in agricultural exports in 1987 after a 1 per cent drop in 1986, but they immediately went on to stress that the reasons for this upturn were not encouraging: world agricultural production, for its part, dropped by 3 per cent for the first time since 1980, and the 'quite considerable subsidies' spent on the export of various products – sugar, cereals, milk products and meat – has influenced this kind of trade.

It is clear that Cuba, as a country whose main product for export is sugar, has particularly suffered from this situation. In 1983 and 1984 the Cuban economy endured the effects of an unprecedented deterioration in

Table 3 Self-sufficiency* in Sugar of Particular Developed Capitalist Countries (average %)

Country	*1951–55*	*1981–84*
United States	55.3	65.9
EEC	66.8	132.8
Japan	4.0	30.2

* Defined as the percentage of consumption covered by production.

Source: International Sugar Organization, *Sugar Year Book*, London.

its terms of trade with the capitalist countries. Between 1983 and 1985, according to the National Bank of Cuba, the transfer of resources due to the difference in sugar price was set to reach $642 million (taking the 1977 international sugar agreement as a reference point, with the price of 13 cents a pound).

Table 4 Estimated Transfer of Resources to Market-Economy Countries Due To the Low Price of Sugar (millions of pesos)

	1983	*1984*	*1985*	*Total*
Revenue from sugar exports at market prices	263	250	238	751
Revenue at the minimum price fixed by the 1977 international sugar agreement	387	489	517	1,393
Difference	124	239	279	642

Source: *Report of the National Bank of Cuba*, February 1985.

This means that, in the period 1983–85, Cuba lost $116.72 in convertible foreign exchange revenues for each tonne of sugar exported to the market-economy countries.

In such circumstances it is understandable that Cuban protests have not been isolated, as the declarations of President Sarney of Brazil have shown: 'The costly and artificial protection of the domestic producer leads to a fall in imports and encourages the tendency to use substitutes; on the other hand, the subsidization of exports tends to increase supply on a world scale.'[23] To deal with this crisis, Cuba and Brazil have attempted to finalize a joint strategy aimed at reaching a new international sugar agreement (which has not been renewed since 1984) in order to stabilize prices. In existence since 1978, the international sugar agreement foresaw export quotas and regulating stocks. 'In fixing limits on the stocks of different countries, the accord in effect involves an indirect control of production. ... The success of the accord [and its subsequent failure] must be relativized because the European Community and the United States have not abided by it.'[24] For the secretary of GEPLACEA, the aim is to 'try to win a change in the sugar policy of the

United States and the EEC' and to 'try to control the supply of sugar on the international market, so as to better distribute the costs of production'.[25] It is not surprising that Fidel Castro's accusations, denouncing dumping and the brazen, unfair competition which is ruining the peoples of the dominated countries, should have received a wide audience in Latin America, including governments like that of Brazil; or that Cuba's 'pioneering role' in this battle should be recognized by the secretary of GEPLACEA.

The recent rise in sugar prices on the international market has not changed the overall picture. On the one hand because, even at 10 cents a pound, prices remain below production costs in the majority of Latin American countries;[27] and on the other, because the causes of this rise do nothing to invalidate the general prognosis: some of the most important sugar-exporting countries have suffered long droughts (Brazil, the Philippines and Cuba, for example), leading to falls in production and serious delays in deliveries.[28] In some countries (India and Pakistan) imports could increase, hence a certain reduction of stocks.[29]

But the disorganization of international markets has deeper roots. Price-support policies have led to the appearance of increasingly large agricultural surpluses, thus leading to a fall in prices which ends up backfiring on the beneficiaries of subsidies. When EEC bodies accumulate stocks of butter, cereals or sugar through their price-support operations, they can be said to have acquired false riches in that they will be unable to resell these goods at a price at least equivalent to the cost of production (plus storage costs, insurance premiums etc.). Guaranteed revenues and prices have played a full role in stimulating production and encouraging technological innovation. Bit by bit, stocks and overcapacity have accumulated; and from 1980 they have begun to weigh heavily on international markets. The agricultural war has not stopped raging since; and in a few years international prices have collapsed, even when the fall in the dollar – the main currency in which prices are expressed – is taken into account.[30]

The Development of Synthetic Sweeteners

Just as worrying for the elaboration of a long-term economic strategy has been the development of sugar substitutes. To the sharp increase in the use of high fructose corn syrup (HFCS), and the development of synthetic sweeteners associated with changing eating habits in the industrialized countries, a new sweetening product[31] has just been added – corn-based crystalline fructose, which, for the time being, is being used for medical or paramedical purposes[32] and is still very expensive. As with other agricultural raw materials, the trend towards the replacement of natural sugar with synthetic substitutes is developing; the uncertain nature of agricultural harvests (the effects on sugar-cane of drought followed by torrential rains in 1988, for example) and their effects on supply and prices have been one of the causes for this.

In spite of the fall in natural sugar prices, the consumption of artificial sugars, especially corn syrup, has not stopped growing since the beginning of the 1970s, particularly in the major importing countries (Japan, Canada, the EEC and the United States). In the United States, sugar took 76 per cent of the local market ten years ago; but it now represents a mere 48 per cent, the use of corn syrup having gone up in the meantime from 0 to 30 per cent.[33]

Table 5 Production Costs of High Fructose Corn Syrup in the United States (US$ per tonne)

	Low	*Medium*	*High*
Capital cost	110	110	110
Conversion cost	95	95	95
Net cost of raw materials	58	87	95
Total cost	263	292	334
US cents per pound	11.9	13.2	15.2

Source: *Cuba socialista*, November 1986.

The average cost of production of HFCS is 13.2 cents a pound, which is well below the stabilization price for raw sugar, hence its growing use: in 1985 the two most important US soft drinks companies – Coca Cola and Pepsi Cola – decided to replace completely the sugar in drinks with HFCS.

To this can be added the dietary campaigns to reduce sugar consumption for health reasons. The production of aspartame-based low-calorie foods and drinks is increasing. The UN-linked Food and Agriculture Organization (FAO) estimates that the substitution of sugar by aspartame will reach 950,000 tonnes in 1990 in the United States, Japan, the EEC and Canada.[34]

The future is thus problematic for the sugar-producing underdeveloped countries, even if one must be wary of making generalizations from the trends now mainly affecting the industrialized nations. China, for example, has had to ration its sugar consumption and the government may take measures to develop cultivation and thus attain self-sufficiency.[35] This is also the case with certain African countries now attempting to meet their own domestic consumption needs.[36] But such measures run the risk of increasing production capacity on markets that are already saturated.

The notion that commodities – in this case sugar – could facilitate industrialization through the acquisition of crucial imports has been in question since the moment that the purchasing power of commodities in relation to manufactured goods began to fall.[37] The development strategy based on increasing sugar exports to build the foundations for a rapid industrialization has been shaken.

A Change of Economic Policy

The Cuban economy has nevertheless been relatively protected since 80 per cent of its sugar production is exported to the 'socialist' countries (of which 60 per cent goes to the Soviet Union under long-term agreements). The portion sold on the open market[38] has gone down from 32 per cent in 1975 to 22 per cent in 1986, hence the deficit in external trade and the debt with Western countries. But production targets have not been met and supplies to CMEA countries have been short of targets set when, as part of the division of labour within CMEA, the cultivation of sugar-beet was to be reduced in favour of sugar-cane, whose yield is greater. The inability to honour export obligations during the first half of 1988, even after the effects of drought had been allowed for, led Cuba to postpone deliveries due at the beginning of the year (not just to the CMEA, but also to Japan): talks took place in Havana with Soviet officials and international traders. The financial agreement reached at the end of this meeting[39] resulted in the purchase by the Soviet Union of 750,000 tonnes of brown sugar on behalf of the government of Cuba so that the latter could meet its contractual obligations. The most striking feature of this move, noticed by several observers,[40] was that it was the Soviet Union which made these purchases directly, Cuba lacking sufficient funds to buy the sugar on the open market to cover its contracts.

Impelled by the crisis, a reorientation of policy discussed at the time of the Third Congress of the PCC was to be implemented to encourage industrial diversification and a better industrial use of cane. Bagasse was to be used as both fuel and raw material in the paper-cardboard and other industries.

Thus, twenty-seven years after Che's speech in Punta del Este[41] anticipating the transformation of Cuba into one of the most industrialized countries of Latin America – in which sugar would represent merely 60 per cent of the value of exports instead of 80 – the Cuban economy still faces the effects of sugar dependency; and no alternative solutions exist in the short term which can provide the crucial resources in foreign exchange to import goods needed for industrialization.

To change economic policy – and thereby escape dependency and the notorious ups and downs of agricultural raw materials – has thus become a question of survival; and there is no shortage of pundits preaching the need for freedom from the sugar dependency 'at the root of the present crisis'.[42] According to these commentators, such inability to diversify is the result of a 'perpetually incompetent administration'[43] which is responsible for the rigidities of an antiquated, hyper-centralized planning system unable to take the path of economic liberalization in the image of China or other countries of the Eastern bloc.

Fashionable in Western economic circles, such judgements are suspect to say the least. They generally do not say a word about the still dramatic effects of the US blockade (on nickel, for example, whose price is rising on the world market, as the United States opposes the purchase of any material containing Cuban nickel), with every attempt being made to persuade Western banks against granting further credits. They do not deal with the crucial remaining problem of how, at what speed, and by what, sugar is to be gradually replaced as a provider of foreign exchange. Or how a debt in foreign exchange, contracted in the very different conditions of high sugar prices and easy Western credits, can be repaid. More generally, does Cuba have an alternative to economic links with the Soviet Union, in so far as US pressure means that the natural outlet of the Latin American market is not accessible for the foreseeable future?

Beyond this discussion of Cuba's medium-term possibilities, there is a difference of opinion over the actual state of affairs. French analysts[44] consider that the structure of industry has changed little and is still dominated by sugar and the conversion of oil imported from the Soviet Union. They note a slow-down in industrial growth at the beginning of the 1980s (although high sugar prices had allowed significant Western credits to be obtained, the fall in prices led to the abandonment of several industrial projects anticipated under the plan), and conclude that

> changes from the past continue to be minimal. Cuba was and still is a semi-industrial supplier of raw materials and semi-finished goods, and lacks the means to go on to create a diversified processing industry. ... Since 1972, Cuba has had to repay credits granted by the Soviet Union through increased deliveries of sugar. The increase in deliveries of sugar, nickel, citrus fruits and tobacco ... to the Soviet Union and its CMEA partners takes away any

> possibility of Cuba settling its bill with the Western developed countries, hence its inability to obtain the numerous consumer goods and industrial products needed to develop its industry.[45]

Such an analysis has been the subject of long polemics between US and Swedish economists and academics.[46] As well as the problems raised by assessing Soviet aid and Cuba's integration in CMEA, opinions also differ over the growth of industrial production and the relation between growth in sugar production and the development of industry.

For C. Brundenius, 'there has been vigourous industrial growth in almost all industrial activities during the 1970s. The sub-sector of manufacturing industry has seen an annual growth rate of 7 per cent, and the capital goods industry one of 15.5 per cent. The most spectacular growth sector has been construction, which rose by an annual 14.2 per cent during this period.'[47]

In 1981, 34.9 per cent of investments were made in industry, as opposed to 16.7 per cent in 1966.[48] The engineering industry is based on agriculture's technical requirements. Confirming C. Brundenius's assessment, R. Turits believes that there is no contradiction between the efforts to increase sugar production and the development of industry, as the development of sugar production and that of engineering are linked. He invokes in particular the impressive results of the mechanization of the cane harvest: in 1985 two-thirds of the harvesting was mechanized, and since 1970 the loading process has been totally mechanized as well. Whereas in 1957–58 it needed 370,000 workers to harvest 5.9 million tonnes of sugar-cane, in 1980–81 it took only 100,000 to harvest 7.4 million tonnes.[49]

Mechanization has been accompanied by a considerable effort in terms of the education, qualifications and technical skills of the workforce. This has led to an uncontrolled movement of the agricultural workforce into industry and services. As a result, the age-old fear of sugar workers that mechanization – which they had always opposed before the revolution – would lead to unemployment, has been eliminated. The importance of industrial efforts is equally illustrated by the fact that Cuba is one of the world's leading producers of cane-cutting and harvesting machinery, and this should play a significant role in future industrial exports. The development of the sugar industry has also enabled significant energy savings to be made through bagasse. Oil consumption in the production of sugar has been eliminated to a large extent; and the production of ethanol provides the prospect for diversification, as is the case with other sugar-derived products.

Nevertheless, the main issue continues to be the growing inability of sugar to guarantee a sufficient amount of foreign exchange on the open

Table 6 Structural Changes in the Cuban Economy 1961–81 (%)

Sector	*Contribution to GDP*			*Average annual growth*		
	1961	*1970*	*1981*	*1961–70*	*1970–81*	*1961–81*
Agriculture[a]	18.2	18.1	12.9	1.5	3.6	2.7
Sugar cane	7.9	9.2	4.9	3.2	1.0	2.0
Others	10.3	8.9	8.0	0.0	5.8	3.1
Industry	31.8	38.4	46.4	3.6	8.4	6.2
Manufacturing industry	24.4	29.7	30.7	3.6	7.0	5.5
Machinery	1.6	2.5	6.6	6.5	15.5	11.5
Sugar and derivatives	4.7	4.8	3.0	1.8	2.2	2.0
Construction	5.2	5.7	13.0	2.4	14.2	8.9
Total from sugar[b]	12.6	14.0	7.9	2.7	1.4	2.0
Total material production	50.0	56.5	59.4	2.8	7.1	5.2
Gross material product	82.2	79.9	73.2	0.2	5.9	3.3
Services production	17.8	20.1	26.8	2.9	9.3	6.4
Gross domestic product	100.0	100.0	100.0	1.5	6.7	4.3

[a] including forestry and fishing; [b] sugar-cane and sugar refining.

Source: Brundenius, 'Cuba, Crecimiento con Equidad', Managua, INIES, 1984.

market, in spite of Cuba's frequent infringement of 'socialist' solidarity by selling on the open market cargoes of sugar reserved in principle for the Soviet Union. Such a practice has recently earned Cuba severe criticism.[50] And the transfer to the open market of part of the quotas reserved for CMEA is now all the more limited as a result of the fall in production. Cuba must devote a share of future harvests to the repayment of its debt, in order to make up for the insufficient deliveries of recent years.

The fact that Cuba has made progress in building a modern industrial infrastructure linked to sugar production and has developed an agro-industrial sector based on sugar products, has led the general secretary of GEPLACEA, José Antonio Cerre, to say that 'the sugar agro-industry of that country is one of the most developed in the world' – so developed that he envisages 'a transfer of technology to other countries in Latin America'. But this would mean controlling the supply of sugar internationally and 'gaining the unity of the Latin American and Caribbean countries so as to reach an international sugar agreement with economic clauses ... and to change the sugar policies of the United States and the EEC'.[51]

There is not a shadow of doubt in his mind that the Cuban leadership attaches the utmost importance to such efforts. As with the debt, the Cuban leadership is seeking the greatest possible unity at the Latin American level against imperialist domination, if only to counterbalance the uncertain dynamics of the division of labour within CMEA: Cuba's role is laid down by 188 multi- and bilateral accords and it is committed to providing sugar, nickel, citrus fruits and tobacco in exchange for machinery, equipment and fuel,[52] the quality and technological level of which is far from satisfying the country's needs.

The Debt Burden

In 1979 the Cuban debt in relation to exports was the fifth highest in Latin America. In 1982 the National Bank asked for payments falling due between 1982 and 1985 to be rescheduled. The debt in convertible currency was then around $3,000 million, in other words around three and a half times the value of exports to Western countries. Interest payments alone to the latter represented 45 per cent of the value of exports to the West.[53]

While Cuba had been granted very few loans in the 1960s, the situation was to change in the 1970s, due to the gradual restoration of diplomatic and commercial relations, easy access to international credit as a result of oil surpluses, and, above all, the spectacular rise in sugar prices, which reached 64 cents a pound in 1974. Imports were to quadruple between 1973 and 1975 and trade with the West amounted to 40 per cent of total trade in 1970, but less than 14 per cent in 1983. From 1977 the sugar price per pound fell to 8 cents. This collapse was as damaging in its effects as it had been unexpected in its scale, coming at a time when high anticipated credits were supposed to finance investments related to industrialization.

The rescheduling granted in 1982 was over ten years with three years' grace, with payments to be resumed from January 1986. The Cuban leadership was relying on the 'stabilization of sugar prices at reasonable levels as a result of a world agreement'.[54] But in 1984 sugar exports to the market-economy countries dropped from 35.5 to 20.3 per cent in volume, and from 25.5 to 4 per cent in value.

Other products' share in exports fell in comparison with 1983. The production of tobacco, citrus fruits and sugar was affected by climatic factors, and coffee production was hit by 'rust', a disease caused by fungi. Meanwhile, the production of nickel[55] and cobalt dropped by 15.4 per cent between 1983 and 1984 as a result of modernization work on factories and accumulated delays in the organization of production. Moreover, the US embargo on nickel sales explains why a portion of production originally earmarked for the market-economy countries had to be renegotiated with the Eastern bloc countries (with 50 per cent of production exported to the Soviet Union).

The conditions attached to long-term contracts with the Soviet Union are not always favourable to Cuba. According to R. Turits: 'until 1976 the cumulative subsidy from the Soviet price for Cuban sugar was less than what the island would have obtained if it was still receiving the US import price.'[56] The value of nickel exports did not go up, even though there had been a very significant increase in prices in 1987 (in 1979 and 1980, Cuba had already lost \$32 and \$37 million respectively in nickel sales to the Soviet Union[57]).

But Cuba has mainly suffered from the fall in oil prices. Re-exports of oil supplied by the Soviet Union (or at least the portion saved by Cuba through energy economies[58]) have represented a very significant share of foreign exchange resources. In 1985, according to the National Bank of Cuba,[59] 40 per cent of export revenues came from re-exports of oil, representing a \$728 million increase on the projected figure for 1982. This increase partly made up for the reduction in foreign exchange revenues from sugar.

The profit was sufficiently large for the Cubans to be able to finance purchases of sugar on the open market in 1984 and 1985, and so fulfil contracts with the Soviet Union, and, above all, to take the profits related to transactions in oil.

Table 7 Distribution of Cuban Sugar Exports by Country (%)

	1978	*1979*	*1980*	*1981*	*1982*	*1983*	*1984*
Value							
Soviet Union	79.7	76.1	61.8	58.7	72.7	75.9	77.4
Rest of East	11.7	14.0	12.7	13.9	18.4	17.5	18.2
Rest of world	8.6	9.9	25.5	27.4	8.9	6.6	4.4
Volume							
Soviet Union	54.4	52.9	44.2	45.4	57.3	50.5	52.1
Rest of East	17.3	18.8	20.5	20.8	22.3	26.8	27.6
Rest of world	28.3	28.3	35.5	33.8	20.4	22.7	20.3

Source: *Economic Report on Cuba*, United Nations 1984.

The profitability of oil re-exports and the decisive role they have played is illustrated by table 8.

Table 8 Cuban Exports in Convertible Currencies from 1983 to 1985 (millions of pesos)

	Forecast	*Results*	*Difference*
Sugar	1,253.9	751.5	–502.4
Other exports	1,871.5	1,404.4	–467.1
Oil re-exports	682.1	1,409.9	+727.8
Total	3,807.5	3,565.8	–241.7

Source: *Report of the National Bank of Cuba*, February 1985.

Until 1986 Soviet aid was therefore linked to oil supplies, which in turn were linked to sugar quotas. The fall in oil prices was translated into a sharp drop in foreign exchange revenues. In 1985 foreign exchange from oil was three to four times higher than in 1981. In 1986, on the other hand, the fall in oil prices reduced expected foreign exchange revenues by 50 per cent; and the total value of exports showed a fall of 37 per cent instead of the 26 per cent forecast.[60] In other words, the advantageous subsidies linked to trading oil against sugar suddenly fell, and the Gorbachev leadership has given no indication whatsoever of intending to compensate for these losses. This reveals some of the complex workings of Soviet aid, notably the arbitrary and unstable nature of subsidies, which are at the mercy of the fluctuations in Soviet–Cuban relations and can be totally reversed.

Table 9, showing imports/exports with the market economies for 1983 and 1984, which was published by the National Bank of Cuba, indicates a surplus for 1983 and a deficit for 1984.

While the value of exports fell between 1983 and 1984, imports rose significantly and debt servicing used up 58 per cent of export earnings in 1984. One might ask why Cuba had to pay for oil in 1987 at the same price as 1986, when Poland and Bulgaria benefited from reductions of 10.6 and 13.2 per cent respectively for the same year.[61]

Although 1984 was characterized by one of the highest per capita growth rates in Latin America, Cuba's financial situation was to lead to a drastic revision of economic prospects, as well as to sharp criticism of

Table 9 Balance of Trade in Convertible Currencies at Current Prices (millions of pesos)

	1983	*1984*	*1984/83 (%)*
Exports (including re-exports)	1,287.4	1,098.2	85.3
Imports	831.7	1,164.7	140.0
Balance	455.7	-66.5	

Source: *Report of the National Bank of Cuba*, February 1985.

Fidel Castro because of uncontrolled growth, gained at the price of an excessively high level of imports.

There has been no improvement in the negative factors at work in 1984. Debt renegotiations took place in 1986 and 1987. Cuban economists themselves admit that the economic situation was much more difficult in 1987 than 1986: 'Imports in freely convertible currencies have been reduced to approximately $700 million. ... The Cuban foreign debt has risen by 377 million pesos in the first nine months of 1987, following the devaluation of the US dollar.'[62] The growth of the debt is shown in table 10.

Table 10 Cuba's Foreign Debt in Freely Convertible Currencies (millions of pesos)

1986	*1987*	*Increase*
3,944.2	5,551.1	1,610.9

Source: *Report of the National Bank of Cuba*, 31 December 1987.

Japan, Spain, France and Canada are among the major creditors. Cuba is particularly affected by the devaluation of the dollar in that its exports are valued in dollars while its imports and debt payments are valued in hard currency. Thus, in spite of its close integration in CMEA, Cuba continues to be highly subject to fluctuations in the world market and dependent on Western capital, as pointed out by S. Ekstein who stresses the capitalist constraints on Cuban socialist development.[64]

A kind of vicious circle is thus established: to industrialize, imports are needed; to import, foreign exchange is needed; and to obtain foreign exchange, whatever is immediately available must be exported – first and foremost sugar, but in increasingly large quantities to make up for the fall in prices and debt interest payments.

In order for the island to be able to release trade surplus earnings and correct its balance of payments, a number of measures were contemplated in 1983–84. These were to 'limit imports from the West, even at the cost of economic growth, with hard currency imports to be maintained at the lowest indispensable level'.[65] For the 1986–90 five-year plan the Cuban Central Bank thus envisaged 'limiting growth in consumption, given the standard of living already achieved by the Cuban people'.[66] Strongly suggested by the Paris Club following debt renegotiations, such measures met with the initial opposition of the Cuban government. But, willingly or reluctantly, it finally had to accept them.

The year 1986 was thus a turning point. As well as the debt annually renegotiated with the Paris Club, there was the debt with the Soviet Union and CMEA, where it had been decided in 1972 (the date of Cuba's admission to Comecon) that payment of debit balances in non-convertible currency[67] would, from 1986, be made interest-free and in kind (nickel, sugar etc.). Such a method of payment meant a drop in exports and a loss of hard currency earnings, required for the purchase of goods that the countries of the East could not supply. That is why Fidel Castro has been calling so insistently – and for a short while now, publicly – for the cancellation of the debt pure and simple.

For 1986 was also the planned settlement date following the rescheduling of the Western debt with the international banks. Afer a period of three years' grace the total amount of half-yearly payments due from 1 January 1986 was $125,130 million accompanied, of course, by interest rates.[68] In spite of repeated Cuban protests, the granting of fresh credits was made conditional on the settlement of interest repayments and fell well below the country's needs. In September the director of the National Bank of Cuba, Hector Rodríguez Llompart, complained that Cuba was in fact being denied access to international credits, and threatened creditors with a further supension in debt service payments if new money was not forthcoming.

The level of foreign exchange imports dropped from $1,200 million in 1986 to $740 million in 1987, with a $500 million limit envisaged for 1988.[69] This lent a certain degree of credibility to the statement that 'the Cuban economy is in the throes of one of its worst crises since the 1959 revolution because of a shortage of hard currency, failure to meet export targets and the poor performance of its import substitution policies.'[70]

The Second Debt

In February 1985 the National Bank of Cuba referred to the debt with the Soviet Union in the following terms: 'The servicing of the debt with the Soviet Union, which is to begin in 1986, should not affect the balance of payments during the five-year period beginning this year, as it has been refinanced on favourable terms.[71] Cuba can also rely on guaranteed and adequate supplies of oil which, added to growth in domestic production, should lead to a high level of income in convertible currency as a result of hydrocarbon sales.'[72] Such hopes, however, have not been supported by reality. The Gorbachev leadership is giving priority to domestic economic activity, is demanding better economic performance from its partners, and is embarked on a process of global negotiation with the United States, thus relativizing Third World demands.

In May 1987, the Soviet government therefore decided to reduce oil deliveries to Nicaragua – to which it was the major supplier – forcing that country to launch an appeal for international aid (Iran has delivered oil to Nicaragua[73]). Yet Soviet oil production was up 3.4 per cent on 1985 and sales have increased to two CMEA allies, Romania and Vietnam.[74] As far as Cuba is concerned, there has not only been a fall in the price for sugar paid by the Soviet Union; the prices demanded by the Soviet Union for its oil have remained above those on the world market, whereas Cuban re-exports have been made at current prices. Cuba has thus amassed a fall in sugar resources and oil revenues.[75]

At the same time the servicing of the debt in relation to exports in convertible currency has risen sharply.

Table 11 Indicators of the Cuban Foreign Debt in Hard Currency (millions of pesos)

	1979	*1980*	*1981*	*1982*
Total debt	3,267	3,227	3,170	2,694
Service of debt as % of exports, goods and services	45.3	28.7	35.9	64.7

Source: Acciari, *Courrier des Pays de l'Est*, May 1984.

This situation was made worse in July and August 1982 when foreign banks withdrew short-term credit lines for a total of $370 million.[76] Such circumstances further increased the importance of trade and financial relations with the member countries of CMEA, particularly the Soviet Union.

Brezhnev's visit to Cuba in 1972 and the joining of Comecon were marked by the signature of agreements over the payment of the accumulated debt since 1960. Though repayable in kind, from 1986 the debt was to be amortized through twenty-five interest-free annual payments.[77] The debt in 1982 was valued at $4,500 million by some,[78] and at $8,000 million by others.[79] Estimates are extremely variable in the absence of official figures. In November 1985, the figure of $7,000 million to $10,000 million was advanced,[80] while in 1987 Fidel Castro stated it was $10,000 million.[81] Other estimates are much higher.

Other agreements concerned the granting of credits to finance various projects, as well as the introduction of a system of indirect subsidies through fixed preferential prices for exported products as part of long-term agreements.

On the whole, the exact scale of Soviet aid is difficult to assess. The importance of indirect subsidies is much debated and the forms of aid very complex. Would certain Soviet products be able to find buyers on the market, given their more than mediocre quality? According to a Swedish economist, 'even if the [cane-harvesting] machines were given to Cuba free – which is not likely – it was probably a very costly enterprise'.[82] How should one therefore assess the value of Soviet products traded for sugar?

The agreement on oil re-exports (in a situation where sugar prices were low and the price of oil high) could be seen as a desire on the Soviet Union's part to compensate for the deterioration in the terms of trade. According to R. Turits, these subsidies protected the Cuban economy from the devastating effects that the rise in oil prices had on other underdeveloped countries;[83] but they were only particularly considerable in years following significant rises, and, notably, between 1980 and 1982.

As to the rest of the agreements, Turits stresses the conditional nature of aid (export credits) – and this was the case well before Gorbachev came to power – as well as the difficulty of assessing the quality, range and competitiveness of Soviet products in relation to similar products on the world market. In particular, he points out that until 1976 subsidies (included in the price paid by the Soviet Union for Cuban sugar) were well below those the island would have obtained if it had still benefited from the price of US imports. For Turits, this is why precise calculation of Soviet subsidies to Cuba would require the creation of 'an economic model for overall terms of trade, foreign balances, and derived exchange rates'.

Other US authors are similarly inclined, considering that Cuba may have been forced to buy Soviet capital goods 'that are not readily saleable on the world market. ... If that is the case ... what is apparently only a subsidy to Cuba in fact also accrues benefit to the USSR. Who gains the most is impossible to determine.'[84] An old joke from Eastern Europe that is told in Cuba sums up the situation well: a husband tells his wife he has just sold his dog for a thousand dollars. 'Wonderful!', she exclaims, 'but what are you doing with these two ugly cats?' 'Well,' he explains, 'in order to sell our dog for 1,000 dollars, I had to buy the two cats for 500 dollars apiece.'

It is also inappropriate to compare the sugar price paid by the Soviet Union with the price offered on the world market, for sugar sold on the latter only represents a fifth of world production. Whether for political reasons or because of protectionism, most sugar is traded within the framework of quotas whose prices are high. The price paid by the Soviet Union would therefore have to be compared with the average price based on the different markets within the preferential agreements.

Moreover, this aid is not granted in convertible currency – unless it is a small proportion – but is tied to the purchase of Soviet goods. Calculations are made on the basis of official exchange rates, which, according to Turits, can lead to the value of aid in dollars being overestimated. The priority given by the Cubans to sales of sugar on the open market to the detriment of those at a preferential (Soviet) price is a further indication of this. That is why 'any convincing estimate of Soviet subsidies will thus have to evaluate carefully the complex nexus of hard and soft currency transactions, and the context in which Cuba responds to both market and socialist forces.'[85] On the one hand, the importance of subsidies is shown by the key role of sugar and oil in trade: Turits claims that Cuba would not have been able to buy – at the world market price – its oil products through sugar revenues alone, at least in recent years. But the exact value of imports from the Soviet Union on the world market should be determined. This could relativize the importance of Soviet aid which is much more unstable than it appears.

The same author makes a comparison between Cuba and other highly subsidized countries. The difference with Israel is remarkable (in 1985, Israel received the equivalent of three and a half times the annual aid provided by the Soviet Union; also it was in foreign exchange and without conditions), though Israel's unique situation and the aid it receives from the diaspora makes this parallel questionable. More interesting is the case of Puerto Rico, which received at least twice the equivalent amount of aid to Cuba.[86]

All things considered, it is true that in the early years Soviet aid enabled the island to survive in very difficult circumstances, when the violent break with the United States imposed emergency solutions on the revolution. Within the context of an economy dominated by sugar-cane monoculture and the absence of energy resources, a change in partner was needed to ensure the flow of sugar production and guarantee oil deliveries. It is undeniable that the social gains and the 'growth with equality'[87] that has characterized the Cuban Revolution are due to Soviet aid, especially in the first decade. From this perspective, no other country in Latin America bears comparison, in spite of the severe effects on Cuba of the United States' draconian economic blockade.

But the requirements of economic development have made it clear that Cuba, in spite of its trump cards, is paying an economic and political price for Soviet aid. As part of the 'socialist' division of labour within CMEA, the export of sugar in exchange for manufactured imports has made the country highly vulnerable. In the final instance, Turits notes 'the dynamics of the Cuban economy are conditioned by decisions made in Moscow over subsidies and trade patterns ... and the particularly convoluted mechanisms by which the Soviets relay assistance remain far from clear. Why not just give the Cubans the aid, whether in hard or soft currency?'[88] Could the emphasis on sugar production and the various activities related to it not lead to a structural dependence on the Soviet Union and hinder autonomous economic development, given the far from optimistic prospects for sugar production? The precariousness of the Cuban situation stems from its double dependency: on sugar and on the Soviet Union.

Such vulnerability has been revealed by recent data. According to a report of the National Bank of Cuba[89] published in March 1988, imports from the Soviet Union for the first nine months of 1987 fell for the first time in thirty years. This information was provided on 18 January by Cuban officials in Paris for talks on the rescheduling of the debt (with Japan, Great Britain, France, Spain and West Germany).

This fall in imports came at the time of a very difficult economic situation[90] and confirmed the changes that had taken place in Soviet–Cuban relations. It would seem that the Soviet Union had already imposed very tough economic conditions[91] on Cuba in 1986 during the signing of the bilateral agreement of economic and commercial co-operation for the 1986–90 period. And it is significant that the Soviet reduction of purchases from Cuba[92] (–8.2 per cent) coincided with the signing in August 1987 of its first commercial agreement with Honduras, from which it will receive coffee, sugar and palm oil exports. Given Honduras's role in Central America as the military fortress of imperialism, as well as the products it will export (the same as Cuba), the significance of the agreement is far from slight.

Fidel Castro presented his recent demand for the cancellation of the debt as an obvious fact: 'All debts must be abrogated and cancelled. And for reasons of principle, that includes this one, even though it is theoretical.'[93] But there are particular reasons: 'A socialist country in the Third World must develop; it must not only postpone indefinitely – or even eternally – the payment of its debt, but also receive new credits and resources for its development.'[94] But is the debt with the Soviet Union really 'theoretical'?

It is as a leader of the Third World that Fidel Castro addresses the Soviet Union and the 'socialist community', appealing for their solidarity in the struggle for just economic demands. But twenty-five years on, the appeal occasionally takes on the meaning of an implicit denunciation. Che had already denounced in Algiers 'the tacit complicity of the socialist countries with the exploiting countries of the West. ... Foreign trade must not determine politics; on the contary it must be subordinate to a policy of fraternity with peoples.'[95]

In 1987, at the meeting of parties held in Moscow for the seventieth anniversary of the October Revolution, Fidel defended the cause of the Third World ('our Third World') in terms which associated peaceful co-existence with the struggle against the inequalities of development and the 'poverty which kills as many children in the Third World as a hundred nuclear bombs each year'. 'Such inequality must be eliminated if the world is to be free from violent social explosion,' he said.

He denounced the increase in the Third World debt and 'the price differences which have cost [us] hundreds of thousands of millions over the last ten years, and yet they continue to pressure us'. 'We must all take up the defence of a new international economic order as an integral part of our struggle for a durable peace. ... We cannot sit back and fold our arms.' Albeit veiled, the point was clear: nuclear disarmament and peace talks should not leave anyone under any illusions. The super-exploitation of oppressed peoples would continue to cause war and revolutions.

A fateful year, 1986 was to be historical. In Cuba itself, it was marked by growing social and economic difficulties. And internationally, Gorbachev's policy threw the Castro leadership off balance. In response to the deepening of glasnost and perestroika, Fidel Castro introduced the process of 'rectification of errors and negative tendencies'. The significance of this process was to develop as the months went by, but its first effect was to take the bureaucratic apparatus back in hand.

Notes

1. Fidel Castro, speech to the Confederation of Cuban Workers (CTC), 1 February 1987.

2. 1980: 83.6 per cent; 1981: 79.1 per cent; 1982: 77.1 per cent; 1983: 73.8 per cent; in *Comparative Economic Studies*, vol. 27, nos. 1–4, 1985; ibid.,41, vol. 24, no. 4, 1983.

3. Sanguinetty, introduction to the report of the National Bank of Cuba, published by the Cuban-American Foundation, 1985.

4. *Pensamiento Propio*, Managua, January 1987.

5. B. Pollitt, 'El azúcar en la economía cubana, la nueva independencia', in *Pensamiento Propio*, Managua, January 1987.

6. *Le Monde*, 2 and 3 August 1987.

7. *Le Monde*, 26 and 27 June 1989.

8. *Marchés tropicaux*, 23 June 1989.

9. *Marchés tropicaux*, 25 August 1989.

10. Report of the National Bank of Cuba, 1985, p. 24.

11. Marcelo Fernández Font, in *Cuba Socialista*, no. 24, November–December 1986, p. 65.

12. *Marchés tropicaux*, 9 September 1988.

13. *Marchés tropicaux*, 23 June 1989.

14. *Le Monde*, 2 August 1987.

15. An enzyme capable of turning glucose into fructose was discovered at the beginning of the 1960s and gave birth to the sweetener, high fructose corn syrup (HFCS).

16. *Granma*, 21 February 1988.

17. *Marchés tropicaux*, 26 December 1986.

18. *Marchés tropicaux*, 27 November 1987.

19. *Marchés tropicaux*, 23 June 1989.

20. *Granma*, 21 February 1988.

21. *The Economist*, 10 August 1985; *Marchés tropicaux*, 19 December 1986.

22. *Le Monde*, 1 March 1988.

23. *Granma*, 23 November 1986.

24. *Problèmes économiques*, Documentation française, 22 February 1984.

25. *Granma*, 21 February 1988.

26. Ibid.

27. Ibid.

28. Ibid.

29. *Marchés tropicaux*, 26 February 1988. GEPLACEA fears that the rise in sugar prices might cause a sharp increase in production in the different national economies, thus leading to a fall in prices with all its known effects (*Marchés tropicaux*, 24 June 1988).

30. *Le Monde*, 2 June 1987.

31. Perfected by the firm Tate & Lyle.

32. *Marchés tropicaux*, 6 February 1988.

33. *Marchés tropicaux*, 27 November 1987.

34. *Cuba Socialista*, December 1986, p. 104.

35. *Marchés tropicaux*, 11 December 1987 and 29 January 1988.

36. *Africa Analysis*, November 1986.

37. From 1980 to 1986, this cumulative fall reached an average 30 per cent for agricultural primary goods, and 27 per cent for food products. In 1987 the purchasing power of raw materials reached the historical low of the 1930s.

38. *Courrier des pays de l'Est*, Documentation française, November 1987.

39. *Marchés tropicaux*, 24 February 1988.

40. *Marchés tropicaux*, 8 January 1988.

41. Speech at Punta del Este, 6 July 1961, quoted by Jorge Pérez López, 'Two Decades of Cuban Socialism', in *Latin American Research Review*, no. 3, 1983.

42. Sanguinetty, introduction to the report of the National Bank of Cuba, published by the Cuban-American Foundation, 1985.

43. Ibid.
44. *Courrier des pays de l'Est*, Documentation française, November 1987.
45. Ibid.
46. See the debate between C. Mesa-Lago and J. Pérez-López, authors of reports for the US Department of Labor, and Zimbalist and Brundenius, in *Comparative Economic Studies*, nos. 1,3, and 4, 1985.
47. Brundenius, *Cuba, Crecimiento con Equidad*, p. 10.
48. R. Turits. 'Trade, Debt and the Cuban Economy', in *World Development*, vol. 15, no. 1, 1987, p. 168.
49. Ibid., p. 168.
50. In July 1983 Cuba had to buy 1.5 million tonnes of sugar on the open market to fulfil its commitments with the Soviet Union (*World Development*, vol. 15, no. 1, 1987, p. 72).
51. *Granma*, 21 February 1988.
52. *Courrier des pays de l'Est*, Documentation française, November 1987.
53. *World Development*, vol. 15, no. 1, 1987, p. 163.
54. *Granma*, 21 February 1988.
55. National Bank of Cuba, February 1985.
56. Turits, 'Trade, Debt and the Cuban Economy'.
57. Horst Brezinski, 'Cuba's economic ties with the Soviet Union and the CMEA in the mid-eighties'.
58. The way this agreement works is contested; a former Cuban official, now a refugee in Spain, believes that it was not a case of actual re-exports, but of revenues granted in foreign exchange by the Soviet Union equivalent to savings made.
59. National Bank of Cuba, February 1985.
60. *Latin America Weekly Report*, 21 May 1987.
61. Brezinski, 'Cuba's economic ties with the Soviet Union'.
62. *Granma*, 21 February 1988.
63. In 1987 the debt stood at US$5,657 million, according to the report of the National Bank of Cuba (31 December 1987).
64. S. Ekstein, 'Capitalist Constraints on Cuban Socialist Development', in *Comparative Economic Studies*, April 1980.
65. ECLA, in *Courrier des pays de l'Est*, Documentation française, May 1984, p. 58.
66. Report of the National Bank of Cuba, February 1985.
67. A part of the debt with the Soviet Union is payable in foreign exchange, but the amount is believed to be very limited.
68. 'La dette cubaine envers l'Ouest', in *Courrier des pays de l'Est*, Documentation française, May 1984.
69. *Caribbean Report*, February 1988.
70. *Financial Times*, 29 October 1986.
71. Only capital was to be repaid.
72. Report of the National Bank of Cuba, 1985.
73. *Le Monde*, 7 July 1987; *Latin America Weekly Report*, 25 June 1987.
74. *Courrier des pays de l'Est*, Documentation française, May 1987, p. 40.
75. *Caribbean Report*, 2 October 1986. *Latin America Weekly Report*, 11 September 1986.
76. Ibid.
77. *Problèmes d'Amérique latine*, Documentation française, April 1982.
78. Ibid.
79. Acciaris, in *Courrier des pays de l'Est*, Documentation française, May 1984.
80. *Le Monde*, November 1985.
81. Interview with *Veja*, Brazil, 18 March 1987.
82. Edquist, in *World Development*, vol. 15, no. 1, 1987.
83. Turits. 'Trade, Debt and the Cuban Economy'.
84. Theriot and Matheson, 'Soviet Economic Relations with non-European CMEA: Cuba, Vietnam, Mongolia', in *World Development*, vol. 15, no. 1, 1987, p. 173.
85. Turits. 'Trade, Debt and the Cuban Economy', p. 174.

86. Ibid., p. 176.
87. Brundenius, *Cuba, Crecimiento con Equidad*.
88. Turits. 'Trade, Debt and the Cuban Economy', p. 177.
89. *Herald Tribune*, 17 March 1988.
90. Investments fell by 30 per cent.
91. *El País*, 15 August 1986.
92. *Courrier des pays de l'Est*, Documentation française, May 1987.
93. *El País*, 25 September 1987.
94. *Le Monde*, 25 September 1987.
95. Ernesto Che Guevara, *Ecrits d'un révolutionnaire*, pp. 165–6.

2

Economic Reforms and their Consequences

The planned target of 10 million tonnes of sugar for 1970 was not achieved, in spite of huge efforts and the cost in socio-economic tension. This setback was to place in question the mode of economic organization in the 1966–70 period, which was from then on characterized as 'idealistic and voluntaristic'[1] by Fidel Castro. A new stage began: a different economic policy was to be applied in the second decade of the revolution. Following the joining of Comecon in 1972, this policy was aimed at a more thorough reorganization of planning under the auspices of the Central Planning Board (JUCEPLAN), thus bringing an end to the anarchy of the 'special plans', decided on the basis of Fidel Castro's chaotic urges. The target of a 10-million-tonne sugar harvest had been the culmination of such bouts of voluntarism. The main thrust of this move was inspired by the reforms advocated by the Libermann school in the Soviet Union around 1965, as well as the variations being implemented in the Hungarian economy.[2]

With the First PCC Congress in 1975, the first five-year plan got underway, as well as a new system of management. Measures allowing for partial decentralization aimed to give the organs of people's power a limited degree of responsibility in the management of services and local activities.

The introduction of the System of Economic Management and Planning (SDPE) was carried out amid general references to the law of value and 'monetary-market relations' as regulators of production. The increased autonomy of enterprises and the personal responsibility of their managers; the emphasis on profitability and the development of material incentives; the priority given to the fight against absenteeism; and the promulgation of a law on compulsory work in 1971 (which contrasted remarkably with the place given to voluntary work during the time of Che): all marked a break with the undoubtedly voluntaristic, but egalitarian approach of the 1960s.

The implementation and effects of this process of economic reform have been one of the causes of current social tensions and the present crisis. The 'process of rectification of errors and negative tendencies' begun in 1986 was supposed to correct the economic, social and political effects of reform – increased inequality, sectoral tensions and contradictions, the development of corruption and privileges, growth in bureaucracy – as well as their repercussions on the working class: cynicism and absenteeism, the development of a black market and a fall in labour productivity.

But it was only in 1986 that this situation was violently and publicly denounced, on the occasion of the twenty-fifth anniversary of the victory over imperialism at Playa Girón and at a time when Gorbachev was launching a new course, both for the Soviet Union and internationally. Since then, there has been no end to the scope of this campaign, both in the party (it was at the root of the report of the Third Congress) and in the mass organizations. It has led to significant upheaval and confrontation in the ruling apparatus.

The introduction of the SDPE took the form of wage reform, opening up free farmers' markets, liberalizing particular private activities (commerce, crafts and services), generalizing private-property housing, as well as spreading certain opportunities for the purchase, sale, lease and decentralization of state enterprises: the number of such enterprises went up from 300 in 1968 to 3,000 in 1979.[3] The considerable growth in management personnel that took place as a result had a major effect on the composition of the state apparatus. According to a director of the Centre for Studies on the Americas, Martínez Heredia, 'the number of bureaucrats went up two and a half times between 1973 and 1984'.[4] A significant number of the technocrats subsequently challenged by Fidel Castro came from this period.

Under the SDPE's plans, one part of an enterprise's profits would be paid into the state budget and another used for the repayment of loans, while the third would be spent on social security payments, the rest going on the stimulation of economic activity. This latter portion was to be divided into three parts: the first would be for the various bonuses and monetary incentives to be paid individually to the workers and managers; the second would be for collective needs (crèches, restaurants etc.); and the third for the acquisition of equipment needed to modernize the enterprise. Emphasis was placed on the profitability and efficiency of the enterprise, with the establishment of a set of indicators by which to assess its performance – sometimes with quite ludicrous results.[5] In terms of its internal functioning, the state enterprise would be accountable to a manager appointed by higher authorities, aided by a management council with trade union participation.

Priority was henceforth given to the individualization of wages, and cuts were made in social services. To the detriment of the most popular aspirations, use was made of the prices weapon; and money and market mechanisms, as well as economic profitability, were developed. This gave rise to a greater social stratification and the growth of inequalities. Yet it is precisely the spectacular reduction in social inequalities, with the poorest groups benefiting from increases in the lowest wages, full employment and free social services (education, health and housing), which has turned Cuba into the country with the most extraordinary and egalitarian social gains in Latin America.[6]

Recognized by all, this fact has been a key element in popular support for the regime in a country located ninety miles from the United States. The Cuban people have so far triumphed against all forms of imperialist aggression, defending not just national dignity but unprecedented social gains. It is therefore not suprising that the reemergence of inequalities should weaken the popular support on which the leadership has always been able to rely; and this social base of support has been crucial not only to confronting imperialism, but also to the influence of, and support for, the Cuban Revolution in Latin America.

Wage Reform

In 1973 the thirteenth congress of the Confederation of Cuban Workers (CTC) had rejected 'petit-bourgeois egalitarianism' and reasserted the value of individual material incentives linked to productivity. In June 1980 such views were reinforced by the wage reform that came into force. Despite a 27 per cent increase for agricultural workers and the lower paid, the wage range was widened. Indeed, from then on wages were adjusted through a system of various bonuses, linked to the productivity of the enterprise and differentiated according to the work sector and its importance. Following the unsuccessful labour-productivity result of 1979 (0.8 per cent growth instead of the planned 4 per cent[7]), the links between productivity and wages were further reinforced: an enterprise could now distribute a part of its profits to workers, whether in the form of money or consumer durables.

If Cuban statements are to be believed, 1979–80 salary differentials were quite narrow. The remuneration of highly qualified technicians and managers had fallen in relation to 1965. This assessment, however, has been challenged, contradicted in fact, from several quarters. According to the economist Carmelo Mesa-Lago, the tendency since the 1960s has been for an increase in wage differentials.[8] As is shown in table 12, there was a great difference between the average wage of a middle-level employee and that of an agricultural worker on a state farm or an industrial worker, with the former earning twice as much as the latter, in spite of infinitely easier working conditions. (This was also to lead to a significant expansion of administrative personnel.) The advantages enjoyed by state employees must be added: housing priority, use of a state car, trips abroad, extra funds in foreign exchange, access to rationed goods, and so on.

Table 12 Estimated Average Monthly Wages in Cuba 1975–79 (pesos)

Activity	*Salary*	*Activity*	*Salary*
Agriculture	**128**	**Commerce**	122
Worker on state farm	80–100	Tourism	117
Private farmer (tobacco)	630	Small business	126
Cane-cutter	800		
Fisher	151		
Fisher (private co-op)	500–600	**Services**	**121**
		Cleaning lady	75–80
Industry	**136**	Child-minder	98
Tobacco	109	Cook in small hotel	140
Lighting	132		
Food	138	**Education**	**136**
Construction	143	School-teacher	100–190
Sugar	152	Head-teacher	230–300
Mining	153	Academic	325–500
Oil	166		
Power stations	188		
Metallurgical industry	190	**Culture**	**167**
Chemistry	198	Famous musician	700
Electrician	120–220		
Cemeteries	100–250	**Health**	**127**
Engineer	300–400	Laboratory assistant	150
Highly qualified technician	700–999	Doctor	300–600
		Bureaucracy	
Transport	**162**	Middle-level employee	200–300
Merchant navy	177		
Aviation	180	Cabinet minister	700

Source: C. Mesa-Lago, *La economía en Cuba socialista, 1984*.

The situation was grave in 1987. The number of administrative employees had gone from 90,000 to 248,000 in the space of ten years and of managerial personnel from 148,000 to 250,000.[9] Such distortions, due to the new wage structure, had severe effects on production. The journal *Juventud Rebelde*[10] mentioned that 50 per cent of posts at the Vanguardia Socialista and Enrique Varona mechanical iron and steel factories were workers involved in production, and the other 50 per cent administrative or technical posts. The situation was such that factories lacked sufficient workers to cover all shifts, and an appeal had to be made to the conscience of young engineers for them to come and work in production.

The opportunity given for enterprise managers to have a certain leeway in the use of resources and in fixing work norms had the effect of doubling, and, indeed, sometimes tripling, the basic wage through bonuses and productivity incentives.

> Out of 1,200,000 workers paid according to productivity, almost 400,000 have a 130 per cent achievement rate. ... The payment of bonuses was often unrelated to extra efforts by the workers. ... In order to hide the over-achievement of targets, enterprises would give a working time higher than actually carried out in their statements. ... Profits have occasionally been redistributed to workers in order to hide particularly high wages, or wage rises have been spread over a longer period.[11]

The links established between the profitability of enterprises, or of particular sectors, and wages produced a staff surplus in some workplaces at the expense of others, thus disrupting production and increasing costs. The low wages in agriculture resulted in a major shortage of labour in agricultural co-operatives[12] where the working day is estimated at four to five hours a day for an average twenty days a month.[13]

Wage rises did not correspond to actual profitability. In Pinar del Río province alone, for example, 53.7 per cent of enterprises were stated in 1987 as being profitable;[14] that is a lower percentage than in 1985 and one which did not square with the rises granted. Problems of absenteeism and carelessness at work worsened. The 1980 reforms, which were precisely aimed at linking wage rises to increased work productivity, led to wage differentials without increased productivity. The other aim – to improve the distribution of the workforce by attracting workers to the most crucial regions and sectors for economic development – also failed. Around 70 per cent of the population is urban and there is a shortage of labour in agriculture.

There have been aberrations and flagrant injustices: workers at the Mambisa enterprise, for example, who transport goods between different

Cuban ports, receive part of their wages in foreign exchange.[15] When one is aware of what the shortage of foreign exchange represents for the Cuban economy, it is easy to imagine the corruption that such dealings can engender.

The growth in wage inequality between workers and management (see table 13) has had negative effects on mass mobilization. It has encouraged a lack of respect for work standards and all kinds of violations of the legislation in force. Workers, already stripped of the right to control production, have often responded by changing jobs irrespective of industrial priorities.

Table 13 New Wage Scale following the 1980 Reforms (pesos)

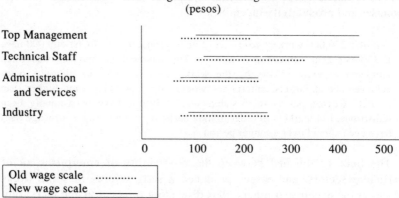

Top Management

Technical Staff

Administration and Services

Industry

0 100 200 300 400 500

Old wage scale ....

New wage scale ______

Source: *Latin America Regional Reports Caribbean*, 9 May 1980.

Following the conclusions of the Fifty-Third Plenum of the CTC, Fidel Castro made a critical assessment of the situation, challenging the persistence of very low wages, of 'less than 100 pesos a month' for 100,000–150,000 workers. Similarly, he said:

> Agriculture was expected to work with ridiculous wages in a social system where men and women have a whole range of job opportunities. Who was going to farm the land ... for a ridiculous wage? In this process of rectification, the lowest agricultural wages have been increased 40 per cent, in the same way as there have been increases in the hospitals for those who are not doctors or nurses, but who wash and clean the premises. ... There is a will for social justice in this process: the tendency to increase the highest salaries, to allow certain people to earn up to 1,000 pesos when their work did not deserve it and

when a modest worker was earning 100, 102 or 103 pesos, has been reversed.[16]

In 1987 rises were given to 186,000 workers who would now have a minimum wage of 100 pesos,[17] and then to 200,000 workers (group number two in the wage scale), whose basic wage rose from 100 to 110 pesos.[18]

But wage rises for the most disadvantaged social groups have had little effect on the gap in real incomes, as income inequalities do not just come from the size of the wage scale: far from it. Fidel Castro has identified 50,000 peso incomes in sectors where private initiative had been authorized (agriculture, artistic work). While private peasant landowners had lost 60 per cent of their income in the 1960s, at the time of the great economic debate instigated by Che, they were now part of the most privileged groups.[19]

The Free Farmers' Markets

Free farmers' markets were legalized in 1980, allowing private farmers to sell off their agricultural surpluses (except meat, tobacco and coffee) once they had met their obligations to the state. The prices, fixed on a supply and demand basis, were much higher than those of subsidized products, but lower than those on the black market. They coexisted with another distribution system, the parallel state markets (MPE). This offered fixed prices, according to the law of supply and demand, for both consumer goods and national and foreign food products that were either unattainable or available only in small quantity under the state rationing system. The parallel markets had been introduced to fight the black market and to encourage effort at work.

The creation of free markets was a response to the desire to stimulate private agricultural production by raising the prices paid by state purchasing bodies, the aim being to overcome supply dificulties and to correct the effects of the previous policy in the countryside. In 1970 several areas of land, notably those devoted to the rearing of livestock, were allocated to the planting of sugar-cane in order to meet the 10-million-tonne sugar target. The result was disastrous for essential agricultural products: milk and meat. Farmers were forced to produce cane in return for particular economic subsidies, but were left with just a plot of land for their own subsistence. This sparked considerable resistance,[20] in spite of the special plans devised by Fidel Castro for the cultivation of basic foods.

Pressure was then exerted on private-sector farmers to sell their produce to the state for low prices. They were encouraged to give up their land to the public sector in order to work part-time on state farms. The leasing of private-sector lands by the state in order to increase land cultivated for sugar was gradually replaced by a reduction in the rents paid:[21] they were fixed below the minimum level so as to encourage farmers not only to surrender their land to the state, but also to work for the latter. Thus, by restricting the activities of small farmers and by dispossessing workers employed on state farms of their individual plots, the government sacrificed the production and profits that could have been obtained in the short term on individual units for the maximum production befitting an economy geared to exports. The last independent smallholders had preferred to produce for the internal market rather than the external market, since producing fruit and vegetables for the internal market did not require machinery and they made more profit from it. (This was particularly due to the black market which had developed as soon as the government forced small farmers to sell their produce at a low price to state purchasing bodies.)

The result of these measures was to reduce the confidence of the small farmers in the revolution, all the so more because the industrial products they needed were not available. The supply of food was very difficult during this period and it is known that protests took place (notably at the Santiago carnival). This was to lead to a change of agricultural policy from the mid-1970s. The prices paid by state purchasing bodies rose; the pressure on farmers to work on state farms dropped; emphasis was placed on the creation of production co-operatives; and finally, in May 1980, authorization was granted for farmers to sell their agricultural surpluses. At the same time, the aim was to increase farmers' incomes in order to eliminate the consequences of the previous period, improve the distribution of food products and wipe out the black market. But prices rose quickly and, from 1982, tensions emerged, leading to the arrest of certain sellers and the requisition of produce at exorbitant prices.[22]

While the law only allowed farmers to sell their output in their local area, sellers could market produce without any controls across the whole island, through middlemen. The latter, nicknamed the 'bandits of Rio Frio' by the people (after the name of a television programme), pocketed handsome rewards; in order to mask the size of the profits made, they helped disguise the quantities sold. But they were indispensable in so far as they helped the farmers avoid wasting huge amounts of time because of transport difficulties. In such circumstances, excessive prices did not solve supply problems, except for particular consumers, and farmers' incomes increased rapidly. Even before the opening of the free market, certain private producers could already make annual profits of between 10,000 and 20,000 pesos.[23] This was why the congress of the National

Association of Small Farmers (ANAP) in 1977 proposed a tax on private co-operatives, in order to reduce the considerable income differentials with farmers working on state farms.

By May 1986, farmers' growing wealth had reached exorbitant levels. Fidel Castro quoted the case of garlic growers with an income of 50,000 pesos.[24] A stratum of rich farmers began to emerge, aided by powerful commercial middlemen and the corruption of local administrators. Protests against the development of this 'new class' began to grow and were to lead to the end of the free markets. 'It was as if the revolution had a new slogan: not "Workers unite", but "Workers and peasants get rich" ', declared Fidel Castro, paraphrasing Bukharin. With the end of the free markets, the state was from then on to buy the co-operatives' above-quota production at dearer prices, so as not to reduce incentives for agricultural production. The parallel markets (controlled by the state) were supposed to fill any gap in distribution left by rationing. In practice, it would appear that the black market spread, as did the rise in prices. The elimination of the free markets was a challenge for the state distribution system. The most difficult problems were transport and the capacity to store stocks in order to guarantee satisfactory distribution.

Although the measures taken met with general approval, at least at the time of the ANAP congress in June 1986,[25] the difficulties remain far from solved. Nevertheless, it would seem that the social tensions and contradictions caused by the existence of the free markets had made their elimination inevitable. The parallel markets were increasingly less well supplied;[26] the number of small farmers rejoining agricultural co-operatives fell; rural divisions worsened; and social inequalities sparked several popular protests. 'The people bought on the free market and that did not not stop them regarding the farmers as thieves. The free market has created a division between the farmers and the rest of the population.'[27]

In his speech to the second meeting of production co-operatives, Fidel Castro stressed the need to fight against 'neo-capitalist elements': 'The free market was hindering the development of co-operatives and was arousing the hostility of the farmers. ... If an individual with a hectare of garlic can earn 50,000 pesos in a year, how is he to be expected to rejoin a co-operative?'[28] In the debate over the economic priorities of agriculture, as well as over the property structure stemming from the agrarian reforms decided by the revolution, this is one of the key questions. The agrarian structure is very different from that of Eastern Europe, in that there is far less private property. The agricultural output of farmers, whether working the land as individuals or in co-operatives, does not exceed 20 per cent of total production. The bulk of agricultural production destined for consumption or for export has come from state concerns where mechanization is highly advanced. Nevertheless, although most land was nationalized, the second agrarian reform law limited property to 65 hectares and many farmers 'have 5, 10, 15, indeed 65 hectares, a sizeable difference from the situation in other socialist countries, as a farmer with 20 hectares can become very rich. ... And what happened? The farmer stopped selling his produce to the state, in spite of the resources he received from the latter, to sell it as he pleased at a higher price. As a result, the development of the co-operative movement essential to economic life was held back.'[29]

Since the mid-1970s the emphasis has been on the development of agricultural co-operatives. In 1980, 11 per cent of lands were organized as co-operatives; and at the time of the national meeting of production co-operatives in May 1988, 61.3 per cent of lands belonging to small farmers had been integrated. Between 1986 (when the free markets ended) and 1987, the total area of co-operatives rose by 41,633 hectares, and currently there are 1,418 production co-operatives bringing together 69,604 farmers. Credits for the purchase of machines and equipment have increased considerably.[30] With certain crops, the importance of the co-operative and private sector is decisive. In 1984 it produced 75 per cent of the tobacco crop, 40 per cent of the coffee crop, 65 per cent of the cocoa crop, 63 per cent of vegetables, 52 per cent of bananas, 16 per cent of citrus fruits and 10 per cent of cereals.[31]

These figures highlight the problem the government ran up against when small farmer sugar production began to fall in 1984. This was due to inadequate state prices for sugar cane[32] and the possibility of selling alternative produce on the free markets: the enormous profits to be made from the possession of a plot of land delayed the process of the farmers' 'co-operativization'. In 1986 smallholders were granted subsidies on the condition that they increased the area of land cultivated and, above all, that they retained the same area for sugar-cane as in 1984. Such measures were inadequate, and it was at this point that the decision was taken to eliminate the alternative outlets given to the farmers by abolishing the free markets. The economic background to the decision was to check the fall in sugar production, as well as the delay in the development of co-operatives. Then came the arguments on social grounds: the need to take measures 'against the kulaks subsisting here – to use a historical term – for there are a few of them ... to put an end to all forms of absentee property-owning [there had been instances of land being rented out], to put an end to all undue or incorrect use of land ownership'. Taking advantage of the material support afforded by the state, the farmers had been able to increase production and get rich. A shortage of labour began to occur in the co-operatives, and in 1985 30 per cent of the latter were judged to be non-profitable. In addition to social divisions in the countryside there was the discontent of those in the towns who could not afford expensive produce. The government decided to replace an abundance rationed by the pocket with a shortage that would be less inegalitarian.

The Legalization of Particular Private Activities

The legalization of particular private activities (in the small-scale craft industry, repair services and the quite different area of the arts) was brought about in 1976 to overcome public-sector shortages in domestic services or indispensable mechanical repairs. Such activities were allowed on payment of a licence fee. But the most important decision was the approval by the National Assembly in 1984 of a housing law, allowing tenants to become house-owners from 1 July 1985. The law encouraged construction by the population itself, the aim being to compensate for the housing shortage and to foster individual responsibility for the upkeep of property. It also authorized, in particular circumstances, the letting of houses or rooms. The ownership of two flats per person, however, was banned, except in particular cases in agriculture.

Of the 37,000 flats erected in 1984, half were built by state enterprises and the other half by individuals, co-operatives or enterprises not belonging to the construction sector. Also completed were 80,000 buildings of various kinds which did not meet state standards.[33] At the same time, large quantities of construction materials began to be stolen from public enterprises, and workplace absenteeism became generalized. Instances of corruption, the theft of materials from enterprises and the unauthorized use of machinery – all within a context of falling imports – led to the abolition in 1986 of private construction and related activities, as well as to the banning of flat and private-house sales. New legislation was introduced limiting property inheritance and the letting of rooms.[34]

Economically, these measures quickly produced an overall decline in construction, with local people's power organizations building 25,041 houses instead of 34,085 as planned.[35] To make up for this fall, the leadership of the Cuban Communist Party decided to reactivate the system of microbrigades. Released by their enterprises from which they continued to draw their wages, groups of workers would build flats (half for themselves and half for the state) and carry out various social works. Meanwhile their work in production would be taken on by the rest of the staff in the enterprise, thus allowing the rationalization of surplus workforce. Spectacular success stories did occur in particular cases (the building of crèches, for example), and were celebrated by the Cuban press. But the acuteness of the housing crisis, particularly affected by the fall in imports, meant that the results were not adequate.

Once again, competition between the private and the public sector took place to the detriment of the latter, with private activity combining the unauthorized use of public materials with the private initiative of buyers. The perverse effects of the reform were also felt in terms of their neutralization of social incentives in several areas. For example, the prospect of receiving a good flat by being a member of an agricultural co-operative was no longer that attractive to farmers. As Fidel Castro pointed out:

> Someone with an annual income of 50,000 pesos [thanks to the free market] can get cement anyway; or rather he bribes someone with cement at the co-operative – a storeman, a lorry driver transporting it, or a watchman on a building site. ... As to the bureaucrats with good flats, they don't care that there might be hundreds of thousands of people living badly or tens of thousands living in unhealthy houses. ... Under the circumstances they don't care that the number of flats recently built in Havana was between 4,000 and 5,000 a year. Some of these go to army officers carrying out difficult assignments. ... That leaves 4,000. But 4,000 become dilapidated each year. So how many does that leave for the workers?[36]

The halt of private construction (as with the ending of the free market) was thus an attempt to prevent the formation of a stratum of rich house-owners and prosperous land speculators, aimed at putting an end to competition between private activity and the public sector. Unfortunately, the latter's inability to resolve the numerous problems in the construction sector has not eliminated the social tensions arising from the housing crisis. In terms of social gains, it is in this area that delays have been the greatest. Such was the demand that workers pressured for the right to build on an individual basis. And it is in this area that official privileges have been the most conspicuous. Fidel Castro devoted his 26 July speech to the issue in 1987.

The offensive against the private sector had contradictory results. On the one hand, it satisfied the very strong egalitarian aspirations of the regime's base of social support. The privatization of flat construction had highlighted income differentials; goods had been available, but at exorbitant prices; and once again the dilemma of rationing either through the pocket or through the *libreta* (rationing book) had reappeared. But on the other hand, the microbrigades were unable to provide a solution for the housing problem, in spite of their efficiency.

Craft activities were suppressed, but within certain limits. Repair work such as joinery, plumbing, locksmithing or dressmaking was authorized through the award of a licence. Fifty thousand workers were registered with a licence – approximately one per cent of the active population. This was judged to be a high proportion by C. Andana, ideology secretary of the PCC's Central Committee.[37] Carlos Aldana, while acknowledging the complaints of consumers expressed in *Juventud Rebelde* (over the shortage of standard articles such as clothes, shoes, furniture and various household goods), stressed that private activity was not a solution. He based his opinion on the failure of the socialist countries to avoid crises and conflicts, in spite of their attempts to coexist with small traders and to give considerable space to the private sector.

An Abortive Attempt at Price Reform

Introduced as part of the SDPE, an attempt at reform in food prices was to lead from 1982 to strong discontent. The first effect of the reform, decided in January 1981 and announced in December, was an increase in restaurant, bar and café prices. Much frequented because of the frugality of meals subject to the constraints of rationing, these establishments (or at least some of them) charged relatively affordable prices, in order to soak up surplus monetary liquidity.

According to the *1984 Statistical Yearbook of Cuba*[38] the increase forecast was between 10 and 30 per cent, but in most cases prices doubled. Rationed and subsidized items (milk, rice, beans, oil, meat, chicken, clothes, soap, cigarettes, petrol) were also affected by the increases.[39] The cost of these goods was still moderate in that the previous subsidized prices had been very low; but as the first rise since 1962, it was significant. Food prices went up between 10 and 12 per cent;[40] and subsidies, while maintained, were at a lower level. The reform was also to remove what government officials called 'unjustified gratuities': free items for schoolchildren, free museum tickets, free meals and snacks at work, schools and crèches, public services at derisory prices, etc.

For Cuban economists, the aim of the price reform was to check the pressure from excess liquidity in relation to available goods and services. It was based on a more 'realistic' vision of monetary–market relations during the period of transition and broke with the 1967–70 period described as 'idealist'.[41] Indeed, the reform went hand in hand with the reform of wages. With the aim of increasing labour productivity, priority was given to material incentives and the reduction of government subsidies.

The increases provoked a storm of protests which were relayed back, particularly by the trade unions, to the Provincial Assembly of Havana. The increases were suspended and two ministerial officials – the Minister of Foreign Trade, Serafin F. Rodríguez, and the chairman of the Prices Committee, Santiago R. Hernández – 'resigned', both judged to have committed 'serious errors'.

Well before the start of the process of rectification, the incident simultaneously bore witness not only to the problems linked to the introduction of the SDPE and the economic reforms, but also to the effectiveness of the popular response and its ability to mobilize. It was an alarm signal for the ruling group, for this was not yet a period of crisis and the level of imports was still high.

In an underdeveloped country so dependent on its external resources, stimulating labour productivity through the offer of consumer goods came up against major difficulties. This was underlined by a popular joke: Cubans had enough paper money to cover the walls of their flats.

What was true in the 1970s and in 1981 remains the case today when the burden of the debt, as well as the shortage of foreign exchange and fresh credits, have led to a sharp fall in imports. Indeed, the promotion of a particular form of private consumption requires a higher level of imports. And in the present situation that means squaring the circle. The Cuban leadership has frequently emphasized the workers' insufficient 'economic awareness'. Absenteeism and lack of enthusiasm at work stand in contrast to the maintenance of a strong capacity for mobilization when it comes to defending the revolution; or even reaffirming their support for the revolution without any material reward. It was this situation that was to justify, for Fidel Castro, the process undertaken in 1986. The reasons stemming from the distinctive features of the Cuban process must also be added: by highlighting injustices and privileges, the reforms went against the population's highly egalitarian aspirations and sensibilities. Injustices and privileges existed in spite of the reforms, but it was the latter which brought them to light. Moreover, rightly or wrongly, the majority of workers felt that the central core around Fidel Castro did not benefit from them. They blamed and held responsible the technocrats and the middle management strata for errors and dislocations – harsh and public criticisms that Fidel Castro successfully used to his advantage.

The Topicality of the Great Economic Debate of the 1960s

Begun with Che more than twenty years ago, the debate over the law of value, the relationship between state planning and the market, the autonomy of enterprises and the form of wage distribution, has today sprung back to life, induced by the process of rectification. Fidel Castro today openly invokes the positions defended by Che before his final departure from Cuba (officially in 1965, though it is known that he subsequently returned to Cuba for several months[42] to write *Socialism and Man,* a political and economic synthesis of the positions – minority positions – he defended before his departure).

It is necessary to put the record straight on this point. In official texts – particularly since the turning point of the First Congress in 1975 – criticisms of 'idealism', 'voluntarism' and 'extremism' (the terms used to describe the period when priority was given to moral incentives) generally cover the whole of the decade 1960–70, and thus lump together Che's stance between 1963 and 1965 with the practice of the so-called 'revolutionary offensive' between 1967 and 1970. These later years were characterized by an unbridled voluntarism in the area of wages, as well as the extension of the no-charge principle in particular services. Seen as part of an accelerated march to communism, such measures were not advocated by Che who intended, among other things, to foster professional training through a certain degree of wage hierarchy.

This period was marked by a dismantling of central planning in favour of the special plans advanced by Fidel, the aim being to compensate for the misuse of land and to reach the voluntaristic target of 10 million tonnes of sugar. These special plans were intended to protect consumption of essential agricultural products, suddenly under threat from extensive cane cultivation. Che had come out against such a drive to specialization (he did not come to be minister for industry by chance) and had always supported a diversification of the economy to reduce dependency on cane monoculture. He was a fervent defender of centralized (yet thorough) planning, an approach he took in the setting up of his ministry and which was at total variance with the practice followed in the period 1967–70 when 'Cuba could no longer be considered a centrally planned economy'.[43] Che's opposition to the so-called 'economic calculation' system (which meant enterprises having financial autonomy) did not lead to any lax accounting. On the contrary, he demanded precise accounts for industrial enterprises and a meticulous control of production costs, avoiding the bureaucratic pitfalls of which he was aware. It was public knowledge that the Ministry of Industry was the best organized in Cuba.

> If there was one thing Che paid absolute attention to, it was accountancy and the analysis, cent for cent, of expenses and costs. Che saw the construction of socialism and the management of the economy as nothing less than proper organization, efficient control and strict accounting. He could not conceive development without increasing labour productivity. He even studied mathematics to improve control of the economy and measure its efficiency. Che used to dream of using information technology to gauge economic efficiency under socialism and saw this as essential.[44]

He certainly would not have approved of the brusque nationalization of small shopowners in 1967. He declared to *Hoy* in 1963 that there was no need to 'centralize small shops and coffee stalls ... whose management would lead to serious administrative problems'. Only the owners of small- and medium-sized enterprises who were leaving the country should be expropriated.

The economic debate in the 1960s on the problems of the transition to socialism was highly significant. First, because it was a public and contentious debate between Cuban leaders (the only one in this case) on theoretical issues, but whose political significance was immediate. Also because it was a debate on the problems of the transition to socialism that was more topical than ever. As Ernest Mandel pointed out (a participant in the discussion whose contributions were published in the magazine edited by Che)[45] the controversy related to four issues. Two were of a theoretical nature: the exact role of the law of value during the transition period and the nature of the means of production (is or is it not a question of producing goods?); and two were of a political and economic nature: the organization of enterprises and the centralization of their management, and the role of material and moral incentives in the construction of socialism in an underdeveloped economy. Those emphasizing the regulating role of the law of value gave a major place to market mechanisms in the planned economy, calling for considerable financial autonomy in enterprises and a greater role for bonuses and material incentives. Che and his fellow supporters, defending the budgetary system (the financing of industrial enterprises through the national budget exercising financial control at the level of the Ministry of Industries and Finances), argued that centralized management was better suited to Cuban reality: the small number of enterprises and managers, the existence of sufficiently developed means of telecommunication and, above all, the need for strict control of the resource economy. According to the Finance Minister of the time, who was a fervent supporter of Che:

> In this system, the principle of commercial performance in the state sphere is strictly formal and is governed by the plan, merely in order to allow economic calculation, accounting and financial control, etc. But it will never manage to govern, in a fetishistic way, the social content of production. For as the enterprise does not have its own capital independent from the state, it does not accumulate or retain, in its own funds, the proceeds from production and returns on its costs. In the budgetary system, buying and selling only occur where the state sells to other forms of property.[46]

Che's opponents criticized this approach on the grounds that necessary financial discipline was compromised by the fact that 'the expenses of those enterprises are covered, and for them that means bringing in nothing for the state'.[47] In order to force enterprises to be profitable, they thus felt that they should be granted financial autonomy and subjected to strict economic criteria. This obviously meant a much greater use of material incentives, mainly by interesting managers and workers in increasing labour productivity and enterprise profitability.

Recalling this debate is useful in many ways, not just to highlight the validity of Che's theoretical approach – one of the few Third World leaders in power to have dealt in Marxist terms with the problems of transition in an underdeveloped economy – but also because the subsequent practical experience sheds further light on the discussion.

Che put forward three considerations that were fundamental in his view. First, he asserted that 'communism is an objective of humanity that can only be achieved consciously; education and the elimination of the defects of the old system in people's conscience are of huge importance, not forgetting, of course, that such a society can never be achieved without simultaneous progress in production.'[48] Secondly, he considered that the financial autonomy of enterprises (which he compared with self-management) ran the risk of questioning national priorities to the benefit of sectoral choices, and also of increasing the autonomy of managers in terms of investment. And finally, he was afraid of the effects of basing the organization of work on financial inducements: 'One goes back to the theory of the market. ... The whole organization of work relies on material incentives ... and it is the managers who always earn more. One should look at the last plan in the German Democratic Republic with the importance that management takes on, or rather the remuneration of the managers.'[49] It is Che's anti-bureaucratic conscience that is speaking, even though it is true that he had an incomplete understanding of socialist democracy. His defence of centralized economic planning against the extension of market categories left aside the crucial political question: who decides, how are key production decisions to be taken, and who is in control?

In the struggle against bureaucracy – whether within the framework of hyper-centralized planning, the extension of market mechanisms or, as in Cuba, a combination of both – Che relied on the revolutionary example, training and awareness of the leaders in particular. He stressed the role of moral incentives, conceived as collective and social incentives, in avoiding the disintegrative effects that generalized competition between workers would have on the awareness of the masses. From his ministry he promoted a reorganization of the wage system based on the setting of work norms. In this system, the setting of wages was based on an assessment of qualifications and of jobs. A portion of wages varied according to productivity; and in order to foster aspirations to professional development, increases granted would not go above the amount corresponding to the highest qualification. Five years after the seizure of power, the average level of schooling was at best elementary and, as recounted by the great Cuban writer Jésus Díaz,[50] it was not rare to see young people who were practically illiterate being catapulted overnight to the management of agricultural or industrial enterprises.

We are thus a long way from the caricatures of Che's positions, although subsequent events were to confirm his fears. After 1966 (when Che was already in Bolivia) economic measures were indeed taken – the famous 'revolutionary offensive' – that he had never proposed, not to mention the wave of repression at that time. With the updating of economic debate, this has been recognized for the first time: articles published in Cuba have corrected previous confusions and distortions; a book on Che's economic thought which took several years of preparation has been given an award.[51]

Another Cuban economist, Alexis Codina Jiménez, clearly recalls that the most unrealistic measures were decided from 1967 onwards: the elimination of bonuses and overtime payments. Work was no longer rewarded according to difficulty or actual results and overtime hours became 'conscience time'. The organization of work patterns advocated by Che was abandoned. It was also at this time that the total abolition of rent, free use of telephones and other measures were decided. The context of these events was the preparation of the 10-million-tonne *zafra* (sugar harvest). The failure to achieve this goal, as well as the disappearance of practically any planning and the disastrous results of non-sugar production, was to lead to a deterioration in the internal economic situation; and to a serious demoralization, which caused a significant drop in labour productivity and a growth in absenteeism.

The seriousness of the economic and political crisis as well as the loss of credibility of Fidel Castro (who offered his resignation) explain the turning point of the 1970s. In 1975, at the time of the First PCC Congress, an assessment of the period was made which favoured a complete reorientation along Soviet lines and which was totally opposed to Che's approach. Schools and universities were flooded with 'orthodox' manuals of political economy. It was only in 1987, at the time of the twentieth anniversary of Che's death, that Fidel Castro, by way of self-criticism, was to declare: 'Some of Che's ideas were, for a time, misinterpreted and badly introduced. It is true that no attempt was ever seriously made to put them into practice, and that for a while ideas diametrically opposed to Che's economic thought were spread.'[52]

The self-criticism was clear enough not to leave any ambiguity, especially when Fidel paid emotive homage to Che's economic thought in the same speech:

> My modest request on this twentieth anniversary is for Che's economic thought to be known; for it to be known here; for it to be known in Latin America; for it to be known in the world, in the developed capitalist world, in the Third World and in the socialist countries. For it to be known here as well! Along with all the other texts and manuals we read, Che's economic thought should also be known in the socialist camp! ... and in particular our abundance of economics students, who ingest all kinds of brochures, manuals and theories of capitalist categories and capitalist laws, should deign to enrich their culture by acquainting themselves with Che's economic thought. ... I think many of Che's ideas are highly topical. And if we were acquainted with Che's economic thought, we would be a hundred times better equipped to lead this horse and hold its reins.[53]

Well into the Gorbachev era, the Cuban leadership (or at least its most restricted inner circle) thus took a stand in the debate over economic reform – on the eve of the October Revolution anniversary celebrations in Moscow in 1987 in which Fidel Castro could only briefly participate.

But was not this homage suspect? 'If we were acquainted with Che's economic thought', said Fidel. But where did this 'if' come from? Or rather, why was there this 'if'? Did the party secretary and premier want to give the impression that he had not taken any position over the great economic debate? What did this 'sacralization' of Che's thought mean? Was not the aim to make everyone forget and to 'piously cover up ... that Che came off worst in this polemic with ideological enemies at the heart of power; and that the defeat of his ideas in this area led him to move on to another, namely that of the tricontinental struggle? In other words, even if there was an agreement, and more probably a strategic agreement, between himself and Fidel, Che left Havana with his economic policy defeated.'[54] Even if it takes away from the hypothesis, such an explanation does enable this period of relations between Fidel Castro and Che Guevara, until this day obscure, to be understood.

In these times of crisis and corruption, it is not superfluous to contrast Gorbachev (and those in Cuba who invoke him) with other values – the values that were, and still are personified by Che: intransigence, disinterest, internationalism and an alternative socialist identity. The author of *Socialism and Man*, who denounced the illusion of building socialism with the 'blunt arms passed on by capitalism' (the market as an economic cell, profitability, private material interest as the incentive) would have been stupefied to read, from the pen of a fashionable Soviet professor of philosophy, that 'between the worker and the state (represented by the management of the enterprise) relations based on wage labour appear that can only take the form of market relations';[55] or to hear Gorbachev's right-hand man, Yakovlev, declare before the workers of a large Moscow car factory that the market is merely 'an economic device, whose function is to ensure exchange and distribution', but that this function is 'not just economic, as the market is the economic foundation on which democracy is based'.[56]

A Critical Assessment

Initially, the new economic policy gave positive results. First because it was accompanied by a revitalization of the mass organizations: old leaders had been pushed aside in trade union elections, and numerous collective debates were held in workplaces. Secondly because the introduction of the first market reforms was able to take advantage of a highly favourable economic juncture, with very high sugar prices on the world market. Cuba benefited from significant foreign exchange revenues, substantial loans, and sizeable aid from the Soviet Union. The standard of living of the population improved and the social promotion of the first generations of students was assured by the country's cadre requirements. And at first the economic reforms were credited for such improvements.

The absolute priority given to financial incentives has now become the object of criticism. The fall in imports and economic difficulties have placed limits on goods available on the market. The conditions for wages becoming a tool with which to stimulate the economy have not been met: 'The problem stems from the fact that the population's monetary income outstrips the supply of goods and services. Part of the income received thus finds no use, and this destroys the incentive to make extra efforts to raise labour productivity or improve the overall performance of the enterprise.'[57] Monetary incentives were linked to enterprises' financial autonomy, which was seen as evidence of efficiency and profitability. With enterprises subject to criteria of profitability, workers were to be interested in raising labour productivity through the device of bonuses linked to the enterprise's performance; and managers and administrators were to be the main beneficiaries.

During the introduction of the SDPE, the emphasis was placed on the 'objective economic laws at work in the construction of socialism', as well as the central relevance of the law of value, 'monetary-market relations', the 'economic-operative autonomy in the management of enterprises'[58] and the latter's greater autonomy in terms of the use of funds provided by the state. Profit and profitability became the essential categories in carrying out the plan. Although investment had been decided through budgetary means within the context of the main decisions taken during the preparation of the plan, the door was left open for 'managers to demand increasing autonomy in terms of investment' and also to try, given 'their own criteria of profitability, to obtain supplies from abroad'.[59]

In February 1985 the report of the National Bank of Cuba stressed:

> A 4.2 per cent fall in income took place in 1984. This was due to the fact that the process of decentralization of economic management led state enterprises to allocate resources to the financing of their investments, when previously they would have been transferred to the budget. With this fall in revenues, an 18 per cent reduction in costs was also recorded in the productive sphere. This was possible in so far as the budget did not have to finance the investments made by the state enterprises. As we have said, the latter finance their own investments through their own means.[60]

Finally, at the deferred session of the Third PCC Congress, Fidel Castro indicated that it was necessary to 'rectify the errors in the approach to investment policy'[61] and reduce the level of imports. The dangers of self-financing investment in a country so dependent on the outside world were thus confirmed: 'With bonuses for staff, and particularly for management, depending on performance, enterprises will inevitably tend to seek conditions that enable them to make the most profit. One of the factors in profit growth is quite clearly the efficiency and scope of investments. In so far as they have a material interest, managers will increasingly seek to control and determine the scope and aims of such investments.'[62] In 1980 this same analysis emphasized that the opportunity for enterprises to make their own decentralized investments in production from their profits could have serious consequences, by increasing inequalities between enteprises in terms of their development and orienting their investment 'so as to increase the production of the goods they lack most or are lacking the most locally. ... Criteria of sectoral or local interest could quickly gain the upper hand and impose on national priorities, thus introducing the law of value; inequalities between sectors of activity and thus between sections of the working class might also grow.'[63]

In fact the positions defended by Che had since 1964 foreseen the dangers that were to be confirmed twenty years later: the risk that, by leaving enterprises free to choose 'their criteria of profitability', they would be pushed into 'obtaining supplies from abroad';[64] and a risk 'because a better national profitability is never the sum of the optimum potential of each unit'.

In response to Charles Bettelheim's proposal of absorbing surplus demand through the legalization of free markets, Ernest Mandel countered that replacing the rationing of basic goods and services with rationing according to spending power invited the possibility of great social injustices being committed, not to mention speculation and corruption. In short, in an underdeveloped economy 'the less available capable, experienced, and truly socialist technical cadres are, the more it seems wise to retain centralized decision-making power over investment and all financial problems above a certain limit'.[65] Cuban economists expressed themselves in almost identical terms in 1987. Cuba's low level of development requires the centralized control of mobilization and the allocation of resources:

> Since underdevelopment in a small country entails structural imbalance and international dependence, strong central controls are necessary for restructuring the domestic economy and changing its relationship to the international economy. They are also necessary to correct inequalities between regions. Second, international political–economic hostility also necessitates centralization, especially given the US blockade and fears of political subversion and economic sabotage. ... Heavy military demands on the economy strengthen the rationale and the reality of centralization.[66]

But the struggle (underlying the debate of the 1960s and especially that of today) for increased labour productivity and performance cannot be resolved in terms of an alternative between hyper-centralization, on the one hand – based on single command (*mando único*) and so-called 'democratic centralism' (often more bureaucratic than democratic) – and the introduction of market mechanisms which exacerbate social differences and inequalities, on the other. As in 1964 it is the issue of workers' self-management – even in a situation of shortage – that must be resolved, not just in the enterprises but throughout production as a whole, granting workers truly executive functions. That was the Achilles' heel of the position defended by Che, even if subsequent events largely confirmed his predictions and, above all, his fears. Fidel Castro's reference to his ideas has not just come up against the same limits, but also against the traditions inherited from the Soviet Union that are solidly entrenched in the party apparatus.

Notes

1. *Granma*, 15 November 1987.
2. *Problèmes économiques*, Documentation française, July 1987.
3. C. Mesa-Lago, *La economía en Cuba socialista*.
4. Martínez Heredia, *Desafíos del socialismo*. Martínez Heredia was cultural attaché in Nicaragua from 1979 to 1984; he was editor of *Pensamiento Crítico*, a non-dogmatic magazine of debate which ceased publication at the beginning of the 1970s.
5. Alberto Recarte, *Cuba, Economía y Poder*.
6. C. Mesa-Lago, *La economía en Cuba socialista*, p. 214.
7. *Latin American Caribbean Report*, 15 January 1982.

8. C. Mesa-Lago, *La economía en Cuba socialista*, p. 230.
9. *Financial Times*, 29 October 1986.
10. *Juventud Rebelde*, 7 May 1987.
11. Fifty-third CTC plenum, Graphic Propaganda Unit, 14 January 1987.
12. *Granma*, 11 May 1987.
13. *Granma*, 29 March 1987.
14. *Granma*, 7 May 1987.
15. Fidel Castro, closing speech at the provincial assembly of the party in Havana, 13 December 1987.
16. *Granma*, 13 December 1987.
17. *Granma*, 1 March 1987.
18. *Granma*, 21 June 1987.
19. C. Mesa-Lago, *La economía en Cuba socialista*, p. 289.
20. Félix de la Uz, 'Personal letter to P.S.', 20 August 1970.
21. *Problèmes économiques,* Documentation française, 8 July 1987.
22. *Caribbean Regional Report*, 26 March 1982.
23. C. Mesa-Lago, *La economía en Cuba socialista*, p. 234.
24. Ibid., p. 234.
25. *Latin America Weekly Report*, 30 May 1986.
26. Ibid., 30 May 1986.
27. Interview with Fidel Castro in *l'Humanité*, 25 May 1987.
28. *Granma*, 1 June 1986.
29. *L'Humanité*, 25 May 1987.
30. ECLA report, August 1985.
31. Ibid.
32. H.C. Feuer 'The Performance of the Cuban Sugar Industry' in *World Development*, vol. 15, no. 1, 1987, p. 73.
33. ECLA report, August 1985.
34. *Caribbean Report*, October 1987.
35. Ibid.
36. Fidel Castro, 14 January 1987.
37. *Latin America Weekly Report*, 12 November 1987.
38. *World Development*, vol. 15, no. 1, 1987, p. 84.
39. *Caribbean Report*, 15 January 1982.
40. R. Turits, 'Trade, Debt, and the Cuban Economy' in *World Development*, vol. 15, no. 1, 1987, p. 172.
41. Falsely attributed to Che, as we shall see later.
42. Gianni Miná, *Habla Fidel*; or *Un Encuentro con Fidel*.
43. 'We have limited ourselves to formulating partial plans at sector or factory level. ... Our plans are continually challenged by other economic emergencies in the country.' Che once again confirms, five years after the seizure of power, the absence of real planning (*Ecrits d'un révolutionnaire*, p. 60).
44. Fidel Castro in *Granma*, 18 October 1987.
45. *Nuestra Industria*, Ministry of Industries, June 1964 (Che was accused of 'Trotskyism' by the pro-Soviets).
46. Luis Alvarez Rom., quoted by Che, *Ecrits d'un révolutionnaire*, p. 48.
47. Ibid., p. 49.
48. Ibid., p. 47.
49. Ibid., p. 75.
50. Jésus Díaz, *Los Iniciales de la Tierra*.
51. Carlos Tablada, *El Pensamiento Económico del Che*.
52. *Granma*, 18 October 1987.
53. Speech for the twentieth anniversary of Che's death, 1987.
54. François Maspero, 'Cuba', in *Autrement*, January 1989.
55. Viktor Kisselev, in *Revolution*, April 1989.
56. *Le Monde*, 24 June 1989.
57. Alexis Codina Jiménez, in *Economía y Desarrollo*, Institute of Economics of the

University of Havana, March–April 1980.

58. First Congress of the PCC, 1975.

59. Ernest Mandel, 'Le grand débat économique' and 'Les catégories marchandes dans la période de transition', in *Ecrits d'un révolutionnaire*.

60. National Bank of Cuba, Cuban National American Foundation, 1985, p. 19.

61. Main report to the Third Congress of the PCC.

62. Jean-Pierre Beauvais, in *Inprecor*, no. 94–95, 1981.

63. Ibid.

64. Ernest Mandel in 'Les catégories marchandes dans la période de transition', in *Ecrits d'un révolutionnaire*.

65. Ibid.

66. Quoted by G. White, 'Cuban Planning in the mid-1980s: Centralization, Decentralization and Participation', in *World Development*, vol. 15, no. 1, 1987.

3

Social Crisis, Bureaucratization and Rectification

According to the National Bank of Cuba 'the national economy grew ... by 7.4 per cent[1] in 1984, but in a context marked by a deterioration in the terms of trade with the market economies. ... This growth, registered in certain areas of production, was not always economically justified, among other reasons because the cost was a level of imports based on a higher energy consumption, as well as a greater use of the means of production than would have been required under conditions of maximum efficiency.'[2]

From late 1984, the third five-year plan was challenged by Fidel Castro. At the end of that November, a meeting of members of the PCC Politburo, vice-presidents of the government Executive Committee, provincial party secretaries, presidents of the People's Power assemblies and leaders of mass organizations, questioned the plan envisaged from top to bottom. It was decided to create a 'central group' under the direction of Osmany Cienfuegos to revise the plan as a matter of urgency.

Fidel Castro's criticism focused on the 'sectoral spirit' prevailing in ministries and enterprises; and on the fact that the plan was merely the sum of the different sectors' needs, with each one considering its own as essential. In his opinion, the plan was at the time becoming 'a war to grab the limited resources we have at our disposal', when a collective approach was needed towards the economy as a whole. The head of government also attacked the pre-eminence given to the 'importer' and 'consumer' mentality at the expense of exportation. The pressure exerted by enterprises, organs of people's power and ministries to obtain funding for their respective investment programmes was matched by the need for a greater control and intervention by the party. The party was to supplant JUCEPLAN, as well as officials from Finance and from the Central Bank, whose report of February 1985 and its conclusions were challenged. Leaders were stripped of their responsibilities and occasionally faced serious allegations, as was the case with Humberto Pérez, excluded from the Central Committee at the body's Sixth Plenary.[3]

The SDPE, conceived as an act of economic reorganization and restructuring, was placed in question. Criticism was made of the growing use of bonuses in the salary structure, especially for cadres and technicians. The financial autonomy of enterprises was similarly contested, on account of the distortions it had introduced into overall decisions.

At a time of austerity, the proposals announced by the Central Bank to limit consumption (during debt renegotiations with the Paris Club) were potentially explosive, and ran the risk of calling into question that famous 'growth in equality'[4] that has been the essential strength of the Cuban Revolution. The relation between productive investment and social costs, as well as the spectre of the Polish crisis, were to become the subject of numerous debates.

Beyond these socio-political aspects, the process of rectification challenged the quite unrealistic economic forecasts presented by the Central Bank and those responsible for the plan: difficulties in obtaining new bank loans, the persistent stagnation in sugar revenues, the constraints of the debt and fear of a liquidity crisis, the fall in revenues previously gained through Soviet oil, and the fall in Soviet subsidies. According to R. Turits, 'The combined Western and socialist debt in 1984 was the highest in Cuba's history.'[5]

Such are the premises of the process of rectification, leading as it has to a global debate on both the problems of the transition to socialism and the respective roles of the party and officials from the economic institutions. Tensions have intensified within the apparatus between the Castroite group and the 'technocrats' (as they are called by Fidel Castro), the 'second-rate capitalists' who talk only of 'economic mechanisms' and believe money can solve everything.

In a few years social inequalities have grown and social tensions have appeared. Economic difficulties have been reflected in an increase in the daily struggles of the population, suffering from the lack of particular consumer goods and often without access to products sold on the black market, whose high prices highlight differences in income.

Corruption and Speculation

Waste and corruption have led to a feeling of discontent among the regime's base of support, the wage-earning strata, faced with the growing wealth of certain sectors of farmers, as well as the privileges enjoyed by the administrative bureaucracy and top officials of the economic and state apparatus. Signs of economic inefficiency, waste, theft and the misappropriation of goods have been joined by the black market and currency trafficking, the spread of prostitution,[6] and a growth of petty delinquency near tourist centres. All such phenomena had fallen considerably – disappeared, in fact – in the years following the seizure of power.

From June 1986, the Politburo of the PCC undertook an 'exhaustive analysis of the problem of crime and anti-social behaviour', particularly in Havana, highlighting 'instances of aggressive conduct, violence against the person, and "hooliganism" displayed in the capital'.[7]

Just over a year later several top officials fled to the United States, either by using considerable resources in foreign currency which they had embezzled or by taking advantage of special facilities, thus pointing to the importance of certain privileges. In 1986, Manuel Sánchez Pérez, vice-minister in charge of purchasing technical supplies from abroad, deserted to Spain with US$ 499,000. According to his declarations, 'While still in Cuba I did some business deals with foreign firms and accumulated funds for the purpose of creating [abroad] an institution which will prepare a strategy for a return to democracy in Cuba'.[8] This gives some idea of the facilities available to leading officials. In May 1987, General Rafael del Pino, a former fighter at Playa Girón, managed to reach the United States in a small Cessna 402 aeroplane, taking off from an air base with his wife and three children 'under the pretext of taking a trip round the island'.[9] The mind boggles at the ease with which this general had access to a private runway. In June 1987, Luis Domínguez, the president of the Institute of Civil Aviation (INA), was arrested, accused of corruption and the misappropriation of resources; he supposedly had personal bank accounts to the tune of $500,000.[10] This arrest was followed by the desertion of Commander Florentino Aspillaga Lombard, the head of Cuban counter-espionage in Czechoslovakia,[11] and then by that of Gustavo Pérez Cortt, vice-president of the State Committee for Technical and Material Supplies (CEANT), in January 1988 following a CMEA meeting.[12]

Even before the Ochoa affair, this desertion of top officials was a symptom of the exacerbation of social and political tensions, particularly among the most privileged strata who felt insecure and threatened by the current direction being taken by Castro. Corruption, the misappropriation of funds from enterprises or using the latter for private ends have been repeatedly denounced.

Fidel Castro had already put enterprise managers misusing state funds in the hot seat in 1982. These 'thieves',[13] he declared, were a very widespread species. It was significant that it was at this time that he began to denounce the illegitimate profits made by middlemen on the free farmers' market. He would later claim that his advice had not been heeded on this issue.[14] The fact that it took him four years to get round to eliminating this private market gives some indication of the battles and divisions running through the state apparatus which were kept secret.

During the twenty-fifth anniversary of the Bay of Pigs in April 1986, the offensive was resumed 'against those who confuse income from work and speculation, fiddlers who are little better than thieves, and indeed often are thieves.' This theme reappeared during the CTC Congress: denunciation of the huge profits made, thanks to the existence of a significant private sector, by the *nouveaux riches* (truck owners, farmers, middlemen in charge of selling works of art, etc.); by administrators linked to external trade[15] or enjoying privileges gained in trips to Western countries (also denounced by the Young Communists at their 1987 congress);[16] by 'bureaucrats with comfortable homes';[17] and by technocrats who build 'two huge nickel-processing factories and only provide accommodation for the manager and the thirty or forty top cadres, while the workers are put up in makeshift huts'.[18]

Condemnation of 'bureaucratism', of course, is not new. From 1965, commissions had been charged with the rationalization of surplus administrative staff. Armando Hart, now Minister of Culture, recalled at the time[19] that 'bureaucracy is the petty-bourgeois spirit in the proletarian state', and that 'its historical and ideological roots must be analysed'.[20] But there is no comparison between what was being denounced then and the current situation. The 1970s were a decade in which the Soviet Union regained a dominant influence in all areas – institutional, political, economic and ideological; and this dominance, followed by the introduction of the economic reforms, gave further impetus to the spread of bureaucratization in a country where basic goods are still rationed.

Privileges and Social Differences

The autonomy and room for manoeuvre enjoyed by enterprise managers after the introduction of the SDPE accentuated social differences. Such privileges were the focus of an analysis by Ariel Hidalgo, a prisoner for seven years[21] and author of a pamphlet devoted to the study of the *gerentocracy*: 'The manager's unrestricted control of the means of production allows him to determine not just production, but the goods produced. If the state's only link with production is through the managers, and if the latter are in effect its most legitimate representatives, how will the state be able to prevent them from using part of surpluses for personal ends? ... How can it be explained that the vast majority of enterprise managers enjoy a whole range of prerogatives that are denied to nearly the whole rank-and-file working population?' Hidalgo called into question the financial autonomy of enterprises which allowed managers to return nothing to the state except 'the difference between the sum total of production and the share appropriated by him'. 'The managers', he concluded, 'represent a new exploiter social class, a gerentocracy that dominates the mass of wage labourers.'[22]

Written in 1984, this pamphlet was symptomatic of the state of mind prevailing in the 1980s and of the growing crisis affecting the relations between the apparatus and the masses. Several of the problems raised by Hidalgo were to be taken up by Fidel Castro, particularly in his attacks on managers, from the time of the launch of the process of rectification in 1986. Given the deterioration of the economic and financial crisis and the austerity measures, such inequalities could have a divisive effect on the social strata forming the mainstay of the leadership.

All the more so because they have been joined by another aspect of the crisis: indeed, for the first time, Fidel Castro has denounced serious inadequacies in the social services, questioning the 'petty-bourgeois' spirit of choices made by technocrats in terms of the relation between accumulation and consumption. According to Turits, non-productive investment fell significantly between 1962 and 1981, from 29.3 per cent of total investment to 15.6.[23] Fidel Castro challenged 'the promoters of reactionary ideas in the revolution, the advocates of bourgeois or liberal ideas ... the technocrats and bureaucrats ... the partisans of reaction and counter-revolution who do not support the process of rectification and who merely want one thing: to deny the people any success'.[24]

'With socialism there can be no economic development without social development.' In spite of health being one of the revolution's priorities – and one where progress had been spectacular – the secretary of the PCC challenged

> the dilapidated polyclinics, set up in buildings in a poor condition, which provide appalling services, centres which do not have the minimum of material resources. In terms of education, there is already a shortage of playschools and crèches; there are not enough schools for weekly boarders, or for the handicapped. ... The promoters of reactionary ideas in the revolution allege that building a playschool involves social expenditure and that social expenditure is of no use. The only useful thing for them is investment in the productive sector; as if those going to work at the factories were cattle, horses or mules rather than human beings, men and women with problems – especially women with problems. Those people reason like this: no social costs, only investment in material productive goods. As a result, they end up all alone with their factories because there isn't any form of production that can do without people.[25]

Rectification was to bring progress in social justice. According to Martínez Heredia, social provision increased by 10 per cent in 1988 with 49 per cent of planned expenditure earmarked for health care and education as well as social security payments.

Within a context of crisis and a relative fall in living standards, the shortcomings of social services – in spite of free health care and education being the most important gains of the revolution – have led to a deterioration in the popular masses' living conditions. Unlike officials trained in the Soviet school, the core group around Castro has understood that in lean times existing disparities must be reduced if one wants to achieve productivity gains, rationalize working practices, reduce bonuses, fight absenteeism, reduce surplus staff, stabilize the rural workforce, and relaunch voluntary work. The reference to Che and, above all, his ideas, gives some indication of the debate underway.

> Voluntary work, an idea inherited from Che ... was seen as a stupid idea. ... Problems were to be solved through overtime hours, without bothering to turn the working day to good account. ... We have become bogged down with bureaucratism, surplus staff, anachronistic working practices, trickery and lies. ... Che would have been horrified if he had been told that one day enterprises would steal to be profitable ... that they would steal building materials instead of using them for building, in spite of entering them in the books. ... Che would have been horrified. ... And yet this is what has happened in fifteen boroughs of the capital where fifteen house-maintenance enterprises gave a production-figure of 8,000 pesos a year when it was really only 4,000 pesos. ... If Che had been told that the attitude of our workers would become more and more corrupt each day and that the hallmark of men was to be money instead of their brain, he would have been horrified ... for he knew that that path could only lead to the eventual loss of any idea of human solidarity, or even of internationalism.

Che was the victim of a long silence for several years, to such an extent that his name was not even mentioned at the First PCC Congress in 1975. Today his positions serve as a reference point, confronting the advocates of market reforms and supporters of Gorbachev with another conception of socialism. But as well as acting as a dividing line in discussions, such a reference point has another advantage: Che has become such an emblematic figure that it is difficult to take an anti-Guevarist stance in the eyes of the popular masses. In short, Che has rehabilitated the idea of an honest, austere and incorruptible leader. At a time of austerity when sacrifice and duty are called for, this is far from irrelevant: for the difficulties of everyday life qualify many speeches, and the people are not worried about passing comment on privileges and favours.

Indeed, differences in living standards are apparent in housing and supplies, particularly in towns where there is a shortage of certain foods that can nevertheless be found on the black market or in tourist shops. The elimination of free markets has not solved supply difficulties; and problems in the organization of distribution have not been solved: agriculture and construction always suffer from a shortage of labour that voluntary or seasonal workers cannot replace.

Bohemia magazine has quoted the case of eight workers on a 600-hectare agricultural unit who were unable to cope with preparations for sowing, and considered that sixty additional workers would have been needed to solve the problem.[26] Labour shortages have often prevented fruit and vegetables from being harvested, with produce left uncut to rot, in spite of shortages in the shops. The recent wage rises given to agricultural workers (100 pesos at the bottom of the wage scale) do not seem to be high enough to attract youth to the countryside. This situation has fed speculation. Quite recently, a huge police operation was carried out against speculators in essential goods. Two years after the banning of the free markets, middlemen were buying large quantities of goods to resell on the black market, to the detriment of the parallel state markets.

On the whole, a kind of double network works in favour of the privileged, who are either linked in one way or another with the tourist, diplomatic or commercial circuits, or benefit from high incomes from their private activities. Popular discontent has been provoked by the existence of the Intur shops, which are very well stocked and officially aimed at tapping foreign exchange from tourists in hotels. It is the same with official cars, highly visible near beaches, which drivers now conceal because the people take down the registration numbers and report them to the ministries.

Top officials feel threatened. The most compromised are haunted by job insecurity, fearing a purge which, before the Ochoa trial, had already affected some of them (leaders from JUCEPLAN, accountable to PCC ideology). The prevailing uncertainty increases the paralysis of the technocratic strata, in spite of Fidel Castro's guarantees against a 'cultural revolution'. Such fears explain the unusual wave of desertions witnessed in the recent past. The risks of the 'job' are significant: bureaucratic posts are subject to the vicissitudes of the ruling group's decisions, and positions gained remain fragile.

At the beginning of the process, the popular masses were on the alert; rectification had given them back the initiative, albeit carefully channelled. Criticism was encouraged in enterprises and instances of managers resigning under the pressure of the workers, as well as public denunciation of waste and neglect, were not uncommon. The campaign in the enterprises was aimed in particular at remobilizing and homogenizing a disoriented working-class rank and file; a rank and file that was cynical in some cases, but above all divided and atomized as a result of the wage policies followed, as well as inequalities and the reign of the arbitrary. The magazine of the Confederation of Cuban Workers has highlighted the damage being caused to the economy by the pervasive atmosphere of carelessness and, worse still, the harm done to the 'moral integrity of the workers'.[27] *Trabajadores* plays an important role in denouncing fraud, as does the State Finances Committee (CEF) which revealed[28] that economic fraud had reached 19 millions pesos in six ministries and several municipal organizations – those most involved being the ministries of Finance, Internal Trade, Light Industry, Agriculture, Construction, Food and Civil Aviation. Petty crime has been frequent in the case of rare goods: the robbery of shoes or toothbrushes, for example, when there is a shortage on the market. It is striking that *Juventud Rebelde*, the Communist Youth journal, has denounced cases of stealing by railwaymen[29] or in particular enterprises, thus proving that petty delinquency is not just widespread among the marginal or 'semi-lumpen' strata as they are called in official vocabulary.

'What's the point of working? With a hundred pesos a month I can't get what I want,'[30] says a nineteen-year-old black joiner who lives from various fiddles. Even though it is true that everyone is guaranteed essential services such as health care and education, it is a meagre existence with several children and a wage at the bottom of the scale.[31]

The setting of standards and bonuses bearing no relation to work done has introduced distortions and sharply felt injustices. 'In the mid-1980s only half of employees in the productive sector were rewarded on the basis of task specifications. Out of three million such specifications, 23 per cent are technically based. Most bonuses therefore bear no relation to any objective reality.'[32] The reorganization of wages and standards has led in a number of cases to loss of income. 'Perhaps the most difficult aspect of rectification,' stated *Granma*, 'has been to convince workers with excessively high wages – stemming from the application of out-of-date standards or erroneous criteria – to give them up.'[33]

In spite of difficulties and errors, the working masses remain firmly behind the revolution, as has been witnessed by journalists who can hardly be suspected of pro-Castro sympathies. But they do have a sceptical wait-and-see attitude; and their doubts and questions do not get a response. 'We are aware of the problems, the workers say, but we would like to know how to solve them.'[34] 'It's not the system we dislike. It's the fact that it's working badly,' certain activists placing their hope in rectification commented significantly.[35]

On the eve of the introduction of important austerity measures in 1987, the rectification process was able to appear as a way of making a virtue out of necessity; and Cuban workers wondered whether it was yet another case of the 'hara-kiri technique' – the nickname given to party officials' hypocritical practice of criticism and self-criticism. In spite of displays of scepticism, rectification has often led, at least initially, to criticism of cadres. The Castro leadership has needed to close ranks around itself in a difficult economic situation; and this social support has been all the more necessary because of the hostile reactions manifested in the apparatus: 'Some officials ... fear a purge is on the way, but do not know who will be purged and who will emerge on top. This state of uncertainty has led in some officials and departments to partial paralysis.'[36] This has been accompanied by the discontent of those, like the middlemen or beneficiaries of private activity, who are hostile to rectification. Forced into austerity, the leadership cannot be the butt of every resentment.

Lean Times

This was the context for the announcement of twenty-five to thirty austerity measures on 11 January 1987 in response to the financial crisis. Varying in importance, their main implications were: the reduction of powdered-milk imports, and thus of (often free) milk supplies in the communities; the (also limited) reduction of meat consumption; the strongly resented (!) elimination of the traditional snack-break at 10 a.m. and 4 p.m. in public services, which would lead on average to two one-hour interruptions (which says a lot about the room for manoeuvre of rank-and-file workers in the enterprises); the reduction of sugar supplies to local organs of people's power and to the Ministry of Food, as well as the replacement of rice (a staple food) with potatoes; the limitation of supplies to canteens at the Ministry of the Sugar Industry and the Ministry of Agriculture; the replacement of evening meals at playschools with a substantial snack; an end to free meals in canteens; public transport price rises; the self-financing of popular festivals; the revision of supplies provided for medical reasons; a reduction by half of the time spent on meetings and sport and leisure activities at the workplace; and price rises on the parallel markets.

Some were energy-saving measures: the volume of petrol earmarked for public services fell by 20 per cent; television programmes were cut by five hours a day; electricity charges were increased. Other decisions affected cadres, for 'it is with them that one must begin',[37] Fidel Castro declared. The use of public vehicles was to be regulated and the number of vehicles awarded for professional reasons, officially estimated at 20,000, was brought down to 5,000. Expenses for administrative staff were cut as part of a staff rationalization policy, and expenses in foreign exchange for trips abroad were to be reduced by 15 per cent. Two years later events were to show that such decisions continued to be a dead letter.

The measures were significant for their effort to balance the distribution of austerity between population and bureaucrats, showing that the Castro leadership was not at all unaware of the perks enjoyed by the nomenklatura. The review of the lowest wages (which Fidel Castro described as 'ridiculous') and the 'reversal of the tendency to increase the highest wages' were similarly inspired. At the same time they sought to overcome labour shortages in sectors such as agriculture or construction. Staff rationalization (notably of over-abundant administrative staff) was aimed at fighting staff surpluses, officially estimated at at least 50,000 people,[38] a figure certainly well below the real one. Simultaneously, labour reorganization included the revision of wage rates and qualifications and this led to a fall in purchasing power.

Since June 1981[39] the system of evaluating workers' qualifications was supposed to be working towards the implementation of the principles of 'socialist distribution'. But the evaluation commissions in charge of systematizing the different jobs and respective qualifications, as well as promotion grades, came up against the insufficient qualifications of their own members, and also against their lack of time and the difficulty of establishing a precise definition of duties at the top of the hierarchy.

The Ambiguities of Rectification

The rectification process was presented in 1987 not just as 'a duty, but as a vital necessity'.[40] It arose, in its early stages, from a critique of the economic market reforms (SDPE); a critique directed at the competitive relations that the reforms had introduced, as well as the rivalry between workers and the questioning of the right to work and of social gains. In terms of social relations, such market mechanisms were not neutral (as Fidel Castro pointed out) and their introduction had begun to provoke tensions and conflicts; not just between management and workers, but between workers themselves, even though the economic reforms accompanying the introduction of the SDPE have been limited in comparison with countries in Eastern Europe.

As a process, rectification has thus gone against the grain in terms of the economic policy advocated by Gorbachev; and the past experience of a certain perestroika (but without glasnost!) led the Castro leadership to criticize Gorbachev-style conceptions.

Fidel Castro claimed in any case that Gorbachev had adopted

measures aimed at 'reinforcing discipline at work, fighting the corruption that is displayed in certain areas and in certain cadres. It's a policy with high moral principles, similar to the one we're practising in our country.'[41] False naïvety or really a manoeuvre? This declaration already represented a shift from initial ojectives.

Ever since the halt in Cuban payments to the Western banks in summer 1986, the Paris Club had recommended the introduction of austerity policies similar to those advocated by the IMF. While Fidel Castro has always denied any link between such directives and the austerity measures he adopted, it is difficult not to make the connection.

As well as these economic features, the process of rectification has a specific political dimension, aimed in particular at restoring a broader consensus between the Castro leadership and the masses. The denunciation of capitalism – of its 'cruel instruments of pressure on workers', of a system 'whose driving force is individual enrichment', a system 'which divides men, a system of inequalities and selfishness'[42] – as well as the declaration of the will to struggle against injustices, are both linked to the particular geopolitical situation of the Cuban Revolution: ninety miles from the United States, thousands of kilometres from the Soviet Union and without a common border with another workers' state. Any weakening in popular cohesion and mobilization could threaten – in the short or long term – the revolutionary process. In spite of the secret commitments between Khrushchev and Kennedy at the time of the missile crisis[43] in 1962, no one can guarantee that US imperialism – faced with a spread of revolution in Central America, for example – would not try to attack Cuba if it felt the situation was right.

The increase in privileges, corruption and inequalities was weakening the unity and cohesion of the workers and breaking their revolutionary spirit and confidence. That is why Fidel Castro asserted: 'We were weakening the revolution.' And that is why the errors of the previous decade were described as 'strategic' rather than 'idealistic' as in the 1960s. 'If we lose this [revolutionary] awareness and this spirit [of solidarity], what will we have left? What will be left of a country facing the empire? What will be left of a small country trying to build socialism from underdevelopment, poverty, ignorance and the lack of education? What would be left? How should we defend ourselves and develop?'[44]

The Mariel trauma was terrible: more than 100,000 emigrated[45] to the United States in 1980 and hundreds of thousands have since lived there with their descendants in the area of Miami nicknamed 'Little Havana'. The effect of authorized visits of Cuban exiles on their families was to increase the discontent caused by material difficulties. The example of the Polish workers' rebellion in 1980 was present in the minds of leaders. Once again, this explains the leaders' current will to affect as little as possible the population's minimum standard of living, as well as the social gains which have been the revolution's strength.

The current ideological campaign is therefore not just a pretext, even if the efficiency of the methods used might be doubted. There is the denunciation of the 'mercenaries seeking privileges and profits', of those who want to 'pocket the money they have not earned with their own sweat but through fiddles and speculation ... these technocrats and bureaucrats are infected with a kind of ideological Aids, a kind of Aids that was destroying the defence of the revolution'.[46] In spite of being one of the most dubious of metaphors – as is the case with anything related to homosexuality in Cuba – this denunciation strongly conveys the idea of a battle against a process of divisions and bureaucratization that would be fatal for the revolution.

The difficulty of the task is considerable. It is a battle being fought mainly from 'above', and to a small extent from 'below', within the limits set by the ruling group. Patriotic rhetoric and appeals to a sense of duty irritate sections of youth and intellectuals, who see such discourse as a poor blanket substitute for ideology and politics, and as incapable of responding to their desire for openness or to their cultural needs. It is true that aspirations to a Western-style consumption model – which is out of reach given the economic situation in Cuba, at least in the short or medium term – do not go well with austerity.

The Scepticism of the New Generation

The new generation born after the revolution has not known poverty and dictatorship. The classic sociological phenomenon, it is therefore less sensitive to the experiences of the revolution. And its demands have increased as a result of the raising of cultural standards and the school boom. Indeed, the number of students in secondary and technical schools rose from 28,000 in 1970–71 to 300,000 in 1983–84; and for the same years, university enrolment went up from 35,000 to 200,000. More than half the population was born after 1959.

Some young people are tired of hearing about the past when they are mainly concerned with current difficulties, with their career progress – in other words with rising socially. While the first generation of university leavers enjoyed real social promotion because of the lack of cadres, the situation is different today. The existence of surplus staff in firms, and particularly in administration and among party cadres, is already a brake on the prospects for professional development of university-trained young people in certain areas. Yet it is in production that labour power, particularly technicians, is most needed. In May 1987, for example,

Juventud Rebelde cited the case of two Havana firms where half the workers were in production and the other half held administrative or technical posts. The result, according to the journal, was that it was not possible to work a double shift system; and that there was an under-utilization of productive capacity, even though costly equipment that had been paid for in foreign exchange was often being used. In other cases, sophisticated machines were handled by inadequately trained workers. This is why young workers in administrative posts are asked to change jobs and work in production. The journalist ends his article with an appeal to young people in the mechanical iron and steel industry to leave their desks.

Fidel Castro's criticisms point in the same direction: research and development centres have not been established to 'raise wages and produce doctorate candidates, but to resolve problems of production. There are people fresh out of university who work hours and hours preparing to qualify ... the proliferation of centres of this kind and the race to qualify are negative phenomena.'[47] There is therefore a massive contradiction between the level of training of young people and available outlets, especially for those with university qualifications.

The deficiencies of the education system have been underlined by the Minister of Education, José Fernández: one of the most worrying signs is academic cheating which applies to 34 per cent of secondary schools – carried out by teachers and pupils in order to meet the targets of education plans.[48]

Such sociological transformations have produced conflict, including at the political level, within the PCC where the younger generation continues to be marginalized. According to José Raúl Viera, First Vice-Minister of Foreign Affairs, 'the promotion of young people must not be interrupted. It is the retirement of comrades who have been in leadership posts for a long time that must go ahead.' Easier said than done! During the last PCC Congress in February 1986 (first session), 40 per cent of the Central Committee was renewed. But while 55.5 per cent of the population are less than thirty years old,[49] only 9 per cent of the Central Committee are less than thirty-five years old, 50 per cent being more than forty-six years old.[50] Three members of the Politburo have been replaced (Guillermo García, Sergio del Valle, Ramiro Valdés, the latter having been Minister of the Interior and the other two commanders of the Rebel Army). But in the main it is the old guard who hold the key party and state posts.

Moreover, a certain political demobilization – indeed, a certain cynicism – can be perceived in some sections of youth. There is a clear reluctance to do compulsory military service, occasionally seen as 'a punishment or a sort of purgatory'[51] according to *Juventud Rebelde*.

Enthusiasm for internationalist missions (principally Angola) has similarly decreased. While his declarations must be treated with the utmost caution, Rafael del Pino (the former Cuban army general who fled to the United States) has suggested that the participation of Cubans in the fighting in Angola came up against several difficulties, claiming that 56,000 soldiers had deserted during the last three years of the war and that 10,000[52] had died since 1976. Though such figures are probably highly exaggerated, the pursuit of the war has led to tensions and a definite ill-feeling in a section of youth.

The phenomenon of school desertion and truancy has got worse. The practice of moonlighting and the various forms of trafficking near tourist resorts have developed, as has juvenile delinquency. The development of tourism, a big provider of foreign exchange, has contradictory effects. Foreign tourists display an inaccessible model of consumption: 'Tourism plunders. Brazilians will go there with their jeans, they will smuggle and sell dollars on the black market',[53] says a Brazilian journalist. Such instances of petty crime are limited and are especially concentrated in Havana. But they have been worrying enough for *Granma* to stress the problems posed by this 'idle youth'.[54] Likewise the journal of the Young Communists has stressed the existence of 'anti-social petty crimes'.

Political incidents have been multiplying for several years. The publication of an article on prostitution led to the withdrawal of the *Somos Jovenes* magazine from newsstands. The affair gave rise to a stormy meeting with officials of the Young Communists in the presence of the Ideology Secretary, Carlos Aldana. The cult of Fidel Castro in the media and the slavishness of the press were criticized by those attending. Fidel Castro made an appearance, but kept quiet for the first time![55] The Communist Youth, summoned to discipline the insolent students, procrastinated.

The new generation represents an essential challenge, but the official youth organizations seem too conformist. The leadership's concern was shown by Fidel Castro's permanent presence at the last Congress of the Young Communists.

As we have already stressed, the contrast between the resources devoted to tourism and the relative shortage of consumer goods is strongly resented by the population. The facilities reserved for foreign tourists are of much higher quality than those enjoyed by Cubans and this feeds a certain cynicism. According to individual witnesses, dollar areas, hotels and tourist shops (where goods are paid for in foreign currency) are kept under surveillance.

Faced with this situation, the government seemed, for a brief period, to be moving towards a reinforcement of criminal sentences, lumping major corruption cases together with petty crime.[56] The intensification of conflict at the different levels of the social structure has led to a shift in the government's penal repression policy. Ideological mobilization has been emphasized and the virtues of voluntary work – semi-abandoned in the previous decade – have been insisted upon. But as an old farmer noted: 'Voluntary work helps and relieves, but it is not an answer to the problem. You teach one person one day, and along comes someone else the next. You have to explain everything again to them. ... That's no substitute for a stable workforce.'[57]

While the contribution of the voluntary work brigades cannot be disregarded, it is undoubtedly their ideological aim that counts as much as their economic efficiency. 'The microbrigades movement represents much more than building buildings. It is a reaffirmation that problems can be solved through the mass line. ... It is a demonstration that socialism can provide an immediate solution for emergencies of material production, as it has done in the case of education, sport and health.'[58]

Indeed, the microbrigades movement has tended to consolidate. In Havana,[59] 37,000 brigade members have been organized in workplaces. Each brigade has thirty people and is devoted to building homes or carrying out works of social use, supervised by architects. The brigades are co-ordinated by members of the PCC or the Young Communists, and youngsters from schools participate on a voluntary basis to acquaint themselves with manual work. The brigades have also provided a means of dealing with surplus staff problems and the poor distribution of the workforce. Discussions are held in the workplace as to who can participate in the microbrigades and the workers proposed are then released. Generally 'the conclusion is reached that production targets can be easily met with a numerically smaller workforce. Enterprises working at a loss become more efficient and profitable. There is no unemployment or painful readjustment. On the contrary', says David Deutschmann.[60]

But it is difficult to see how those in power can deal with youth malaise in this way. There was a further manifestation of this discontent recently when various cultural rallies, originally conceived as political/artistic initiatives, were the scene of several incidents[61] involving groups of young people. During recent concerts or sporting events, members of the Young Communists have been booed and dissident minorities have delayed the start of performances; and following the dance and pop music concert for the sixtieth anniversary of Che's birth, spectators wrote to *Bohemia* magazine with shock and indignation[62] at the absence of revolutionary banners and slogans or portraits of Che! Such remarks bear witness to the irritation provoked by the conduct of some non-conformist young people.

Permanent Rectification

Under different names, the rectification campaign has had its precedents. The fight against waste to increase labour productivity had already been accompanied by a powerful campaign on the conception of socialism in 1967, and commissions had been set up to combat bureaucracy. At the time, bureaucracy was correctly conceived in its social sense, and not in the usual sense in Cuba of bureaucratic and administrative red-tape.[63]

Between 1968 and 1970, an ultra-leftist course – baptised as the 'Revolutionary Offensive' – led to the nationalization of all small businesses and private activities (including Cuba's profusion of drink stalls) and to the elimination of all work specifications. Nationalization of distribution was carried out under excessively rigid conditions and led to considerable dislocation. As has already been pointed out, Fidel Castro's higher goal was alien to Che's inclinations, and one only has to refer to Castro's interview with *Le Nouvel Observateur* in 1967 to be convinced:

> I am against material incentives because I regard them as incompatible with socialism. ... We want to demystify money, not rehabilitate it. We even intend to abolish it completely. ... The law of value makes sense in a capitalist society where the economy is based on profit. But it makes no sense in a socialist society. Given that we are in a period of transition to socialism, we have no reason to give way to the economic laws of capitalism, as if our sole aim was to manage the old system more efficiently. We have discussed this issue at length and have decided to free ourselves as quickly as possible from the constraints of the market. Our planning must be based on 'labour value' and not on the deceptive calculations of profitability or profit. We are going to eliminate all financial accounting of trade between socialist enterprises.

At the political level, it was a time of the hard line. The 'microfaction' trial, which challenged the pro-Soviet activity of former members of the Popular Socialist Party[64] (organized secretly by the KGB to eliminate Fidel Castro who was clashing openly with the Soviets over his revolutionary policy in Latin America),[65] was accompanied by a climate of intolerance and political repression. Several intellectuals were to lose their jobs and responsibilities[66] during this brief period that has left very bad memories.[67] The rectification process has awoken the same fears.

Then came the dark years – following the failure of the ten-million-tonne sugar-cane harvest in 1970 – with the Soviet Union taking the situation back in hand. In December 1979, almost five years after the First PCC Congress, the introduction of the SDPE, economic liberalization and the first attempt at price reform, Raúl Castro was already denouncing 'the irresponsibility, carelessness and nepotism ... which cause justified anger among broad sections of the population'.[68] He did not blame the workers for labour indiscipline, but 'the enterprise managers and officials who ... falsify statistics ... use and abuse their privileges and the resources of the enterprise to resolve their own personal problems and those of their friends'. He nevertheless emphasized that 'enterprise managers and heads of administration must have the power to take action against workers who are not fulfilling their social duty' in order to do their duty themselves and 'above all to survive materially as a result of the reward received for one's contribution to society.'

Once again, the leadership deflected the irritation of the masses, taking it on board and trying to provide a response; a response that was limited by the leadership's pragmatism and paternalism, as well as by its adoption of a balanced position between the managers and the managed. In so far as it is obvious that there are directors and directed (a concept which, like that of the leader, is at the heart of Castroite thought),[69] the best compromise possible must be struck between the two without denying that their needs are different:

> It is not a case of demagogic petty-bourgeois egalitarianism. For if the managers weren't paid according to their responsibilities and the qualifications demanded by the job, it would conflict with their efficiency. The whole of our people fully understand that officials and cadres at a certain level need the minimum conditions required to do their work, and that often means having a car. On the other hand, they must not abuse the privileges conferred upon them by their responsibility and position in the hierarchy, using them as if they were the owners of goods that the people have created and paid for with their own work and sweat. If those goods are placed under their direction and administration, it is so that they can use them for their work and for the benefit of society as a whole, not as individual or family conveniences.[70]

Raúl Castro's speech was a reflection of the tensions that already existed (particularly in the state apparatus). But it was only seven years later that the SDPE would be challenged, economic liberalization having led the country to 'total disorder and chaos'[71] and criticisms of privileges still having no effect.

It is striking that these top level anti-bureaucratic offensives have often coincided with periods when relations with the Soviet Union have been conflictive. This was the case during the 1960s, a decade marked by serious differences over economic and international policy. In Latin America, a *de facto* break occurred between the pro-Soviet communist parties and the Castro leadership. The revolutionary strategy for the continent advocated by Che Guevara and the conference of the Organization of Latin American Solidarity were accompanied by splits in the communist parties, especially in the Young Communists. But the decade after Che's death saw a volte-face which sanctioned a Cuban rapprochement with the Soviet leadership and its Latin American allies. In 1972 Cuba joined Comecon and the First Congress of the PCC in 1975 consummated the break with Guevarism.

The elaboration of the SDPE dates from that period, which was also characterized by a certain economic and institutional decentralization. High sugar prices on the world market, as well as the substantial credits from Comecon (partly a reward for services rendered in Angola), were to improve the economic situation. But the price was growth distorted by the scale of Western imports, a feature of the period being the easy access to credits in foreign currency. The respite was short-lived, as the effects of economic recession, the debt and the SDPE began to be felt. Simultaneously, the victory of the Nicaraguan Revolution and then the radical changes in Grenada in 1979 reinforced the correlation of forces in the leadership in favour of the Castroite group. The defeat in Grenada in 1983, the Soviet Union's support for Coard – as well as its retreat in the face of the US aggression against Nicaragua – have all provoked new tensions since the beginning of the 1980s.

The peculiarity of the current rectification campaign thus lies not so much in its aims, but in that it is taking place in a completely new context, characterized by the shift in Cuban–Soviet relations since the coming to power of Gorbachev, as well as by Cuba's political position in Latin America after more than twenty years of isolation. Rectification is presented as a 'strategic' watershed. It is true that the 'negative tendencies' to be corrected are part of the revolution's thirty-year record and that the economic situation is very difficult. According to a Cuban American economist,[72] the system has hitherto 'distributed well and produced badly', but has recently begun to distribute badly. Bureaucratization has worsened, giving way to reforms and their specific effects in a country weakened by its dependency.

In several parts of the state apparatus – administration, economic management, planning (JUCEPLAN), parts of the party leadership (ideology officials), teaching, publishing and the press – it is the cadres' long training received in the Soviet Union that is dominant. For years the Castro leadership has been supine, even though its Latin American traditions and origins go against such a tendency. Today, the record of the past is part of the debate involving a reorientation of ideology and overall political choices. An awareness of the insidious rise of bureaucratization does exist; but the problem remains as to what role – and, above all, how much power – the ruling group intends to give the mass movement in the correction of 'negative tendencies'. What economic and political decision-making is the Castroite core prepared to concede?

Fidel Castro's monopoly of power – his leading role more contested than previously and weakened by current bureaucratization – is an obstacle to any advance in the masses' self-organization. The trial of strength – with Castro opposing (and threatening the privileges of) managers and technocrats who base their support on the Soviet Union, and use the novelty of Gorbachev's prestige to consolidate their positions – is still limited. Unlike the past, the problem today is not just of maintaining links with the masses and basing support on their mobilization, but of enabling them to inform themselves first of all, and then to have an influence on both political debate and major economic decisions. In other words, a policy opposed to the Castroite conception of power, illustrated in 1989 by the banning of *Moscow News*.

The economic reforms introduced within the framework of the SDPE have not solved a single problem. In the sectors where they have been applied, market logic has gained the upper hand; and in a context of shortages, this has only favoured corruption. From a social point of view, the SDPE has favoured the management apparatus, with enterprise managers benefiting from significant material privileges. It has been a similar story with the agricultural private sector and various commercial activities linked to tourism and imports. The interests of the masses (the regime's social base), on the other hand – with the exception of particular skilled sectors and technical and administrative posts – have often been adversely affected by the new wage scale. The principle of 'to each according to his or her labour' has been given an anti-egalitarian interpretation. A break has also been placed on advances in social services and their quality has deteriorated.

Should one conclude that the current watershed is a return to bureaucratic centralized planning? Things are clearly much more complex. The Cuban leadership is probably involved in a search for original paths (combining planning and the market), based on a critique of the past and present experiences of the Eastern bloc countries. For some, this general reflection on the transition is inspired by Che's thought, but within the limits set by the absence of socialist democracy.

In 1988, Martínez Heredia summed up the aim of rectification in the following way:

> Rather than accepting reversal or stagnation, it is aimed at deepening a process of transition in a small Third World country which is openly fighting, along with the progressive and revolutionary forces of the region, the harassment of imperialism. A country whose economic system cannot provide the accumulation required for rapid development; and which still bears the marks of underdevelopment. We call rectification a process which is born from the clear denunciation of domestic ills, as well as from perceptions that are still only half-clear and even blurred when it comes to the policies that should be

> introduced. In what might be crucial to its success, [rectification] is aimed at resolving, through revolutionary – that is to say, socialist and partly communist – methods, the multiple tensions produced by the relations between the economy and politics, the economy and education, and between the need for a centralized regime and one where there is effective popular participation in management and decision-making; between ideological unity and freedom of thought, between market relations and socialist (and communist) behaviour, between administration in conditions of underdevelopment and the need to avoid bureaucratic red tape and clientelism, as well as between an insufficient control of the conditions of the mode of production and the need for real economic efficiency. ... The process will inevitably be a long one and will take shape, initially at least, within the framework of existing channels [institutions]. Its long duration will have two foreseeable consequences: one concerns the fact that rectification faces a set of problems with relatively deep roots; the other, which is much more important in my opinion, is an understanding that it is only by using the fundamental tools of socialist popular power – in other words, the conscious and organized action of the masses – that one will be able to overcome the logical resistances caused by ideological distortions and established interests. This means proceeding without appeals for violence, without bureaucratic methods, without hastiness, and without the various forms of extremism that might compromise the success, moral strength and permanence of rectifications in a revolutionary society.[73]

This analysis was indicative of the hopes raised by the new political path being taken by intellectuals who were more receptive to Castroite arguments than to the seductions of perestroika, but anxious about the methods used. One year later, the drug-trafficking scandal broke out.

Notes

1. A. Zimbalist, 'Cuba's Socialist Economy Toward the 1990s', in *World Development*, vol. 15, no. 1, 1987.
2. Report of the National Bank of Cuba, February 1985, pp. 6–7. According to government statistics, between 1980 and 1985 the global social product (GSP) rose in constant per capita prices at an average annual rate of 6.7 per cent (Zimbalist, 'Cuba's Socialist Economy Toward the 1990s'. According to Zimbalist, annual industrial growth was 6.3 per cent between 1965 and 1984. But these estimates are contested by C. Mesa-Lago and J. López-Pérez in a very long debate in which the two authors are pitted against Zimbalist, in *Comparative Economic Studies* magazine, nos. 1–4, 1985.
3. Statement of the Sixth Plenary of the PCC Central Committee, in *Granma*, 13 December 1987.
4. C. Brundenius, *Cuba, Crecimiento con Equidad.*
5. R. Turits. 'Trade, Debt and the Cuban Economy', in *World Development*, vol. 15, no. 1, 1987, p. 179, footnote 30.
6. *Le Monde*, 7 June 1987; D. Thorstadt in *New York Native*, 3 August 1987.
7. *Granma*, 1 June 1986.
8. *Latin American Weekly Report*, 20 November 1986. He has since been associated with Hubert Matos, a recently released former counter-revolutionary.

9. *El País*, 30 May 1987.
10. *Latin American Weekly Report*, nos. 25–26, 1987.
11. *Le Monde*, 12 August 1987. Aspillaga is linked with the British secret services. He was wounded in a shoot-out with the Cuban commercial attaché, leading to the expulsion of the ambassador and the attaché from Great Britain.
12. *Le Monde*, 20 January 1988.
13. *Caribbean Report*, 11 June 1982.
14. Interview with *L'Humanité*, 23 May 1987.
15. In 1977 production contracts and joint ventures had been encouraged. In 1982 a new foreign investment code was introduced, allowing foreigners to control 49 per cent of an enterprise's capital, to repatriate part of the profits, to conduct their own policies over labour, prices and production (*Problèmes économiques*, Documentation française, 8 July 1987). But changes occurred following 'rectification', except in tourism.
16. *El País*, 1 May 1987.
17. Fifty-third Plenary of the CTC, Graphical Propaganda Unit, 14 January 1987.
18. *Granma*, 13 December 1987.
19. At the time the PCC had still not been formed. It was the United Party of the Socialist Revolution (PURS), bringing together the 26th of July Movement, the Revolutionary Directorate and the Popular Socialist Party (PSP).
20. *Granma*, 5 March 1967.
21. Ariel Hidalgo was sentenced to eight years' imprisonment in 1981. The charges are not known, but according to Amnesty International, he had been accused of hostile propaganda (Amnesty International report, 6 September 1988). He was freed in August 1988 and lives in the United States.
22. Ariel Hidalgo, 'Cuba, L'Etat marxiste et la nouvelle classe', 1984, mimeographed.
23. Turits. 'Trade, Debt and the Cuban Economy'.
24. *Granma*, 13 December 1987.
25. Ibid.
26. *Bohemia*, 24 June 1988.
27. *Latin American Weekly Report*, 9 June 1988.
28. Ibid.
29. *Juventud Rebelde*, 13 May 1987.
30. *Le Monde*, 7 June 1987.
31. *Le Monde*, 25 June 1988.
32. *Courrier des pays de l'Est*, Documentation française, November 1987.
33. *Granma*, 18 September 1988.
34. F. Pisani, in *Le Monde diplomatique*, December 1987.
35. F. Pisani, in *Le Journal de Genève*, 14 December 1987.
36. *Caribbean Report*, 26 February 1987.
37. Fidel Castro, in *Granma*, 11 January 1987.
38. *Granma*, 15 February 1987.
39. *Granma*, 11 May 1987.
40. Fidel Castro, in *Granma*, 11 January 1987.
41. G. Miná, *Un encuentro con Fidel*, p. 144 and following pages.
42. G. Miná, *Un encuentro con Fidel*, p. 155.
43. In 1962 Kennedy and Khrushchev concluded a secret agreement of non-aggression against Cuba.
44. Fidel Castro, in *Granma*, 13 December 1987.
45. Turits. 'Trade, Debt and the Cuban Economy', p. 172.
46. Fidel Castro in *Granma*, 27 April 1986.
47. *El País*, 1 May 1987.
48. H. Thomas, *La Revolución Cubana 25 años después*.
49. Martínez Heredia, *Desafíos del socialismo cubano*.
50. Tad Szulc, *Fidel*, p. 650.
51. *Juventud Rebelde*, 12 May 1987.

52. *Le Monde*, 2 July 1987.
53. Z. Ventura, in *Jornal do Brasil*, January 1987.
54. *Granma*, 12 May 1987.
55. *The Nation*, New York, 24 October 1988.
56. *Granma*, 5 October 1986.
57. *Bohemia*, 24 June 1988.
58. *Bohemia*, 8 July 1988.
59. More a 'support force' in 1988 with 10,000 members.
60. David Deutschmann, Cuban books editor for Pathfinder Press, in *Perspectiva Mundial*, July–August 1988.
61. *Bohemia*, 8 July 1988.
62. Ibid.
63. Che Guevara, *Ecrits d'un révolutionnaire*.
64. Ricardo Bofill, for example, the president of the Committee for Human Rights, who was imprisoned and then sent into exile in the Federal Republic of Germany in September 1988 (*The Nation*, 24 October 1988).
65. Carlos Franqui, *Vie, aventures et désastres d'un certain Fidel Castro*.
66. Félix de la Uz, for example, or Javier Varona, a Trotskyist sympathizer who committed suicide.
67. On this period, see Jésus Díaz's excellent novel, *Los iniciales de la Tierra*.
68. Anniversary speech to mark the death of Frank País, in *Granma*, 9 December 1979.
69. Gianni Miná, *Un encuentro con Fidel*.
70. Raúl Castro, in *Granma*, 9 December 1979.
71. Fidel Castro, in *Granma*, 26 July 1988.
72. J. Pérez-López, 'Cuban Economy in the 80s', in *Problems of Communism*, September–October 1986.
73. Martínez Heredia, *Desafíos del socialismo cubano*.

4

A Major Absentee: Political Democracy

Thirty years after the revolution, the contradictions and limits of the ruling group's mode of operation are being laid bare by serious economic and social difficulties. Neither the institutionalization of the organs of people's power, the adoption of a new constitution, nor the structuring of the party, have fundamentally changed the leadership's style of operation, despite the existence of a duality of sorts between the bureaucratic apparatus and the pro-Fidel group that frequently short-circuits it. In the final resort it is the ruling group (Fidel Castro and his faithful followers) which takes the essential decisions – overriding those of JUCEPLAN, the Popular Assembly or the PCC Congress – even though it does not have the means with which to introduce, follow and control their direction. This causes considerable disorganization.

It is the same with the judiciary. Long-serving prisoners were freed during the visit of Jesse Jackson in 1984 and of Spanish Prime Minister Felipe González. Gutiérrez Menoyo, for example, who was in charge of setting up armed groups for the CIA following the seizure of power, was simply freed on Fidel Castro's personal orders.

According to Tad Szulc,

> Fidel's impatience leads him to constant changes between goals planned in the short, medium and long term, as well as to endless improvisations. The time needed for an approach to give results (or to prove unsatisfactory) is not even given, overall political co-ordination is absent, and political or visionary pressures push Castro into sudden decisions, as well as to undertaking grandiose projects that the economy cannot stand. ... His compulsive dedication to detail and the conviction that, no matter what the subject, he knows more about it than anyone else, have combined to make Castro an obstacle to an efficient development of both economy and society. ... Therefore, a mutually protective association of bureaucrats has come into being, and the bitter

> Havana joke is that Cuba does have a two-party system after all: the Communist Party and the Bureaucracy Party. The waste of resources and talent is staggering.[1]

In 1970 a Cuban intellectual was already lucidly denouncing the even further concentration of power in Fidel Castro's hands. He stressed the need for the participation of the masses and the different social groups in economic and political decisions, as opposed to the impossibility of managing from a single centre. But he was already expressing doubts as to the likelihood of this occurring:

> I am a bit pessimistic as to the likelihood of such changes coming about. I would like to be wrong, but Fidel's own words show that his idea is to provoke a few changes of individual people, solve a few minor problems irritating the masses, and win popularity through personal visits and conversations at workplaces. But as you can understand, that won't change anything and it's inconceivable that such measures might lead to a reactivation of the economy and to the masses retaining confidence in the leadership.[2]

It was the dreadful failure of the ten-million-tonne sugar-cane harvest which first gave the Soviet Union and its supporters the chance to pull the Castro leadership into line, and to get its men into positions of control. Fidel Castro would henceforth have to read his copy back before speaking and provide a full written submission to the regular authorities of leadership. The writer Gabriel García Márquez has described such 'captive speeches' of Fidel Castro as 'stifled by the strait-jacket of the written text'.[3] Fidel Castro subsequently criticized the excessively 'organized'[4] nature of the First Congress in 1975 where speeches had been prepared in advance.

Seventeen years after Félix de la Uz, Jacobo Timmerman commented: 'The rectification process is lived more as a search for the culprits of errors committed than as a conscious examination of a society which inevitably leads to those errors.'[5] And it is true that Fidel Castro continues to interfere in decisions over medical investments, which breeds of cows should be reared, or even the number of workers needed on a building site for a nuclear power-station.

His behaviour is a product of the revolution's history and the circumstances in which the revolutionary process developed: the speed of military victory and the effectiveness of a limited number of guerrillas, whose dynamism lay in their example and initiative. The absence of a party, of a programme, of political conflicts, as well as of a tradition of work with the masses, did not predispose the 26th of July Movement to an apprenticeship of political democracy, in spite of the exceptional breadth of insurrectional mass struggle in the Cuban Revolution. But particular historical conditions did not allow the leadership of the urban sector to maintain its leading role, as relations between the urban leadership and that of the Sierra Maestra finally were resolved in the latter's favour.[6] Among other things, this explains the underestimation of mass struggles, as well as the subsequent *foquista* rewriting of the revolution's history.

The absorption of the urban leadership has always had a deep effect on the development and functioning of the Castro leadership. One cannot manage an economy in transition as if one were directing a guerrilla war. The *¡Comandante en jefe, ordene!* ('Commander in Chief, we await your orders'), while having some mobilizing power, is no longer enough, even though microbrigade members have the watchword 'Not a minute more, not a second more, we will do it, commander!'

Power at the Workplace

Such a hierarchical approach can be found, to a greater or lesser degree, in all sectors of society, to the point where enterprise managers are often called *el jefe* (chief). The latter's privileges and power in relation to the workers are clear. In 1983, a trade union activist – the social affairs secretary of the light industry rank-and-file section and an attender of the sessions of the *consejos de trabajo* (work councils) – challenged the absenteeism of particular managers and asked the council to deal with the issue. 'The administration was reluctant. I said: "I can prove that of the 24 administrators' time cards in this workplace, 18 showed unjustified absences." But still the management balked at bringing a case. I tried other routes. I talked to the union, but the union would not back me up. It was just too hard for the union leaders to force the issue because it meant going against the *jefes*. The situation was never resolved. The *consejo* could never do anything at all.'[7]

Workers' councils were set up in 1965 to rule on problems of indiscipline and violations of labour law in enterprises. They can only be formed by workers. According to the law of 1965, they were to be composed of five members elected by secret ballot at their workplace for a three-year renewable period. They are charged with the resolution of conflicts between workers and managers over discipline and workers' rights. They mainly deal with conflicts over absenteeism, late arrival at work, the failure to follow tasks, carelessness, the lack of respect for managers, instances of physical assault, damage to tools, as well as cases of fraud and robbery. But wages, working conditions and transfers also form part of their responsibilities.

The status of the councils changed in 1977. A new law approved by the National Assembly of People's Power transferred authority over the councils from the Minister of Labour to the trade unions, which were then made responsible for the administration of labour justice (law number eight on the organization and function of the councils).

Subsequently, in 1980, a new law, law number thirty-two, limited the powers of the council in work conflicts and reinforced the disciplinary powers of managers. In so far as one of the main aims of the SDPE was to encourage enterprises to become more profitable, managers were pushed into reinforcing workplace discipline. 'The danger that, despite increased union strength, a minority stratum of "rationalizers" will go on to acquire more workplace power should not be brushed aside lightly. After all, with Law Number 32, an impressive and longstanding revolutionary tradition which granted Cuban workers a great deal of control over workplace discipline was nullified by a single decree.'[8] This was done by stripping workplace groups and workers of their previous powers.

The *treinta y dos* (the 'thirty-two'), as workers call it, gave rise in the early years to several discipline cases in which there was an abuse of power. This became all the more visible because another law, number thirty-six (promulgated at the same time as number thirty-two), related to discipline applicable to managers. According to a survey carried out by the CTC in 1981, the 'thirty-two' was used twenty-five times more frequently than the 'thirty-six', even though the latter contained a substantial list of offences.[9]

In 1984, the Fifteenth CTC Congress took note of the excessive use of disciplinary sanctions by the *jefes*; and in February 1987, the plenary meeting of the CTC made a similar assessment. In some cases, managers have the right to retain a fraction of profits earned to pay individual or collective bonuses, particularly to cadres.[10] The SDPE led to a strengthening of the enterprise managers' powers, an increase in their resources, a reinforcement of the division of labour, and to a growth in inequalities and arbitrary actions.

Set up on Che's initiative, the councils were initially independent bodies formed by the workers themselves. They had real power to control, even though the scope of their activities was limited by the overall low level of training at the beginning of the revolution. In the recent period it is significant that lack of time has been one of the councils' major problems. The number of conflicts has become increasingly large and the councils have been criticized for not managing to deal with them. To cope, workers had to add this task to their ordinary work, hence the trend towards the councils' decline. The problem could have been solved by a cut in working hours, but intensification of work was the order of the day.

The experience has posed the question of power at the workplace. Who manages? Who is in control? The only counterweight to the power of the managers has been the rank-and-file sections of the CTC. It is undeniable that their role must be taken into account, both because of the traditions of Cuban workers and also because the Castro leadership has made the maintenance of its links with the working masses a crucial element in the consolidation of the regime's social base; the leadership understands that an improvement in labour productivity will only come about through the existence of mass organizations, however slight their representativeness in the enterprise. The CTC and its journal, *Trabajadores*, have become highly critical mouthpieces of the managers' mistakes and criminal practices. The CTC acts as a brake on the arbitrary actions of those *jefes* the workers are hesitant about confronting by themselves; but this support varies from enterprise to enterprise.

The changes in economic policy in the 1970s were accompanied from the very start by a growth in the masses' participation, at the local, municipal and workplace levels. Trade union activities increased – 26,000 new union sections were created – and the election of union leaders gave the latter greater credibility and independence. Eighty-seven per cent of the officials elected for a two-year period had never held office before,[11] which gives some indication as to the scope of the changes. Meetings also became more regular, with workers participating in discussions on production targets, wages and working conditions.

Average national production per worker rose by 21 per cent in 1972,[12] and this was used by certain economists to argue that the increase in productivity was due to the use of material incentives. But this viewpoint has been contested in recent studies. Apart from the fact that it was only in 1974 that wages were linked to productivity, Zimbalist and Ekstein consider that 'the workers were more willing to share responsibility for the policies to which they had given their agreement. ... The development of social relations in the enterprise produces better worker motivation, as well as useful proposals for improving the production system's efficiency, and this led to a a growth in productivity.'[13]

The creation of national plans in the 1970s was the subject of heated debate at the workplace. According to official reports,[14] workers held discussions on the 1980 plan in 91 per cent of enterprises; and in 59 per cent of cases this led to changes in initial figures. Several surveys and polls would appear to confirm real worker participation at the time. In 1975, 85 per cent of workers asked felt that enterprise management should consult the rank and file, and 58 per cent had no doubt about the importance of their opinion. Another poll in 1976 indicated that, out of 355 workers consulted, 80 per cent felt they had a 'significant' role at production assemblies. And in a random selection of 1,000 workers in 1977, the majority said they had an active role in monthly production assemblies; and that they felt able, more often than not, to solve the problems raised there.

It would seem, however, that this situation has changed considerably. According to a commentator from *Bohemia* magazine, 'within the workplaces, democracy is expressed through workers' assemblies and their participation in decisions regarding the production process. But my own experience raises some doubts. I think the project has gone astray – the influence of workers is poor and sometimes merely formal.'[15] More significantly still, a journalist noted, in an article entitled 'Do we really feel like masters?', that the feeling of being a 'collective owner' plays a decisive role in each worker's way of working and in the quality of his or her work, while 'appeals to honour' are not sufficient.

> In the production assemblies where the plan's guiding figures are discussed, however, a certain formalism occasionally reigns as workers discuss the plan collectively and commit themselves to its achievement. They are sometimes badly informed about the proposed aims and distinctive features of the plan. If, instead of having their sense of judgement deepened, workers are regarded with mistrust or ignored when some of them challenge the figures, then they are being distanced from their status as the masters and collective owners of production, rather than being brought closer to it.[16]

Francis Pisani has made similar observations: 'With infinite patience *compañero* Gada [the manager] explains the principle of what could be called the "yo-yo economy" to me. This consists of sending figures, suggestions or demands "upwards" and waiting for answers, directions and orders to come back "downwards", in an endless to-ing and fro-ing between the rank and file and leadership. It is extraordinarily difficult to locate the level at which decisions are taken, even though the correct answer is always to say "above", but without saying from where.'[17]

The situation in the trade unions has also deteriorated noticeably. The workers' scope for decision-making is very limited, as a JUCEPLAN official self-importantly affirmed: 'We do not discuss balance of payments deficits with factory workers.'[18] According to Pisani, 'the participation of those present is real', the worker 'can freely discuss issues that are taboo in capitalist firms and no one is frightened of speaking'; yet 'the workers have lost their taste for those kinds of meetings'.[19] In one small enterprise 75 out of 300 came to the assembly. As to the self-critical attitude of officials, one activist says that it is a case of the well-known technique of pre-empting the accusations to come. Although all issues are dealt with, including the failure to meet targets set by the plan, few young people participate and there is an overwhelming atmosphere of weariness. Two days earlier, a production assembly had discussed the same issues, and, during the course of the second assembly, a worker summarizes the situation well: 'We know what the problems are. Now we'd like to know how to solve them.'[20] This is a good summary of the more general problems affecting Cuba: debate and criticism are open, but this 'eiderdown democracy' does not give any power to those practising it.

A US sociologist summarizes the situation as follows: 'the union might more correctly be considered a supporter of the status quo at the workplace, rather than an advocate of greater assumption of power by the workforce.'[21] The trade union continues to be a tool for the application of the party's central directives; and the party, in return, is responsible for faithfully reflecting the reactions and state of mind of the masses. Concerned with the disaffection of workers, in February 1987 the CTC Plenum resurrected criticism of managers, for whom 'the most important thing was their enterprise, above the interests of society as a whole'.[22] Speakers stressed how much this sectoralization had weakened workers' power of control and had instead reinforced that of managers.

Initially, rectification led to an extension of workers' room for manoeuvre in the workplace, though this space has been limited. Nevertheless, there has been an upturn in trade union activity; and at a time when the revolution is facing unprecedented difficulties, this is crucial if the government wishes to prevent the current process from being regarded as a new way of getting people to swallow the bitter pill of austerity.

The Organs of People's Power and Planning

From the mid-1970s, bodies in charge of local activities (public services and local enterprises) were created with the aim of decentralizing economic management. These organs of people's power (OPPs) are consulted during the preparation of the plan. Their members can collaborate with the national commissions studying economic problems, and in principle they debate with JUCEPLAN and the Council of Ministers as part of the preparation of national plans. In reality, the powers of the OPPs express and, above all, reflect local and provincial interests in the planning process. Economic power is centralized at ministerial level, and the function of the OPPs is to manage the local investment programmes for which they are responsible, as well as to improve the achievement of objectives that have been assigned centrally.

At the local and provincial level the OPPs are elected by direct suffrage. At the grassroots of electoral wards, lists are composed of a minimum of two candidates and a maximum of eight, and 50 per cent of the votes are needed for election, hence the very frequent need for a second round. But this formally democratic procedure is offset by the national system for the election of deputies which was the subject of significant debate in 1975–76. The OPPs are 'capped' by the National Assembly of People's Power, a legislative assembly whose deputies are elected by the municipal assemblies. This assembly is therefore not elected by direct suffrage, which is limited to the provincial level, and this gave rise to considerable debate between supporters of direct elections at all levels and those wishing to exempt regional and national levels. The deputies' mandate involves explaining government policy and providing regular reports to electors. In the case of elections by direct suffrage, election results could give rise to significant fluctuations, to deputies being sanctioned, as well as the emergence of different positions, indeed, different new groupings. But in a one-party system, candidates elected indirectly are more easy to control.

It would appear that debate over this issue was so important that the text submitted to referendum on 15 February 1976 did not specify the electoral procedure chosen! It was only after the elections that the central preparatory commission under Fidel Castro announced that the National Assembly would be composed of deputies already elected by municipal assemblies.[23] Moreover, Fidel Castro maintains a systematic ambiguity on this election procedure, and has failed to make clear its indirect character at the national level.[24]

Nevertheless, in comparison with other socialist economies, the level of consultation and debate is relatively high, with decentralization and participation more important than in the Soviet Union. But the same authors recognize that 'this kind of participation does not entail a significant diffusion of power nor should it be confused with democratic control ... "real" participation is not merely a process of rational discussion of economic objectives, but a political process which involves the airing of opposing views and competing interests.'[25]

The limits of what was initially intended to ensure a true people's power from top to bottom have been highlighted by the simple fact, emphasized by François Maspero, that such structures should have played a decisive role in rectification:

> Why hasn't this structure at least acted as an alarm bell over the last ten years? Today, the grassroots people's power assemblies should be playing a decisive role in rectification. This is precisely the time for the rendering of accounts. What is happening? In Havana, I am told, there are assemblies that should be attended by 150 people but are only attended by 15. The latter debate vigorously and express their discontent. The rest wait. For what? Disaffection? On arriving, I asked the official body – the Cuban Peoples' Friendship Institute (ICAP), which made a number of suggestions – if I could see one thing: the functioning of people's power. I didn't get a reply.[26]

On 30 April 1989, 98 per cent of the population elected delegates to the municipal assemblies. But even the official press had been concerned about the low participation in the preparatory assemblies.[27] The fact that assemblies for the rendering of accounts are held at the same time as the selection meetings for candidates (because too much time should not be wasted in meetings) also tends to make the accountability of those elected a mere formality. But that is not the most important issue. The problem stems, above all, from the criteria for selecting delegates. According to the Electoral Commission, it is a case of electing the best representatives of the people, those most likely to be sensitive to the problems and suggestions of their neighbours, and the most capable and representative: their curriculum vitae is very important. Strictly applied locally, such criteria are emptied of any content at the national level. And is not the best proof of this provided by the corruption cases at the highest level, which are never denounced on the grounds that a particular OPP at a particular level is involved?

According to the party programme adopted in 1975, however, the OPPs have the right to 'dismiss' elected representatives 'when they are no longer worthy of trust'. Deputies 'appoint and replace administrative officials of the state, elect and dismiss members of executive bodies, elect and dismiss members of the popular tribunals'.

Fidel Castro's statements clearly mask the problem:

> If the people were counter-revolutionary, if the majority of the people were counter-revolutionary, it would only need counter-revolutionaries to be proposed in the electoral wards and the majority of delegates would be counter-revolutionary. They would be against socialism. We have two grassroots elections every five years, and delegates can be re-elected by voters. The electoral system of the Cuban Revolution is truly unique! We have nothing to learn from elsewhere. On the contrary, we could say: come here and learn how a democratic electoral system is created.[28]

In 1989 a member of a dissident human rights group, Roberto Bahamonde, stood for the first time against a PCC member in a local election at San Miguel del Padrón near Havana. He was beaten by an official at the Ministry of the Interior, Gerardo Aldama, but his performance (31 votes against 60) was a surprise.[29]

But the issue is not one of counter-revolutionaries opposing revolutionaries; it is one of different approaches to overall political and economic problems. This would mean the elaboration of different electoral platforms, a plurality of candidates nationally, as well as pluralism in terms of information and organization. 'Bad examples' could come especially from the Soviet Union in as far as *Moscow News* gives widespread coverage of that country's new electoral experiences (which is one reason why it was banned in Cuba in August 1989).

In terms of planning, the remit of popular power is extremely limited, including at the level of controlling the execution of plans. Nationally, JUCEPLAN as a body is relegated to a secondary role and occupies an 'awkward position sandwiched between the demands of the party leadership on the one side and the pressures of economic and social agencies on the other'.[30]

In 1984 the draft plan for 1985 was challenged by the party leadership. The reasons given by Fidel Castro in his opening speech at the first session of the Third Congress amounted to a complete indictment of the functioning of the economy, and of the last five-year plan in particular. He blamed inadequate exports of goods and services, the lack of attention given to import substitution, the failure to anticipate possible uses of sugar-cane derivatives, the conception and execution of investments (characterized by sectoral initiatives), the atomization of enterprises and their lack of profitability, and so on. Such a challenge had several effects, reflecting as it did the scope of internal debate within the party apparatus over market reforms and economic policy.

Those supporting an extension of the powers of enterprises and a greater use of market devices are generally considered to be the pro-Soviet wing. Today's Gorbachev supporters are often yesterday's Stalinists, or rather opportunistic bureaucrats who are finding personal rewards in the new Soviet policy. Among them one simultaneously finds old PSP members, like Carlos Rafael Rodríguez, and younger Soviet-trained officials and economists, of whom Humberto Pérez, a former JUCEPLAN official, is a representative.[31] (Dismissed from his responsibilities at JUCEPLAN in 1985, Pérez was also, until the same date, the president of the commission in charge of introducing the SDPE, as well as the vice-president of the executive committee of the Council of Ministers.)

On 19 December 1987 Pérez was directly challenged at the sixth plenum of the Central Committee: 'In order to look more closely into the origin of the erroneous conceptions and practices that have been introduced into the planning of the national economy, as well as the deviations that resulted from the lack of controls during the introduction of the SDPE, the Politburo formed a commission headed by Raúl Castro to examine the specific responsibility that comrade Humberto Pérez might have had.' Having approved the commission's conclusions, the Central Committee was 'to criticize the justificatory position' of the former official of the plan, as well as his 'formal acceptance of errors of a secondary nature, and his refusal to assume responsibility for crucial matters that were incumbent upon him – either directly, alone or with others – and the management of which has given rise to serious errors'. The sixth plenum also ratified the commission's criticisms of his tendency to amass personal privileges. As a result, Pérez was suspended from the

Central Committee in accordance with article eight of party rules on the application of sanctions.[32]

It is useful to refer to the report prepared by Pérez, when he was president of JUCEPLAN, on the implementation of the plan for the national economy for 1982 and on the draft plan for 1983 presented to the National Assembly. It mentioned the problems faced, the high rates of interest on loans, the effects of rampant inflation on imported goods from the capitalist countries, the massive withdrawal of short-term credit facilities hitherto granted by banks in the capitalist countries, the drastic reduction of available funds in foreign exchange, the effects of the fall in sugar prices, as well as the impact of protectionism by the European Community and the United States. In the report, Pérez defended, as a supporter of the SDPE and one of those responsible for its introduction, 'incentive measures through bonuses in national currency for workers concerned with exports' and 'bonuses in convertible currency for bodies and enterprises that achieve or surpass their export plans'[33] – measures, he claimed, that would have given positive results in 1982. Such a surprising initiative in a country where the shortage of foreign exchange is a major bottleneck – and which would have given an exorbitant privilege to exporting enterprises outside of any central control – was violently denounced by Fidel Castro in 1987, as if he had made a discovery. Yet all this figured prominently in *Granma* in 1983 after a speech made to the National Assembly.

How and when did Pérez violate the mandate of the PCC Congress on the implementation of the SDPE? Was the responsibility individual or collective? What was meant by the sentence emphasizing that Humberto Pérez 'is shirking his responsibilities as far as the crucial issues are concerned'? Except for criticism of his personal lifestyle, nothing was really clear, and one can only conclude that he was a scapegoat.

The muffled and elliptic terms of the debate hid other issues at stake in the critical relations with the Soviet Union. As so often in the past (1962, 1968, 1970, 1975), the Soviet Union uses its aid as an excuse for direct interference and multiple pressures.

The Establishment of the 'Central Group' and the Report of the Third Congress

At the end of 1984 a 'central group' was created, composed of vice-presidents and ministers from the Council of Ministers, Central Committee secretaries and heads of department, and presidents of provincial OPPs. Given the new direction being taken, it was this group which restructured the 1985 plan and was to do the same with the 1986 plan, the five-year plan and the prospective plan looking forward to the year 2000.[34]

Headed by Osmany Cienfuegos – the former minister of construction and a PCC leader – the group has since 'capped' all other structures and will be maintained, as Fidel Castro announced in his speech to the Third Congress. It is interesting to note that the party congress, which, according to article 41 of the statutes, 'discusses and approves the directives of medium- and long-term economic development plans', was confronted in 1986 with a *fait accompli.* Equally significant was the fact that the free farmers' markets had been suppressed in April 1986, shortly after the first session of the Congress and before the second.

These divisions at the top without doubt explain why the Third Congress was held in two sessions, one at the beginning of 1986 and the other in December 1986. In February, Congress approved neither the third five-year plan (1986–90) nor the party programme, and for six months the texts were put on ice. Officially, this was to allow discussions to continue and to submit proposed changes to party members. The resolution on the draft programme[35] specified that the document was approved 'as a plan' but would be submitted 'for discussion by the people'; and that after this 'popular consultation', the plan would be presented to a 'special session of the Third Congress'.

Apparently, the project presented to the February session and deferred to December was aimed at replacing the programme that had been adopted at the First Congress in 1975 (to elaborate the party's definitive programme).[36] The new programme could only gain from the deal. The 1975 platform had a strong neo-Stalinist flavour that even the most unmitigated of bureaucrats would not deny. As far as Latin America was concerned, the deliberations on the 'avant-garde detachments of the working class, namely the Latin American communist parties' were startling. Fidel Castro's diatribes on the betrayal of the Bolivian or Venezuelan communist parties had disappeared. Other passages on the defence of the 'purity of Marxism-Leninism ... against the bourgeoisie and its lackeys, against the anti-Soviet campaigns, right- or left-wing revisionists', were reminiscent of the style of the PSP in the 1950s. Nor was Hungary omitted, with references being made to the 'counter-revolutionary activities of 1956 ... checked by the people ... with the direct aid of the Soviet Union'.

What happened in 1986? Why was the Third Congress split into two sessions at the last minute? As Martínez Heredia has noted,[37] this was 'quite unusual'. The same year, the Vietnamese Communist Party was introducing a policy of economic reform in line with the orientations from Moscow that had been discussed within the framework of Comecon. There can be no doubt that the Castro leadership, by opposing the new course, met with considerable resistance from within the Cuban apparatus itself, as demonstrated by the interruption of the Congress and the announcement of the rectification process between the two sessions.

In 1982 Fidel had denounced speculation in the farmers' markets, as well as illegal enrichment, which he intended to penalize by raising taxes.[38] But his proposals did not win support, as he himself pointed out: 'The farmers don't like the idea of this tax. They claim it will lead to price rises, that the population will be unhappy and that they will criticize the farmers as a result.'[39] In 1986, the decision was irrevocable. But the crucial thing was that the rectification campaign – which should have been adopted by the Congress – was launched, along with an appeal to the masses, between the two sessions in April 1986. The target of the campaign was made clear by the virulence of the attacks against bureaucrats and technocrats of any kind. Those most in the firing line were particular strata of bureaucrats in economic management posts. 'For years they have run a kind of tyranny that has been virtually uncontrolled,' a leader declared.[40] 'But one cannot tackle the crisis and create instability at that level. Hence the need to tone down certain criticisms until the situation had been dealt with.'[41]

Nevertheless, Fidel Castro has taken care to clarify that there was no question of a cultural revolution[42] and that 'you can't do without administrative cadres. It is thus a case of controlling the mechanisms [the cadres] have to use. Such mechanisms must be analysed and studied in depth.'[43] Administrative cadres should be given 'the means to manage better'.[44]

It was also significant that rectification was accompanied by a reaffirmation of the primacy of the leading role of the PCC. But it would be simplistic to see the central political apparatus and managers as being on opposite sides. The debate stemmed from a combination of factors and ran through all levels of leadership, in spite of the autonomy of the group around Fidel Castro. The severity of the economic crisis was joined by what Fidel Castro called the 'difficult circumstances that have arisen since the Congress'.[45] Let us remember that 1986 was a decisive year in terms of debt payments to the West and the Soviet Union.

One-Party Rule and Political Rights

The reaffirmation of the leading role of the PCC and its avant-garde position, the emphasis placed on consciousness as the driving force of the revolution, on mass participation, as well as the criticism of market mechanisms – all occurred within the framework of the conception of the single party as the 'guiding force' of society as a whole. According to the PCC statutes adopted at the First Congress, the party is 'the supreme body leading our society. It brings together, organizes, guides and orientates the workers and all working people, as well as the other social organizations and the state, with a view to the realization of the programme's supreme objective: the construction of a communist society.'[46] Accompanying this definition was a ban on factions, which were 'incompatible' with party principles (article 35). Paradoxically, such imported formulas have been used repeatedly against pro-Soviet figures, particular during periods of tension with the Soviet Union.

The deferred session of the Third Congress adopted amendments to the statutes, but the changes introduced are not known. Decisions on statutes are obviously taken by the core of leading cadres in the Politburo and the Council of State, with the Central Committee merely endorsing them. Moreover, 'official' cases of expulsion from the party are rarely made public,[47] and the political life and activities of the rank-and-file levels – the cells – are generally quite limited.

The real exercise of power does not stem from concepts set down in writing. At the very most, the latter reinforce actual practice. The defence of the *mando único* (the single command), as well as unity conceived as a homogeneous whole, are not originally inspired by the practices of the Communist Party of the Soviet Union or the Latin American communist parties, but from a military conception of the party.

It is worth recalling that, in line with the orders and directives of the rebel-army staff, eight 'departments' had been created in the Sierra Maestra for the civil administration of the liberated areas: the departments of justice, health, social security, agriculture and peasant affairs, construction, industry, social construction, services, education and finances.[48] The departments were embryos of the future ministries.

Following the revolution's victory, the rebel army, the backbone of the 26th of July Movement, became the core for the political organization of society, as is borne out by the number of officers in the government: Fidel Castro, Raúl Castro, Che Guevara, Ramiro Valdés at the Ministry of the Interior, Martínez Sánchez at the Ministry of Labour, Omar Fernández at the Ministry of Transport, Machado Ventura at the Ministry of Health, etc. Practically all ministers were former commanders of the rebel army. All area heads of the National Institute of Agrarian Reform (INRA) in the provinces came from the army: 'They represented revolutionary power in the provinces, thus highlighting the authority and competence of the heads of INRA.'[49] According to Fidel, 'they had to have knowledge of war and be the ramparts of the revolution in their areas'.[50] As Che stressed, it was the army which was the unifying and mobilizing factor for the working masses, especially the peasants. In addition to its socio-economic and political tasks in the wake of the takeover, the rebel army was also active in the area of ideology and education and played a decisive role in the campaign against illiteracy.

The pervasiveness of the rebel army was of a particular kind. The 26th of July Movement was a specific military-political organization with a highly limited number of cadres. Following the takeover, its organizational weakness (approximately 2,000–3,000 soldiers), when compared with the distinctly greater forces of the PSP (estimated at 15,000 members), was to complicate the process of forming a new unified revolutionary organization. Fidel Castro himself would make up for this rank-and-file handicap in the name of unity, sealed at the top under his direction, which did nothing to prevent several crises.

The Integrated Revolutionary Organizations (ORI) brought together the PSP, the 26th of July Movement (which was much smaller in numbers but infinitely more prestigious) and the Revolutionary Directorate, the weakest of the groups. Fidel Castro would impose his political leadership at the cost of numerous conflicts. The struggle for influence between himself and the PSP, which drew its strength from its privileged links with the Soviet Union, lasted for years. This experience has undoubtedly confirmed his conviction that he alone can speak in the name of the whole people, refusing to tolerate the slightest dissent. In 1959 the commander-in-chief had recalled: 'What led to the victory? ... Confidence in the leadership, confidence in the *líder*. ... This confidence was total, there weren't any political problems in the Sierra Maestra. ... Our officers did not ask political questions. We were confident and we had the military leadership of the war.'[51]

Much later, he would confirm this deep conviction: 'The ideal thing in politics is unity of opinion, unity of doctrine, unity of forces and unity of command, as in a war. It is difficult to imagine a battle, being in the midst of a battle, with ten different military strategies and ten different sets of tactics. ... The ideal is unity, but reality is something else.'[52]

In his relations with the masses, Castro displays a didactic charisma and sees the education of the masses like a teacher who exercises his authority and spreads the good word. In the early years of the revolution this style of leadership was accepted by the semi-literate masses who received their political education at huge meetings in Revolution Square. But today this 'government by the word' is increasingly unable to offset the sluggishness of a stratified apparatus; it irritates the intellectuals and leaves many sectors of the population indifferent.

It is difficult to define with precision the relations between the party's ruling apparatus and the administrative and governmental apparatus. In some cases, official responsibility is purely nominal. At the Ministry of Foreign Affairs, for example, it is the PCC's foreign relations secretary, a member of the Politburo, who participates directly in the negotiations on Angola; or it is Carlos Aldana, the official responsible for ideology; but not the actual minister. Until recently, Isidoro Malmierca contented himself with opening flower shows.

Officially, the party has 523,000 members, of whom 43.2 per cent are workers in production and services. They are distributed as follows: 37.3 per cent are manual workers (it is not certain that they are still based in production) and 5.9 per cent are in services; 16.5 per cent are academics, professionals or technicians.[53] Twenty-one per cent are women. Out of 1,790 delegates to the Third Congress, there were 526 manual workers, 24 farmers, 222 workers linked to services, scientific activities, education and other social duties, as well as 223 combatants from the armed forces and the Ministry of the Interior. Out of the total, 864 delegates were university-educated and 442 had had vocational training. Four hundred and twenty-three were founder members of the party (less than a quarter of the total, their previous party membership unknown) and 563 members had taken part in international activity in support of other peoples (helping Nicaragua and Angola militarily or acting as technicians in several other Third World countries).[54]

These figures were given by Raúl Castro at the opening of the deferred session of the Third Congress on 30 November 1986. The text giving notice of the Congress stipulated that provincial assemblies of the party and meetings of the armed forces and the Ministry of the Interior should elect delegates on the basis of proposals made directly by a group of grassroots organizations chosen in workplaces and military units. Thirty per cent of the delegates would be workers directly linked to the production of material goods. It would seem that this proportion was respected. Forty per cent of the Central Committee are new members and 28 per cent of these are black or of mixed colour, which is just below their proportion of the Cuban population as a whole. According to Tad Szulc, the distribution of leaders in the Central Committee was as follows: '78.1 percent had a university education; 27.5 per cent were bureaucrats and administrators, and full-time party officials. Twenty per cent of the seats went to the armed forces and the Interior Ministry Security Services.'[55] Workers still in production are almost absent from this level of the leadership and women are also under-represented, in spite of recent efforts. Only one woman, Vilma Espín, has a seat on the Politburo; she is an official of the Federation of Cuban Women (FMC) and a former official of the 26th of July Movement in Santiago.

That is the situation as far as social composition is concerned. Another important factor is that the membership has evolved in terms of size. The number of PCC members rose from 45,000 in 1965 to more than 500,000 in 1988. In 1975 there were 211,642 members; and in 1980, 434,143. The party therefore doubled its membership in the five years after the

First Congress. Such promotion coincided with a period when Soviet influence had been pervasive in every area. This numerical growth then slowed down. The majority of members have thus joined recently. In 1985 the founder members of the party (with 20 years of service) amounted to 5 per cent at the most; more than two-thirds of members had less than ten years of service, while 39 per cent had been members for more than five years.[56] The vast majority of members receive a poor political education, and are under the influence of an apparatus that is imbued with the ideological concepts that prevailed under Brezhnev, passed on by texts which fill the bookshops. The generations in the majority in the party know little or nothing of the debates that took place in Cuba and Latin America during the first decade. Such a background also helps to explain the upheavals caused by the rectification process.

Concern has been growing in the apparatus since 1986. Officials 'admit to fearing for their jobs and have their doubts as to the wisdom of recent economic measures'.[57]

> In government circles President Castro's criticisms have given rise to fear and anxiety; some officials define the present situation as both uncertain and worrying. They fear a purge is on its way – such as the one that preceded the Mariel exodus in December 1979 – but do not know who will be purged and who will emerge on top. This state of uncertainty has brought some officials and departments to a state of semi-paralysis. ... The *Central de Trabajadores de Cuba* and the *Trabajadores* newspaper have been harsh critics of management and labour malpractices.[58]

Indeed, the dismissal of enterprise managers under trade union pressure has not been uncommon. It has been one of the reasons why certain managers are in favour of workers electing managers, as this gives 'greater scope to the person managing',[59] as well as more independence. During the interval between the two congresses in 1986, it appears that 1,200 members or officials were sanctioned.[60] This instability and job insecurity are reinforced by the fact that the discontent of the popular masses is rarely directed at Fidel Castro who is generally exempted from criticism. And once again, the people give a massive response when it is a question of protesting against imperialism and demonstrating their solidarity with the revolution.[61] Such political credit is also extended to particular leaders known for their integrity and selflessness who live in the old parts of Havana, in the same difficult conditions as the workers.

The bureaucracy is not a homogeneous whole that is united in the defence of its interests and privileges. This new phenomenon owes its existence to the fact that a section of the apparatus is beginning to feel strong enough to resist the commander-in-chief, favouring an approach modelled on the Gorbachev reforms which provide some protection. This probably explains the resistance apparently offered by Humberto Pérez to recognizing his 'errors' in the implementation of the SDPE. Everyone agrees about the attraction exerted by developments in Soviet politics. *Moscow News* used to be eagerly grabbed from the newsstands. This certainly did not mean that there was agreement with market reforms, but it did indicate a thirst for knowledge and the need for debate and new ideas.

As to Fidel Castro, he is the permanent guerrilla in a fortress under siege. And just as national unity and unity of action become confused with ideological unity and the homogeneity of thought, the leadership contains any differences internally. This was the case in the past, with the sectarianism trial in 1962, the Marcos Rodríguez affair in 1964, and the micro-faction affair in 1968, etc. Some of these sybilline debates often conceal an implicit polemic with the Soviet Union and are kept under wraps. But a mitigating factor is that arguments with the Soviet Union were never open and still less public. They were expressed only through misleading double-speak. Faced with Gorbachev, the differences have been more clearly exposed, particularly since the speech of 26 July 1988.

Political life had become so impoverished and sterile that no mechanism existed for the 'negative tendencies' affecting the country to be made manifest. Apparently aware of the problem, Fidel Castro protested to the congress of journalists about the insufficiently critical role of Cuban journalism[62] and denounced the 'mystifications' of which journalists were victims. Yet, while admitting that 'all kinds of criteria and tendencies cut across each other in a revolutionary process', Castro could declare shortly afterwards that press denunciation of serious errors committed at a particular enterprise (Mercerón) should have had the prior agreement of the party leadership![63]

As a Spanish journalist commented ironically, this attempt at opening up was due to the appearance of a new 'leader of the opposition' – Fidel Castro himself, who would add this title to the ones he already held. But, the reporter stressed, 'in his attempt to correct errors, the enthusiasm which springs from Castro's intellectual and political power comes up against a buffer which hinders and puts a brake on the renewal required. The arthritic bureaucratic apparatus that has been developed during thirty years of revolution threatens to stifle efforts at renewal.'[64]

The only real opening up has been in relation to the Church following the switch made by the ecclesiastical hierarchy at the national meeting of the Cuban Church in 1986. As the Jesuit father Pierre de Charantenay has written, this meeting marked 'the emergence of the Cuban Church from the ghetto ... for Christians it was both Vatican II and Puebla'.[65] This development was helped by Fidel Castro's personal relations with Frei

Betto,[66] the Brazilian Dominican, as well as by the role played by dignitaries from the US Church in the liberation of political prisoners.

Rectification and Human Rights

The most recent figure given for the number of prisoners held for 'crimes against the security of the state' was 400, according to the assessment given by the Cuban authorities at the Geneva conference in May 1987,[67] and 455 according to Amnesty International[68] (out of a total penal population of around 30,000 people). But included in Amnesty's calculations were 68 *plantados históricos*,[69] imprisoned for their connection with counter-revolution in the 1960s.

It is difficult to ascertain what the exact charges are, particularly if they are related to crimes of opinion or acts committed against the revolution. The international press lumps together terrorists and political prisoners. It is true that the secrecy surrounding trials and sentences prevents the reasons for the sentences or the precise fate of the culprits from being known. Even today, Cuban officials still justify this by stating that 'trials are public unless the security of the state, morality, public order or respect for the victim of the crime demand that they be held in camera'.[70] This was why, for example, the execution of Marcos Rodríguez was concealed for so long. A member of the Young Communists under the dictatorship, Rodríguez had been responsible for denouncing four revolutionaries and members of the Directorate to Batista's police, and had nevertheless been protected by leaders of the old Cuban Communist Party (his trial had been public in 1964). Similarly, the release of Ramón Guin was only discovered in November 1987 (he had been imprisoned in 1963 for an assassination attempt against Fidel Castro, and the length of his prison sentence had never been made public).

A distinction must always be made between imprisonment for actual counter-revolutionary activities and for crimes of political opinion. The Cuban Revolution has been sufficiently attacked – and continues to be sufficiently threatened – by its powerful neighbour for it to have a legitimate right of defence against attacks on its people planned ninety miles from its shores. There is nothing rhetorical about this, as the numerous accounts of CIA-sponsored assassination attempts on leaders have clearly shown.

But the most notorious issue remains the extent of imprisonments for common-law crimes (until recent measures), despite the significant reduction in crime since the revolution. According to UK Labour member of the European Parliament Richard Balfe, 'sanctions are more severe than would seem reasonable ... those guilty of minor crimes could be released after a year or 18 months in prison instead of three to four years'.[71] Such a verdict was belatedly corroborated by Fidel Castro: 'Our society is incomparably healthier than any other and yet the number of people imprisoned for common-law crimes is abnormally high, due to the fact that Cuban law classifies as crimes a number of deeds that would not be considered as such elsewhere.'[72]

This implicit recognition of the excesses permitted under the 1979 Penal Code led to the removal, as minister of the interior, of R. Valdés – an old Castroite suspected of excessive allegiance to the Soviet Union – and, more significantly still, to the adoption of a new Penal Code in 1987. According to R. Mendoza, 'the new code should eliminate crimes which, according to contemporary theories of criminal law, should not be sanctioned by depriving [people] of their liberty ... but should be curbed by a fines system. ... The criminalization of various forms of behaviour which do not entail any real social danger would be halted.'[73]

Out of 30,000 common-law prisoners, 28,000 have been paroled since 1986 (the new Penal Code having been implemented retroactively) and only 2.9 per cent have become reoffenders.[74] Remaining are the political prisoners accused of attacking the security of the state, or of 'enemy propaganda', the latter considered illegal if 'it makes use of written, oral or any other form of propaganda to attack the social order, international solidarity or the socialist state'. It would seem that this article (103) remains unchanged in the new Penal Code[75] and sentences can range from one to ten years. Imprisonment for attempted illegal departure from the country, on the other hand, has been removed from the new code.

In June 1988 Fidel Castro made a proposal to Cardinal O'Connor, the Archbishop of New York, to free prisoners sentenced for attacks on the security of the state (bar forty-four of them) if the United States was prepared to accept them. And on the whole, it would indeed seem that the freeing of these prisoners has been carried out or is in the course of being carried out. This was an important turning-point. Rejecting the evidence, Fidel Castro had in effect contested the existence of political prisoners: 'I do not accept the idea that there are prisoners for reasons of political dissent. What does exist are people imprisoned for their activities against the socialist state and the revolution, by virtue of deeds sanctioned by laws.'[76]

The case of Armando Valladares, freed on the request of François Mitterrand and following the intervention of Régis Debray in the name of the defence of human rights, has been used by Fidel Castro as an example of this kind. Valladares's paralysis as a result of torture was not only shown to be a fabrication, as Régis Debray has confirmed;[77] but the Cuban press had reproduced his card as a member of the Batista police time and time again and had denounced, in the journal *Revolución* on 30

December 1960, his participation in an assassination attempt. Valladares's presence as US ambassador at a meeting of the UN Human Rights Commission, charged with the condemnation of Cuban abuses, has provoked several protests, not just from Latin Americans, but also from French journalists.[78]

But that does not solve the situation of political dissidents. The case of Gustavo Arcos, for example, a figure with a 'revolutionary background'[79] has been dealt with in an extremely offhand way by Cuban leaders. Replying to a question by the Italian journalist, Gianni Miná, Fidel Castro made vague accusations against Arcos, saying that he had 'racist and fascist' ideas and that he had conspired against the revolution. A rather inadequate reply, given that Arcos was a former party member.

Ariel Hidalgo, the author of a 'samizdat' text – 'The Marxist State and the New Class' – was arrested in 1981 and sentenced to seven years in prison, apparently under the terms of article 108–1 of the old Penal Code. He has since been released and is now in the United States. In an interview, he claimed that his home had been searched following the Mariel exodus. He had criticized the way Cubans going into exile had been insulted. After the discovery of the manuscript at his home, he was sentenced, in his own words, for 'ideological deviation'.[80] His denunciations of the way the apparatus worked have subsequently been confirmed. At the start of the 1960s, the poet Herberto Padilla was more lucky: thanks to his 'confessions', he left prison after thirty-seven days.

The case of Ricardo Bofill, the best-known dissident and president of the Committee for Human Rights (founded in 1976 and then reorganized on a different basis in 1984), was more controversial. He has long since been linked with the old Cuban Communist Party and was sentenced in 1967 during the pro-Soviet micro-faction trial. The Cuban press has reproduced manuscripts giving proof of his aid proposals for the Cuban security services during his stay in prison. To our knowledge, Bofill, who now lives in Germany, has never denied such letters.

The silence which, until recently, surrounded sentences and the arbitrariness of rulings have helped campaigns to discredit the Cuban Revolution. The Castro leadership has become aware of this and has expended considerable efforts to combat it, and especially to avoid condemnation of Cuba by the United Nations. Several Euro-MPs have been brought to see the situation for themselves, and numerous articles in *Granma* have set about refuting accusations. A third attempt to place Cuba in the dock took place at the forty-forth session of the UN Human Rights Commission in Geneva; but it failed, as most Latin American countries refused to associate themselves with the US manoeuvres. Instead, Amnesty International, Americas Watch, the UN Human Rights

Commission and the Red Cross were authorized by the government to visit prisons on the island for the first time in thirty years.

The UN mission's report, written by a five-member working group and chaired by a Senegalese diplomat, Alioune Sene, did not present any conclusions or recommendations, in accordance with the compromise that had led the Cuban authorities to disguise an on-the-spot investigation as something they had invited. The investigators were shocked by 1,700 complaints of human rights violations. While they accepted that 'there is no murder or systematic torture'[81] in Cuban prisons, the mission did confirm the existence of ill-treatment. In 1988, fifteen officials, including the director of Camagüey prison, were punished for cruelty to prisoners. Several cases of harassment and humiliation have confirmed the accounts of former prisoners. Such an account is Martha Frayde's book which makes a good job of tracing the itinerary of the early Castroites, confused by the unforeseen radicalization of the revolution.[82]

According to the working group, of the 458 people imprisoned for state security infringements (this figure provided by the Cuban government), only 121 were still in prison. This was due to changes introduced at the political level and in penal legislation. Indeed, the modification of the old 1979 Penal Code, approved by the National Assembly of People's Power, had a real effect. But since November 1988, six human rights activists have been given sentences of up to a year in prison for printing clandestine texts or disturbing public order (attempted demonstrations). Twenty-two people have been arrested since the visit of the UN mission and some have been detained without trial.[83] And after the execution of Ochoa, others have been arrested for spreading rumours which had portrayed the execution as an 'assassination'. The new Penal Code stipulates that socialist penal law must emphasize crime prevention rather than repression, with the deprivation of freedom reserved for crimes considered to be highly serious. One way or another, the exercise of any civil and political right not accepted by the regime falls into this category.

On the other hand, it is a sign of the times that sanctions 'against abuses in the exercise of responsibilities in state bodies' have increased. A new law has appeared – illicit enrichment – which is aimed in particular at 'those who become rich in an undue manner as a result of their work in any body, irrespective of their job or level of responsibility. This enrichment can be revealed by goods possessed, as well as by lifestyle, in so far as expenditure bears no relation to real income.' Made before the scandal of the officers officially accused of drug trafficking became public, these comments by the Attorney-General, Ramón de la Cruz, already indicated the scale of rampant corruption in ruling circles.

The Revolution, Women's Liberation and Machismo-Leninismo

Until 1958 the proportion of women in the economically active population had never been over 13 per cent[84] and their jobs were mainly domestic, except for a minority who had access to administrative jobs arising from urban growth. This situation conformed to the traditional conception of women's role in a neo-colonial society as being in the home, especially since unemployment was very high. Such an inferior status was reinforced by the machismo of Latin American societies.

The revolution led to major changes in terms of women's access to work. In 1986, 1,144,000 women, or 37.4 per cent of the workforce, were working. In Havana, the figure reached 44 per cent; and in 18 other municipalities, 45 per cent.[85] In social and economic terms, there has thus been considerable progress, even though access to responsibility has far from followed the same pattern.

In the early years of the revolution, the incorporation of women into the workplace was due to the literacy campaign and voluntary work, particularly in agriculture where women replaced men being drafted into the factories. Gradually, women achieved a stable position in production. In 1969 the Federation of Cuban Women (FMC) had committed itself to the integration of 100,000 women into the workforce by 1972. Nevertheless, most women continued to have administrative and services-related jobs, particularly in health care and education. Women's integration into the world of work coincided with an increase in their level of education.[86]

At the institutional level, the Family Code promulgated in 1975 replaced the old Civil Code which linked the family institution to private property. The new code based the defence of the family on state ownership of the means of production; and significantly, it established socio-economic equality both between men and women and in their personal relations with their children, unlike the old code which sanctioned the inferiority of women to their fathers or husbands. Children were given equal status, whether born in or out of wedlock. Contraception is widely practised, and abortion freely available.

Officially, then, men and women are equal in terms of rights. As the 'basic unit of society',[87] the family is responsible for the education of future socialist generations.

The overall record, however, has been very different. The family structure has often disintegrated under the impact of social changes, with a very high divorce rate and an estimated one in two marriages ending in separation.[88] Separations rose by 23 per cent between 1977 and 1981. Family instability has increased, with access to employment and guaranteed education and health care making separations less problematic. Women are financially less dependent and divorce more easily.

But the consequences are serious. Women often have the sole responsibility for bringing up children and face a range of everyday problems. Housing is undoubtedly the most serious, in that often several families are forced to live together in cramped, uncomfortable flats. With separation, the situation becomes even more complicated.

In 1986 there were 854 crèches and playschools (for children of between one and a half years and six), used by 100,000 working women. This well-known insufficiency was due to the limits placed on social-services building in previous years. A special effort was made by micro-brigades in 1988 as part of the rectification campaign, but progress has been hampered by the shortage of building materials.

Free school lunches at midday for children of between six and eleven years old are still not universally available; childcare at lunchtimes and in the afternoon is thus a serious handicap for working women.

In spite of the massive development of collective services (restaurants, laundries), women still find it difficult to combine waged work with domestic work and bringing up the children. This double burden continues to be a reality and equality is far from being achieved. There are several reasons for this: initial underdevelopment (Cuba had only one private crèche in 1959, with three others opened in 1961[89]) meant that the huge advances made were still below needs. And in recent years, the impact of the economic crisis and the fall in imports on daily life (queues, transport and distribution problems) have put a brake on earlier progress.

Added to the weight of tradition, all these reasons explain the gap between egalitarian proclamations and reality. Women's liberation also comes up against several, often unexpressed, taboos and prejudices. Massive access to the labour market is far from being translated into equal access to political and professional responsibilities.

At the First PCC Congress in 1975, women represented 13.23 per cent of members; in 1986, 21.9 per cent of members. (In evaluating such data, it must be borne in mind that gaining party membership is based on workers selecting those – more often men than women – they consider 'exemplary'; and this process is a handicap for women in itself.) In party cells, 23.5 per cent of women have responsibilities, but this figure falls to a mere 13.1 per cent in party sections. It was not until 1986 that a woman was elected to the Politburo, thirty years after the seizure of power! In spite of their exceptional revolutionary background dating from the Moncada attack or the Sierra Maestra, neither Haydee Santamaría and Melba Hernández (both participants in the Moncada attack in 1953) nor Celia Sánchez and Vilma Espín (in charge of the 26th of July Movement in Oriente even before the start of the war in Sierra Maestra) had gained a place. Vilma Espín, president of the FMC, thus became the first woman to become a member. There are only three women in the Central Committee and there is not a single woman minister.

What about mass organizations? In the trade unions, women represented 35 per cent of members in 1983; and in the Committees for the Defence of the Revolution they represented 49.4 per cent of members (this higher percentage was due to the kind of tasks performed by these committees: local management and supervision activities based on the neighbourhood and the home).

Thirty-four per cent of deputies at the National Assembly of People's Power were women in 1986. Not surprisingly, the best record was found in the Young Communists where 41 per cent of members were women in 1984.[90] In 1979, 10 per cent of the national leadership were women, and in 1984 the figure was 27.1 per cent.[91] Eighty per cent of women between the age of forty and sixty-five belong to the Federation of Cuban Women (FMC).

These figures confirm the difficulties that the promotion of women's equality has come up against. There has certainly been progress in the right to work and integration into the production process. But as well as this being a double-edged process which has led to conflict at work, and in families, couples and society, the problem now is to eliminate the considerable forms of discrimination that persist: professional discrimination (in terms of access to responsibilities), discrimination in the family (where the bulk of domestic chores and childcare fall on women's shoulders), and political discrimination (in terms of women's occupation of positions of leadership).

The obstacles are manifold. The pervasive military model in society, the weight of military traditions, and the notion of the chief or *líder*, reinforce masculine pre-eminence and make the promotion of women more difficult. The fact of having been in Angola as an 'internationalist fighter', for example, is a criterion in being allocated to responsibilities, and this once again clearly favours men. As far as the older generations are concerned, the image of women is still full of traditional clichés. The resolution adopted at the meeting of the Continental Front of Women in 1988 at Havana stressed the need to 'feminize leadership'. In his conclusions, Fidel Castro judged the term 'feminization' improper and suggested it be replaced with the more adequate term 'humanize', which, according to him, meant the same thing anyway! In this as in other areas, the new generation of women have demands which will not fail to shake pervasive machismo and subjective resistance.

Eclecticism and Ideological Versatility

The contradictions facing the revolution, the narrowness of its room for manoeuvre, the jockeying for position to which it has become subject, have merely reinforced the paternalistic and verticalist approach of the Cuban leader's relations with 'his' people. The full extent of his political and ideological oscillation is masked by his monopoly of power and public speech.

Fidel Castro is not mean with his speeches. And throughout the last thirty years it has been interesting to follow, if not his ideological evolution, at least the twists and turns of his thought; for he is skilled at adapting himself to audiences and new situations. The low value he puts on theory, as well as his tactical and political genius, explain the eclecticism of his terms of reference and his solid pragmatism. The skill with which he operates on the diplomatic front, moving according to the balance of forces, is particularly visible in Latin America: in the name of the unity required to cancel the debt, he has been shifting for several years from confrontation with most governments to a policy of conciliation. There is no question about the correctness of this policy, but it should not be combined with an attempt to conjure away the class nature of the governments concerned.

This permanent confusion between immediate needs and ideological justification, this masking of the slightest policy change, is a characteristic of Castroism. But as the years go by, all these sudden changes and manoeuvres appear for what they are.

This attitude is first and foremost a product of Fidel Castro's determination to rule out not just the slightest debate, but even the mention of different or contradictory positions; and this has led to incredible ideological contortions. Until the departure in 1965 of Ernesto Che Guevara – whose outspokenness and rejection of all diplomatic language contrasted with Fidel Castro – there had been a certain pluralism of expression, of which the great economic debate was the last episode. The existence of three daily newspapers – *El Mundo*, without any specific political alignment, *Hoy*, the journal of the PSP, and *Revolución*, the journal of the 26th of July Movement, edited at the time by Carlos Franqui – favoured the expression of different points of view and, occasionally, polemic and confrontation. As a result, the revolutionary process gained in vitality, all the more so because the Sino–Soviet debate was at its height internationally. The publication of Soviet and Chinese texts was guaranteed, as Che said, 'with as much respect for one side as for the other'.[92] With the fusion of the three organizations to form the PCC, the three dailies disappeared and the single organ of the new party, *Granma*, replaced political debate with stereotypes.

The economic reorganization and political institutionalization of the 1970s was characterized by Soviet influence in all areas: economic, political, institutional and ideological. To be convinced of this, one only needs to re-read Fidel Castro's message of 12 December 1976 to Brezhnev on the occasion of the latter's birthday:

Dear Comrade Brezhnev,

A few months ago, you wrote to congratulate me on my fiftieth birthday. Today, it is my turn to return this friendly gesture. Our party and people share the immense joy of Soviet communists and citizens in seeing you reach seventy, full of health and vigour.

The deep significance of this birthday stems from the fact that, having travelled a long path from the humblest of positions to the greatest of political responsibilities, you have dedicated your life to the noble and just cause of the peoples of the Soviet Union and the whole of humanity. You have been able to live through an exceptional era, marked by the transition from capitalism to socialism, and you have had the triple privilege of being the son of the people who carried it out; of being the pupil of the genial leader who made that enormous victory possible; and thanks to your capabilities and merits, of having been promoted, in remarkable circumstances, to the leadership of the heroic party that makes such an extraordinary exploit possible. You have known how to be equal to such a huge responsibility.

Future generations will recognize and thank you for this exceptional contribution to the cause of peace in an extremely complex and difficult period of history. Your Cuban friends will be proud to have been able to count on your affection and friendship.

I express my wish that you may preserve for many years the youthful outlook, lively intelligence and extraordinary human qualities that have characterized your noble and courageous life, in order that you may continue to serve, for a long time to come, our Soviet brothers, the international communist movement and all peoples of the world.

Please accept on this occasion the most sincere congratulations of a people that admires and loves you, our affection and gratitude for everything that you have done for Cuba, as well as our wishes for your health and peace.

Your comrade in struggle,

Fidel Castro Ruz

Revolutionary history itself was the the object of reinterpretation and the old PSP, once vilified, was rehabilitated. Concessions were even made on this explosive but taboo theme.

The neo-Stalinist ideological overkill in the 1970s did not meet much resistance. In some cases, Fidel Castro even legitimized it, as in 1975 at the fiftieth anniversary of the foundation of the Cuban Communist Party,[93] or following the death of Blas Roca, a former PSP leader, who had accompanied every capitulation of the party (after the fusion into a single organization of the forces that had participated in one way or another in the revolutionary process, Blas Roca, unlike other PSP leaders, did not associate himself with the divisive operations directed by the Soviet Union; he rallied unconditionally round Fidel Castro and handed him the leadership of the new Communist Party). It was nevertheless strange to hear Fidel Castro declare: 'The coup d'état of 10 March 1952 and the energetic revolutionary response of 26 July 1953 opened a new stage in the struggle of our people. ... Throughout the entire process, Blas's party and the founders of the 26th of July Movement maintained excellent and fraternal contacts. ... We did not always choose the same tactics, but even if our paths were different, they led to the same historical objectives.'[94] One can only be surprised at such a rewriting of history. One only has to recall that, following the Moncada attack, the PSP described the members of the 26th of July Movement as 'petty-bourgeois adventurers playing into the hands of the bourgeoisie'. The old Communist Party provided no defence for those who attacked the barracks – not even a democratic defence – in spite of their savage repression by Batista. Was this an example of 'fraternal contacts'? As has been illustrated by several testimonies, the liberation war was accompanied by tensions right up to the eve of victory.

To claim that their historical aims had been the same, when three weeks before the takeover the PSP leadership had been publicly declaring that it was not the time for the proclamation of soviets but for the restoration of bourgeois democracy,[95] must scandalize many a Cuban revolutionary activist.

With his customary rigour, Che had clarified in 1963 that 'the Communist Party did not lead the revolution in Cuba, even though its influence had been felt and its participation was important following the takeover. ... The Communist Party had not seen the situation clearly and had not correctly understood the methods of struggle. It made a mistake and did not correctly assess the movement's chances of victory. The costs of this very serious error were not too high because Fidel Castro and a group of true revolutionaries were there.' For his part, Fidel Castro asserted in 1975 that the PSP 'was teaching communism'![96] One might inquire into the reasons which also led the First Secretary of the PCC to declare that he had been a communist since the Moncada attack, contrary to the historical data available at the time. It is known that he was in contact with activists of the Communist Youth (of which his brother, Raúl, was a member). His prison letters also bear witness to his reading of Marxist texts. But on this point, Che is once again clear: 'Marxism-

Leninism was not the official doctrine of the movement, nor the internal ideology of some comrades. We became persuaded of the Marxist-Leninist programme during the course of the process. Our struggle against imperialism and the exploiting classes enabled us to understand how such problems could be resolved.'[97] And at the height of the guerrilla war in 1957, Che had even written that he considered Fidel to be a 'left-wing bourgeois'.[98] How should such adaptations to history be understood? They must undoubtedly be seen as a way of claiming a legitimate Marxist orthodoxy that was just as old as that of the orthodox mentors who were in fashion in 1975.

Fidel Castro is often guided by an empirical, pragmatic and subjective vision of men and events, and this explains some of the sudden changes of mind to which he is given. Accompanying his allergy to dogmatism, to coded and bureaucratic language drawn from quotes and manuals,[99] is a certain scorn for theoretical issues which he tends to categorize as excessive generalizations. Hence his insistence that other experiences should not be 'copied' and that the 'idiosyncracy' of each people should be respected. Indeed, he is little concerned with historical or theoretical rigour. His flexibility is all the greater because no form of questioning is to be feared. As he himself has said: 'I am neither pragmatic nor dogmatic. I am dialectical. Nothing is permanent, everything changes.'[100]

Today, muffled discussion and argument are developing. Firstly, on the revolution's history. Contrasting with the apologetic and self-justificatory texts published by certain sociology and philosophy magazines are articles by Fidel Castro from 1955 or 1956. Reprinted by the weekly magazine *Bohemia*,[101] they highlight the social and political bases of support for the 26th of July Movement at its foundation. Originally published before the landing of the *Granma* at the Sierra Maestra, they refute the claims of those who would like to minimize the revolutionary clarity of the Castroite project. But it is significant, thirty years on, that Fidel Castro has still not written the history of the liberation war. As he has said: 'Many episodes from the war have been recounted by different comrades; each sees things from his point of view; they are unaware of the tactical or strategic nature of a battle or an event. And I'm aware of the absence of these things myself.'[102] The real reason is that it is impossible to write the history without provoking very sharp conflict between the component parts of the PCC, and without challenging the role of the PSP. Moreover, Fidel Castro attaches great importance to unity as a guarantee of the revolution's survival – he is obsessed by what has happened in Grenada – and considers himself to be the final bastion against division. This leads him either to manoeuvre or to keep quiet.

However, the debate about revolutionary strategy and the comparative experience of the various processes in Latin America has led to a discussion on how the Castroite strategy should be interpreted. The subject is dominated by a certain eclecticism; but unlike the past, the excessive generalization of the different processes' lessons is being avoided. The lessons of *foquismo* have been partially discarded and Régis Debray's book has been criticized.[103]

Another subject of argument and debate has been the conception of socialism and the choice as to what the driving force of socialist society should be.

> If competition does not exist, what can the property owner's motivation to defend his own personal interests in capitalist society be replaced by? By nothing but the sense of responsibility of cadres and men, and not just by workers as a group. ... And these men must be communists, whether they are members of the party or not. ... Not a communist playing at being a capitalist ... or a capitalist disguised as a communist. ... Such an alienating path, such a path of selfishness – where values would be forgotten and where, along with values, a spirit of solidarity, a spirit that is as national as international, would be in danger of being forgotten by a people that is so imbued with patriotic and revolutionary virtues as ours – would not have led us very far.[104]

But such a discourse cannot meet the demands of a society in transition, and the absence of a comprehensive approach is manifest. It is to plug this gap that Fidel Castro no doubt uses references to Che.

Popular support exists, as does internationalism, but they are insufficient. It is not enough to work like an army, as if in the Sierra, as Fidel Castro believes: 'Three hundred at the front and four at staff headquarters, that's enough to get problems solved.' The construction of a new society is much more complicated. It is precisely the way 'staff headquarters' currently works that is ill-suited to the needs of the Cuban people today.

Economic and Political Democratization: A Double Necessity

The contrast between Fidel Castro's personal need for political information and the extent to which he is prepared to grant the population the right to know (in the political sense) is striking. It was his personal friend, García Márquez, who recently noted that he 'has breakfast with 200 pages of news from around the whole world ... reads about 50 documents a day ... not to mention the reports of official services and the latest untranslated books he has had urgently translated'.[105] Such a colossal privilege in comparison with the poor quality of the press and publishing (until recently, bookshops were crammed with books and manuals that even the Soviet people no longer buy) is apparently justified on the grounds that it enables Fidel Castro to be 'informed about all the truths that are hidden from him', thus allowing him to hide the revolution's most serious deficiencies and play out his role as the figure people can ultimately turn to. 'The massive bureaucratic incompetence affecting almost all areas of daily life ... has led Fidel Castro himself, nearly thirty years after the victory, to become directly concerned with issues as extraordinary as bread manufacture and beer distribution.'[106] And so the leader of the revolution substitutes himself for democratic planning!

As a party leader has declared: 'Reality demands changes in structure, language, methods and tone. ... We must promote genuine reflection and encourage argument; and we must not always even aspire to unanimity. ... That is the basis for improving our democracy. And if it doesn't take place in the party, it won't take place in society. ... We've tried to build socialism in fifteen different ways – all except the right way. Socialism isn't possible without democracy.'[107] In response, Fidel Castro has said that there is no opposition in Cuba, apart from a small group linked to the US Interests Section. And in reply to Maria Schriver, interviewing him for the US television channel NBC, he gave the stock answer that opposition takes place within the party and mass organizations: 'We accept opposition within the revolution, but we do not accept it against the revolution. ... The rest is just the mythomania of a system that claims to be democratic.' He ended high-handedly: 'Do you think the Soviets are going to create opposition parties in the Soviet Union? If so, you're kidding yourself.'[108]

That is not the way youth sees things. At a seminar on literary and artistic criticism attended by Carlos Aldana, the party's ideology official, a vehement discussion took place and was reported in *Juventud Rebelde* on 29 May 1988. Dogmatism, the 'schematic nature of teaching', and the 'non-Marxist teaching of Marxism' were criticized. A youth protested against the fact that information was not the product of a conflict of ideas. This, he claimed, would provide the people with a greater range of facts and allow it to reach its own conclusions. Another challenged 'methods of organization which hold back the development of things', comrades who were not 'suitable', as well as the fact that there was no opportunity for reply to the arguments expressed in newspapers. In view of the crisis of cinema and television, one of the female participants recalled that Karl Marx had developed in a context of confrontation and that one could not be a Marxist by default, without a knowledge of other philosophies. In reply, Carlos Aldana described the constraints that the need for mass training had placed on Cuban teaching at the beginning of the revolution, as well as the difficulties created by texts 'which are now being challenged by those who published them'.[109] Nothing like this had appeared in the press for years. A more open attitude also seems to have been adopted over moral and social issues: a different approach has been taken over Aids, for example – once presented as a quasi-diabolical invention of imperialism whose symptoms in Cuba itself were denied – although Aids victims are still isolated in sanatoriums.

The National Union of Writers and Artists of Cuba (UNEAC), a moribund association which held its Fourth Congress in January 1988, appeared to have marked a watershed. In his conclusion, Aldana referred to the regrouping of tendencies that had been brought about by the preparation of the congress and criticized the period when UNEAC 'practically acted as an appendage of the party'. He delivered a veritable creed on artistic freedom, paying homage to creative artists who had never 'used their position to launch themselves as writers'.

The main part of his speech took 1975 as its starting point:

> It is clear that, in 1975, we gave in to the temptation to interfere in the area of aesthetic laws and processes and their relation to ideology. ... In any case, the result of our theoretical incursions in 1975 was that they gave way to a sort of illusion of conceptualization, the clearest and most serious effect of which has been the stagnation of the party's thought in terms of comprehension of the specificity of art, which was seen as a simple form of social consciousness. ... What we have the duty to ban, given its damage to the act of creation, is the exclusion of any creative artist from official positions on the grounds that he is a follower of abstract art or surrealism, critical realism, magical realism, marvellous realism or, indeed, socialist realism if that is what he wants. ... This respect for individual aesthetic choice ... in which works achieve recognition through a formal and expressive competition that is truly free, rather than as a result of artistic intolerance, unseemly disputes and intrigues which mainly degrade their authors, would, if fully established, be the best proof of this democratic spirit that is being demanded today.[110]

It was clearly no coincidence that the year 1975 should be highlighted. Tainted with socialist realism, the 1975 programme had once again retreated from the practices current in the early years of the revolution: 'Cultural policy encouraged expressions of art and literature in a class spirit, in accordance with the principles of Marxism-Leninism ... and refused to accept the obsolete and anti-humanist artistic and literary expressions of capitalism.' Vindicating himself through the process of rectification, Aldana attempted to identify rectification with a 'profound renewal', thus responding to the worries of those who might equate it with the accentuation of a dogmatic and sectarian course and dread the effects of increased economic centralization and political control. Certain leaders had become aware of the danger of continued stagnation, and of market reforms being the only vector of the democratization required.

The UNEAC Congress was the occasion for a landmark in rectification. But such an opening continued to be confined to intellectuals.

The upheavals in Eastern Europe and the intensity of debate over the relation between socialism and democracy on the Latin American left have had repercussions in Cuba. In this area, the process of reflection is already much more advanced in the rest of the Latin American revolutionary movement. This has put the Cuban leadership in a precarious position. The fact that, in the midst of a war, a pluralistic political process has been able to develop in Nicaragua, 'in spite of important limitations';[111] that Orlando Nuñez, a director of the Agrarian Reform Research and Study Centre (CIERA) in Managua, has criticized the Stalinist basis of a monolithic society; that he has denounced the fusion of the state apparatus with the party; and that he has advocated collective leadership, as well as the right to criticism and pluralism, as anti-bureaucratic tools – all of this inevitably has a certain resonance in Cuba. In the words of Nuñez once again: 'We are from a generation – the sixties generation – that made many criticisms as far as socialist regimes are concerned. ... We Sandinistas come from many Maoist, anarchist, social-democratic, radical, Castroite, Guevarist, Trotskyist groups.'[112]

While not as advanced, this culture exists in many Latin American revolutionary movements. And events in the Soviet Union, China, the German Democratic Republic and Czechoslovakia can only fuel further questions as to the reasons that have led to such a degeneration. Even a movement as steeped in military concepts as the Colombian National Liberation Army (ELN) has declared support in its programme 'for freedom of expression, of assembly, of organization, of the press, of thought, of mobilization, as well as for the free activity of parties which will respect the new legal order. The new state will be guided by the most wide-ranging and authentic democracy.'[113] For his part, Joaquín Villalobos, the leader of the FMLN in El Salvador, has stated that 'a one-party system does not suit our reality' and that 'the unity of the revolutionary forces must not be confused with a one-party regime. The one-party model is the product of a historical reality. The social structure of our country is more complex.'[114]

The recent tolerance towards youth, intellectuals and artists is probably the product of this environment in that Cuba is part of the Latin American subcontinent. But in no way does it constitute an adequate substitute for the democratization of Cuban society. The missing element is the institutionalization of effective decison-making power and control by the popular masses over economic and social choices; and this decison-making power would involve free political debate, the confrontation of ideas and the expression of different political currents, all of which are crucial to fighting the fusion of party and state as Orlando

Nuñez has said. Only such a choice could provide a solution to the increasingly acute problem of what Cuban officials call the 'poor economic awareness' of workers. The increase in productivity during the missile crisis was a case in point. The combination of revolutionary mobilization and autonomous decision-making by workers – in the absence of 'officials' who were mobilized elsewhere – demonstrated that managers are not always indispensable. The limited period when trade union sections multiplied and workers could actively participate in decisions had a similar result.

'The system distributes well, but produces badly.' This leitmotif is accompanied by a question: the problem being known, how should it be solved? This 'how' cannot be divorced from a radical rectification that would mean a complete change from a situation where the masses, stripped of any control, must shore up an increasingly incompetent and proliferating apparatus, even if the latter is regularly destabilized.

In this three-sided wrestling match, Fidel Castro is searching for a balance between popular support and the apparatus, attempting to neutralize the latter's conservatism while keeping the mobilization of the working masses under control. But in this (perhaps final) struggle, Castro's paternalism, faced with the social inertia of the bureaucracy, is in danger of gradually losing ground.

The period between 1972, the date of Comecon membership, and 1986 has been marked by the revolution's institutionalization and bureaucratization. Castro's counter-attacks have disrupted the administrative and organizational structures imported from the Soviet Union; and under the impact of these blows, the bureaucratic apparatus is sagging and the masses are mobilizing. The correlation of forces would appear to be consolidating in favour of the alliance between Fidel Castro and the masses. But the apparatchiks' social strength has the upper hand. Rectification 'from above', without the masses having the power of control, will not succeed.

In any case, such a style of leadership, perhaps still possible with Fidel Castro, will not survive him. And given the context of the Cuban geopolitical situation, the revolution would not survive the effective bureaucratization of power and its degeneration.

Notes

1. Tad Szulc, *Fidel*.
2. Félix de la Uz, 'Personal letter to P.S.'.
3. Prologue to G. Miná's book, *Un encuentro con Fidel*, out of print in the Cuban edition.
4. G. Miná, *Un encuentro con Fidel*.

5. *El País*, 19 September 1987.
6. Ernesto Che Guevara, 'Une réunion décisive', *Obras revolucionarias.*
7. Linda Fuller, 'Power at the Workplace: the Resolution of Worker-Management Conflict in Cuba', in *World Development*, vol. 15, no. 1, 1987, p. 143.
8. Ibid., p.147.
9. Ibid.
10. G. White, 'Cuban Planning in the Mid-1980s: Centralization, Decentralization and Participation', in *World Development*, vol. 15, no. 1, 1987.
11. *Problèmes économiques*, Documentation française, 8 July 1987.
12. Mesa-Lago, *La economía en Cuba socialista.*
13. Zimbalist and Ekstein, in *Problèmes économiques*, Documentation française, July 1987.
14. Ibid.
15. *Bohemia* 1988.
16. *Bohemia*, 8 July 1988.
17. F. Pisani, report from Cienfuegos, in *Le Monde diplomatique*, December 1987.
18. White, 'Cuban Planning in the Mid-1980s'.
19. F. Pisani, report from Cienfuegos, in *Le Monde diplomatique*, December 1987.
20. Ibid.
21. Linda Fuller, 'Power at the Workplace: the Resolution of Worker-Management Conflict in Cuba'.
22. *Financial Times*, 2 July 1987.
23. Tad Szulc, *Fidel.*
24. On 26 July 1988, for example, during his speech and press conference in Ecuador.
25. White, 'Cuban Planning in the Mid-1980s'.
26. François Maspero, 'Cuba', in *Autrement*, January 1989.
27. *Bohemia*, March 1989.
28. Fidel Castro, in *Granma*, 4 January 1989.
29. *Latin America Weekly Report*, 30 March 1989.
30. White, 'Cuban Planning in the Mid-1980s'.
31. *Latin America Weekly Report*, 11 December 1986.
32. *Granma*, 19 December 1987.
33. *Granma*, 16 January 1983.
34. Fidel Castro, *Main Report to the Third PCC Congress.*
35. 'Resolutions for the Third Congress', *Editora Política*, Havana.
36. M.A. Walters, in *Perspectiva Mundial*, 12 May 1986.
37. Martínez Heredia, *Desafíos del socialismo cubano.*
38. Fidel Castro, speech to the Young Communists, in *Granma*, 4 April 1982.
39. National Association of Small Farmers (ANAP) Congress, May 1982.
40. Francis Pisani, in *Journal de Genève*, 16 December 1987.
41. Ibid.
42. Fidel Castro, in *Granma*, 25 April 1986.
43. Ibid.
44. Fidel Castro, speech to Confederation of Cuban Workers (CTC), 1 February 1987.
45. *Granma*, 27 April 1986.
46. Statutes adopted at the First PCC Congress, 1975.
47. In the case of Humberto Pérez, the decision was announced by *Granma*, given the importance of the event (see previous chapter).
48. Otero, 'Le rôle de l'armeé révolutionnaire dans le processus de la révolution démocratico-populaire', in *Revista de Ciencias Sociales*, Havana, December 1986.
49. Ibid.
50. Ibid.
51. On 14 December 1959 during the trial of Hubert Matos, former commander of the rebel army, accused of military conspiracy.
52. Quote of Fidel Castro, 1971, taken from Marta Harnecker, *Fidel Castro's Political Strategy.*
53. Fidel Castro, *Main Report to the Third PCC Congress.*

54. M.A. Walters, in *Perspectiva Mundial*, 12 May 1986. This was the first session, but 40 per cent of the total were missing.
55. Tad Szulc, *Fidel*.
56. Max Azicri, *Cuba*.
57. Tad Szulc, *Fidel*.
58. *Caribbean Report*, 26 February 1987.
59. *Le Monde diplomatique*, December 1987.
60. *Latin America Weekly Report*, 11 December 1986.
61. On this subject, see the verdict of Jean-Pierre Clerc, *Fidel de Cuba*.
62. *Granma*, 9 November 1986.
63. *Granma*, 15 January 1987.
64. *País*, 14 April 1986.
65. *Etudes*, magazine of the fathers of the Company of Jesus, December 1988.
66. Frei Betto, *Fidel y la religión*.
67. *El País*, 2 May 1987.
68. Report of the Amnesty International delegation invited to visit Cuba, September 1988.
69. A group of prisoners who refused to wear the uniform of the common-law inmates.
70. René Mendoza, the official in charge of legal issues, in *Granma*, 31 January 1988.
71. *Granma*, 14 February 1988.
72. *Granma* 10 January 1988.
73. *Granma*, 14 February 1988.
74. *Cuba Internacional*, October 1988. Amnesty reported 15,000 prisoners being set free in those two years.
75. Report of Amnesty International, September 1988.
76. Gianni Miná, *Un encuentro con Fidel*.
77. Régis Debray, *Masques*, p. 213.
78. Including Françoise Barthélémy, from the staff of *Le Monde diplomatique*.
79. Gianni Miná, *Un encuentro con Fidel*.
80. *The Nation*, 24 October 1988.
81. *Financial Times*, 17 February 1989.
82. M. Frayde, *Ecoute Fidel*; J. Valls, *Mon ennemi, mon frère*.
83. *New York Review*, 15 June 1989.
84. Except 1953 when the figure was 17.1 per cent; Marta Nuñez Sarmiento, 'Les femmes et l'emploi dans la révolution cubaine'.
85. Max Azicri, *Cuba*.
86. Marta Nuñez Sarmiento, 'Les femmes et l'emploi dans la révolution cubaine'.
87. According to the Family Code.
88. Max Azicri, *Cuba*.
89. Marta Nuñez Sarmiento, 'Les femmes et l'emploi dans la révolution cubaine'.
90. Ibid.
91. Max Azicri, *Cuba*.
92. Interview with Che Guevara, in *l'Express*, 17 July 1963.
93. *Economía y Desarrollo*, 1975.
94. Fidel Castro, in *Granma*, 3 May 1987.
95. 'La solución que conviene a Cuba', PSP, December 1958.
96. *Economía y Desarrollo*, 1975.
97. *Hoy*, 27 August 1963.
98. Carlos Franqui, *Journal de la révolution cubaine*.
99. 'There were quite a few sick minds here who did more harm than good. They always knew Lenin's exact words and the exact page and day he had said them; they could find anything for you in the forty volumes of Lenin's Complete Works. But the party member who had to provide for his family whose house was in danger of caving in had nothing to do with that.' (Fidel Castro, in *Granma*, 13 December 1987.)
100. J.-P. Clerc, *Fidel de Cuba*.
101. *Bohemia*, June and July 1988.

102. G. Miná, *Un encuentro con Fidel.*
103. Marta Harnecker, in *Revue de sciences sociales.*
104. Fidel Castro, in *Granma*, 13 December 1987.
105. *El País*, 6 March 1988.
106. García Márquez, prologue to Gianni Miná, *Habla Fidel.*
107. Francis Pisani, in *Journal de Genève*, 15 December 1987; and in *Le Monde diplomatique*, December 1987.
108. *Granma*, 13 March 1988.
109. *Cuba socialista*, theoretical magazine of the PCC Central Committee, March/April 1988.
110. *Granma*, 14 February 1988.
111. Orlando Nuñez, *Quand l'Amérique s'embrasera.*
112. *Inprecor*, no. 268, 20 June 1988.
113. Programme of the Camilista Union-ELN, duplicated, 8 June 1987.
114. M. Harnecker, interview with J. Villalobos, 'Le rôle de l'avant-garde et les défis de la lutte révolutionnaire actuelle', typescript, 1989.

5

The Contradictions of International Policy and National Defence

Cuban foreign policy bears the weight of the contradictions suffered by the revolution itself. Stifled by the US blockade for thirty years and subject to the fluctuations of Soviet policy, the revolution is to some extent 'mortgaged'.[1] And yet the 'first free country of the Americas' occupies a place on the international stage which is disproportionate to its real importance.

Above all, Cuba considers itself a member of the Latin American community and a spokesman for the Third World. Its relations with the CMEA, however close economically, have never replaced Cuba's sense of community with Latin America in terms of history, traditions and points of reference. The roots of the Cuban Revolution are deeply embedded in the continent's struggles for independence. The heroes of the wars of independence like José Martí and Antonio Maceo are the descendants of Bolívar; and the Sierra Maestra struggle is merely a continuation of the great anti-imperialist struggles of the twentieth century. Such Latin American references have also become extended to the Third World in general. This dual affiliation – to Latin America and the Third World – was reaffirmed by Fidel Castro at the meeting organized in Moscow in November 1987 to celebrate the seventieth anniversary of the October Revolution. Speaking in the name of 'our Third World', he emphasized the need to struggle for 'true peace', free from poverty, backwardness and oppression; and recalled that 'each year poverty kills as many children in the Third World as a hundred nuclear bombs',[2] a reminder to Soviet diplomats – engaged in a privileged dialogue with the United States – that peace cannot be bought at any price, and also that the current horse-trading to solve 'regional conflicts' would be null and void if their social and economic causes were forgotten.

The authority with which Fidel Castro can speak on behalf of the

Third World and demand a 'new international economic order' is not a product of his 'megalomania'. Cuban diplomacy has, over the years, been carrying out a policy of co-operation and technical aid – sending doctors, teachers and agricultural technicians; providing study grants to foreign students who have lived on the island for several years; and in some cases, donating free sugar, medicines and tinned milk to Vietnam and Nicaragua among others. Such economic co-operation, which mainly related to Algeria and Guinea in the 1960s, spread in the 1970s to countries in Africa and the Middle East. The policy applied to thirty-five countries in 1988![3]

The Isle of Pines, a former penitentiary centre where Fidel Castro was imprisoned, has been transformed into an international teaching centre. Fifty thousand people, half of them foreign, stay in these educational establishments. Proportionally speaking, it is as if Great Britain took on 100,000 secondary-school pupils and students – a remarkable teaching experience unparalleled in any developing country, according to reporter Robert Graham of the *Financial Times*.

The Cuban State in the Latin American Camp: a Diplomatic Breakthrough

Since the mid-1970s foreign trade with Latin America and the Caribbean has developed significantly. Out of forty countries, Cuba has established relations with twenty, on many occasions before diplomatic ties had been restored. While relatively small and of a low value in terms of foreign exchange, this foreign trade is highly significant for Cuba. On the one hand, it provides employment for students leaving university and whose prospects are uncertain; and on the other, it facilitates the island's progressive integration into the Latin American community. Cuba is already a member of several regional co-operation bodies and sectoral organizations responsible for the promotion of research in the areas of energy, fertilizers, naval construction or sugar production.[4]

As well as the UN Commission on Latin America (CEPAL), a form of observatory which collects information and produces continental analyses, Cuba is a member of the Latin American Economic System (SELA), a body aiming to promote regional co-operation. Initially conceived by Salvador Allende and the Peruvian nationalist generals (including General Velasco Alvarado), the idea was revived by Mexican and Venezuelan presidents Luis Echeverría and Carlos Andrés Pérez (the latter re-elected in 1989) after OPEC became aware of its ability to increase prices following the effects of the first oil shock. The idea then developed that the body – of which the United States would not form part – could be used to repeat the experience with other raw materials (for example, sugar). Cuba joined without hesitation, but SELA has had neither the breadth of support nor the efficiency that had been expected, in spite of encouraging the expression of a common will for action and numerous exchanges.

Cuba has now emerged from the isolation to which it had been confined for twenty years. In 1962 every country apart from Mexico had voted for its exclusion from the OAS. At the San José conference in 1975, member states had the right to restore relations with the island. Sixteen countries voted in favour of the resolution and two, Nicaragua and Brazil, abstained. The Sandinista government, of course, has restored ties since the takeover, and Brazil has done so recently. Of those who voted against – Chile, Paraguay and Uruguay – only the last has changed its position. It is an irony of history that it should be Sarney – the president of the country that initiated and led the break with Cuba – who has proposed Cuba's reintegration into the OAS. The idea has been supported by the governments of Argentina, Mexico, Peru, Panama, Uruguay, Venezuela and Colombia, countries which are part of the permanent consultation and political co-ordination mechanisms with regard to Central America. This is a far cry from the attitude of the Latin American bourgeoisie in the 1960s. The Nicaraguan Revolution is a long way from provoking unanimous condemnation, unlike what happened with Cuba at the Punta del Este meeting in 1961.

A turning point was the Malvinas crisis. Fidel Castro offered to help Argentina 'by all means', even going as far as to suggest that 2,500 Cuban soldiers be sent to fight British troops and reconquer the archipelago.[5] This declaration was noted, and has been useful to Cuba's diplomatic reintegration. Such a development was highlighted in 1983 by the Contadora initiative. Unlike the 'golden age' when the marines would land in Guatemala, Playa Girón or Santo Domingo, the Contadora initiative on Nicaragua favoured efforts at negotiation and did not fit in with the United States' plan to overthrow the Sandinista government.

Another paradox was Argentina's vote at the UN in 1987 which prevented Cuba from being condemned for human rights violations, just as at the Human Rights Commission in Geneva in 1988. It would obviously be absurd to see these votes as stemming from a genuine concern for democracy or as a decision in favour of self-determination and liberation! The Latin American ruling classes have not rallied round to an anti-imperialist stance. Their relative autonomy, however limited, has deep causes: their considerable indebtedness; capital flight and the effects of unequal exchange; the gravity of the economic and social crisis which bears down on and threatens the stability of existing regimes; the profound changes at work in the minds of the peoples throughout Latin America in the wake of the experience of military dictatorships; the crisis of the populist movement; and the enduring presence of revolutionary processes in Central America since the Nicaraguan Revolution. In spite of setbacks, partial defeats and the war financed by the United States, these revolutionary processes remain undefeated and hold imperialism in check.

The system is in crisis, but in the subcontinent (unlike the Central American isthmus), the bourgeois leaderships still have significant room for manoeuvre and this allows them to distance themselves from an interventionist policy that could touch off an explosion.

For the time being their material interests are more affected by the policy of the US administration – as is shown by the effects of protectionist measures – than by the revolutionary action of the masses. They also take advantage of an apparently more autonomous policy, and this gesture to their internal opposition is also a form of pressure on the United States: Cuba has arrived at just the right moment for them to try and win greater concessions from the United States in these times of threatened protectionism (restrictions on sugar quotas, for example). The case of the Dominican Republic speaks volumes. A 40 per cent cut in sugar quotas in 1987 led to the loss of 17,000 jobs in a country where the rate of unemployment is 27 per cent. Three thousand 'illegal' immigrants in the United States were threatened with repatriation. President Balaguer's initial response was to sign a series of trade agreements with Cuba. And in reserve, he has the backing of a resolution in the Dominican parliament to re-establish diplomatic relations with Cuba if the White House continues to turn a deaf ear.[6]

Cuban diplomacy has played subtly on these issues. In recent years the government has been especially concerned with the struggle against the effects of debt. It has aimed to make Latin American unity a concrete reality through a general strike of debtors, searching for economic integration so as to fight for a new international economic order from a better position. This battle has led to a number of exchanges and governmental contacts, and to several diplomatic successes: a reciprocal visit of Sarney to Cuba and Fidel Castro to Brazil was even planned. Following the visit of Ecuadorean President Febres Cordero in 1985, Fidel Castro has visited Ecuador, Mexico and Venezuela. It remains to be seen how such diplomatic changes will affect Cuba's revolutionary strategy in Latin America.

Ambiguities of the Continental Revolutionary Strategy

The 1960s were, to use Che's phrase, the 'hour of the furnaces'. The Organization of Latin American Solidarity (OLAS) was the embryo for international organization in the subcontinent, and the armed revolutionary organizations that had emerged from the various Christian currents, the young communist groups, and, indeed, the communist parties, multiplied. The hour of victory seemed near, at least in some countries. The defeat of Che in Bolivia in 1967 was to have serious effects, not just in Cuba, but throughout Latin America. It put the revolution on the defensive for the first time since the triumph of the 26th of July Movement and the stinging defeat of the mercenaries in the Bay of Pigs landing in 1961. It was only in 1979 – twelve years after the defeat in Bolivia – that the victory of the Sandinista revolution marked a change in the situation. Outside Central America, the prospects for revolution are more unclear. Cuba's foreign policy has been influenced by victory in Nicaragua but also by the defeat in Grenada in 1983. And along with Soviet policy, such events have led to a reflection on strategy, expressed through a return in Cuba to a 'popular war' type of approach, and to an inquiry as to the prospects for socialist revolution in the continent.

The doubts and worries expressed in the ambiguities of Fidel Castro's speeches are not just a reflection of diplomatic constraints; they are the product of a real disarray which the Cuban leadership has been unable to deal with. It is a long way from the time when Régis Debray's book, *Revolution in the Revolution?*, advanced *foquismo* as a strategy for the continent under the dictate of Fidel Castro. Not long ago, Fidel Castro himself declared:

> The person who advocates the Cuban model to promote revolution in Latin America would be advocating a bad strategy. We smashed the army and created another one. But should the aim be to smash all armies? In many countries in the continent progressive currents can arise in the armed forces. ... Nowadays there must be a broad front in the struggle to achieve social change. It should include Christians, Trotskyists, workers, the middle strata and even members of the armed forces. ... The Nicaraguan model is adapted to current international conditions; it is realistic. ... The Nicaraguans are contributing to the struggle of other peoples, because if they radicalized, they would become isolated, scare everyone and provide a justification for imperialism. They would make Reagan's job easier.

And in the same interview, the tone became much more pessimistic and sceptical:

> Nicaragua has had to suffer invasion, a dirty war and the blockade. And the country is isolated. True, it does receive aid from friendly countries. But I ask myself: can a small or medium-sized country have many prospects when it is isolated? Promoting economic development is much more difficult than defeating an army, and Vietnam is there to prove it. ... What will happen the day that there are fifteen or twenty revolutions in countries without any prospects for development or making social change? Certain conditions have to be met before such changes can take place. ... Imagine what would happen in Latin America if a series of drastic social changes occurred and yet one still had to live off charity. It would be an impossible situation. ... The socialist countries do not have enough resources to help so many countries. That is why the countries of the Third World must create resources in order to develop and that means the cancellation of the debt, a new international economic order and the economic integration of Latin America. Revolutions are not made from goodwill alone. Theories of revolution were based on the premise that socialism would be built in the developed capitalist countries. But the experience of capitalism in the Soviet Union, China, Vietnam and Cuba has made socialism a premise for development.
>
> If our ideas had been advanced in the 1960s or 1970s (or even in 1980), their authors would have automatically been sent to the asylum. But the people who should be sent to the asylum in 1985 are those who come along with a manual or a theoretical model and tell us what is revolutionary and what isn't. What is truly revolutionary in the current circumstances and conditions, I think, is what we have suggested: a debtors' general strike.[7]

The adoption of such positions is a reflection of the impasse revolutionary movements face. The effects of the capitalist economic crisis are joined by the crisis in the countries of Eastern Europe and the uncertainties linked to the rapprochement between the Soviet Union and the United States. The Cubans are haunted by the fear of detente leading to a new Yalta at their expense. Fidel Castro told NBC journalist Maria Schriver that he 'suspects that some minds harbour the opportunistic idea of making peace with the great socialist powers and war against the small progressive countries of the Third World'.[8]

The Soviet Union was challenged in an interview with a Brazilian magazine. According to Fidel Castro, the money to develop the Third World should come from the developed countries, including contributions from socialist countries.[9] Twenty-three years after Che's speech in Algiers criticizing the 'tacit complicity'[10] of the socialist countries with imperialism, Fidel Castro challenged the Soviet Union's relations with the dominated countries in the same terms.

On 22 January 1989 he went one step further by denouncing the attitude of the five permanent members of the UN Security Council, including the Soviet Union, which had opposed the stance taken by Third

World countries (from the Non-Aligned Movement) on the application of the tripartite accords between Cuba, Angola and South Africa on Namibia, as well as on UN Resolution 435 of 1978 defining the steps leading to the country's independence. The dispute was about the need to maintain an adequate number of international UN forces to guarantee the peace process and elections in Namibia, the specific aim being to block the activities of South African-linked paramilitaries. The five (the United States, the Soviet Union, France, Great Britain and China) justified reducing the UN peace-keeping forces on the grounds of excessive financial cost. Evoking the fact that 'the Third World countries representing four thousand million inhabitants can see their deepest hopes and interests blocked by any [*sic*] of the five permanent members of the Security Council', Fidel Castro spoke out in favour of the UN's democratization and the establishment of 'new approaches to international relations' – another dig at Gorbachev.

In an effort to reinforce Cuba's position, Fidel Castro has sought to use tensions between Latin American governments and the US government (stemming from the latter's protectionist measures and the payment of the debt) which are at the root of increasing economic difficulties. But fighting for the cancellation of the debt through a debtors' cartel is one thing; it is quite another to secure the real possibility of a common anti-imperialist front as if the Latin American ruling classes had become trustworthy allies. To characterize, as he did, Brazil's suspension of interest payments on the debt as a 'historic event'[11] was an exaggeration which could only lead to disillusion. Indeed, shortly after the resumption of bilateral negotiations, the Brazilian government quickly renewed payments and introduced a policy of greater austerity.

A break with the policies implemented during the 1960s, such an approach goes back to the start of the 1970s. After the checking of efforts at continental revolution, the Cuban Revolution went through an endogamous phase. This was reinforced by Soviet–Cuban rapprochement and was sanctioned by the First PCC Congress in 1975, the resolutions of which were inspired by Soviet texts and orientations. The Latin American communist parties, having been ridiculed for years by the Castro leadership and especially by Che, also regained a certain respectability during a conference held in Havana the same year. As early as the First Congress Fidel Castro had stated: 'The basis of Cuba's foreign policy, according to our programme, is the subordination of Cuban positions to the international needs of the struggle for socialism and the liberation of peoples. ... Latin America is not ready for global changes that could, as they did in Cuba, lead to socialist transformation, even if this is not impossible in some of the countries in the subcontinent.' The Nicaraguan Revolution was victorious four years later.

In the field of international strategy, Castroite thought is characterized by a compartmentalized vision of international processes and their reciprocal interaction, and, above all, by a miscomprehension of the effects of the capitalist crisis in the industrialized countries, as well as by an erroneous view of the contradictions at work in the countries of Eastern Europe.

The Third World is presented as a bloc, class contradictions are conjured away and the world is divided into two: the developed countries and the rest. Castro is thus slipping into an opportunistic stance towards the national bourgeoisies and this is made all the more ambiguous by the coincidence of party and state, both of which find expression through the voice of Fidel Castro. In May 1988, for example, Carlos Rafael Rodríguez, the Vice-President of the Council of Ministers and the Council of State, stated at a conference in Brazil on debt organized by the Third World Foundation:

> The debts were accumulated by military tyrannies without any kind of popular accountability, and must now be assumed by governments elected by the people. Having barely emerged, the reorganized democracies are in danger of becoming increasingly isolated from their peoples in that they are forced [*sic*] to demand social sacrifices, to reject popular aspirations for a decent standard of living, and, indeed, to abandon their efforts to achieve development to which the foreign debt is a major obstacle.[12]

Thus absolved, the bourgeoisies in power come off well and the socialist revolution is put off *sine die*. Admittedly, this stance is mainly expressed at a diplomatic level and revolution in Central America continues to be a serious obstacle to its implementation. But it was also illustrated in the autumn of 1988 by Fidel Castro's personal attendance (the Cuban state is usually represented by a diplomat) at the inauguration ceremony of Mexican President Salinas de Gortari, who had been elected after massive electoral fraud. According to the most reliable opinion polls, it was Cuauhtémoc Cárdenas who should have won; and the Mexican left felt betrayed by the personal presence of the figure embodying the Cuban Revolution.

Such ambiguities can also be sensed in certain texts on the history of the Cuban Revolution where the interpretation tends to rehabilitate the old hackneyed formula of revolution by stages. Such a formula was believed to have been rejected ever since Che's proclamation of 'Either socialist revolution or a mock revolution!' Today, Roberto R. Alvárez, sector head of the PCC Central Committee asks: 'Is socialist revolution possible today in Latin America? Theoretically, yes. ... But victory is very hard. The conditions have become ripe in Latin America for a popular, democratic and anti-imperialist revolution with national independence and sovereignty as its defined aim. Those are the conditions for the political, social and economic transformations that open the way to socialism.'[13] Some authors do not even hesitate to present the takeover on 1 January 1959 as the opening of a radical democratic stage which, they claim, permitted the application of the programme formulated in 1953 in *History Will Absolve Me*, the speech pronounced by Fidel Castro at his trial following the Moncada attack. A very appropriate justification for the old PSP! Socialism was thus born only in October 1960, not after the destruction of the Batista army and the seizure of power by the rebel army, but after the October 1960 nationalizations.

Speaking more generally, Cuba's positive view of Latin American governments, particularly the Cartagena group – formed in June 1984 to look at ways of reducing the burden of the debt (by Argentina, Brazil, Mexico, Bolivia, Chile, Colombia, the Dominican Republic, Ecuador, Peru, Uruguay and Venezuela – in whose hands 90 per cent of Latin America's total debt of $400,000 million is concentrated) – have not always been devoid of an accommodating attitude: articles in *Granma* on Argentina have occasionally been benevolent towards the Alfonsín government. At the conference on foreign debt in São Paulo in May 1987, organized by the Brazilian United Workers' Congress (CUT), the Uruguayan Inter-Union Plenum of Workers (PIT) and the Bolivian Workers' Congress (COB), the CUT's stance was much more radical than that of the Cuban delegation. This was obviously linked to diplomatic relations with Sarney. Moreover, the fact that Cuba supported a vote for Juan Bosch in the Dominican elections several years ago provoked a negative response in Santo Domingo. The Chilean and Jamaican communist parties did not miss the opportunity to register their disagreement with Fidel Castro's excessively broad conception of Latin American unity. This was somewhat ironical in the case of the Chilean party which was an expert in 'opening out' during Allende's Popular Unity government.

There is no evidence, however, that the Castro leadership has come down, once and for all, in favour of 'building socialism in a single island', as is borne out by its attitude to Central America. But the ruling group is prevented by its pragmatism from drawing the lessons from past defeats to define new perspectives. Along with a criticism of Soviet textbooks is a criticism of theory *tout court*. The imbrication of party and state means that inevitable diplomatic manoeuvring and reasons of state tend to influence Cuban analyses of class conflicts. Fidel Castro's militant Third Worldism may stress the threat of economic and social catastrophes and famine facing certain countries; but he underestimates their structural relation with the maintenance of an economy based on the pursuit of profit. The notion that a common front could emerge to eliminate debt and poverty (as the basis for a change in social relations) is quite simply Utopian.[14]

Whatever the case, the real test of the Cuban leadership's policy is revolution in Central America. This involves defending the Nicaraguan Revolution and supporting the revolutionary struggle taking place in El Salvador. The Cuban leadership gave unambiguous support to the Salvadorean revolutionaries during the FMLN's offensive in November 1989; and Cuba has made considerable efforts to help Nicaragua in all areas: militarily, with advisers and instructors[15] (and aid in the form of arms); technically, with the presence of numerous doctors, teachers, technicians, etc.; and economically, with the decision to cancel $50 million of debt, as well as to supply oil under terms which meant that Nicaragua would not have to pay 12 per cent of its oil bill until 1990. Cuba also agreed to provide cement until 1990 and to provide aid for several agricultural development projects. In relation to Cuban resources, this is the most significant aid that the Sandinistas have received. It was negotiated in June 1988 during an official visit by Daniel Ortega to Cuba.[16]

Such gestures are all the more significant because it is not clear that an agreement exists between the two leaderships over the economic and diplomatic policies that should be followed.

On 14 February 1989, the five Central American presidents made a joint declaration as part of the Esquipulas II accords. Relating to the peace and national reconciliation process and the holding of elections in Nicaragua in 1990, it also invited all groups in El Salvador 'to participate in the presidential election', and demanded that governments of the region cease all aid, 'either open or secret' to insurgent movements. It was published in full in *Granma*. In a short commentary entitled 'uncertain diagnosis', one of the newspaper's columnists recalled that 'the contras are far from entering a terminal phase' and 'had not lost their breath'. And on the Central American summit, he wrote that it represented an 'enormous effort in favour of peace', but that its fruits would be seen 'by the extent to which all concerned parties prove their willingness to negotiate'.

Excluded from bilateral negotiations between the Soviet Union and the United States on Central America, the Castro leadership has demonstrated that it cannot be ignored with impunity. Fidel Castro's presence at presidential inauguration ceremonies in Ecuador, Mexico and Venezuela in 1988 and 1989 provided the opportunity for meetings and negotiations on the Central American crisis. Only the future will tell what the conclusions will be, but one thing is certain: the Cuban leadership has asserted its pre-eminence, in spite of being marginalized by the two 'great' powers.

As far as El Salvador is concerned, there have been ups and downs in relations with the revolutionary movement. In January 1984 the Cuban Deputy Minister of Foreign Affairs, Ricardo Alarcón, stated officially that Cuba would not help El Salvador.[17] This was just after the Grenada defeat, but before the change in the direction of Cuban defence policy (Fidel Castro later stressed the influence that El Salvador had had in the swing towards popular war).

In 1987, the Soviet government gave its backing to the Guatemala meeting and the document (already) signed by the five Central America presidents in favour of a 'fair negotiated settlement'.[18] On 9 October 1987 Eduard Shevardnadze visited Havana. A joint statement ratified the support of the two countries for the Guatemala accords and confirmed their solidarity with 'the struggle of the Nicaraguan people for the achievement of their inalienable right to determine their own destiny'.[19] El Salvador was not even mentioned. In so far as the negotiations held within the framework of the Contadora group or the Arias plan were based on the implementation of a so-called policy of 'national reconciliation', the latter could only lead to tensions in the Salvadorean organizations. The linkage between the contras and the Sandinista government was made in such a way that it could be translated in a radically different way in El Salvador. Unlike Nicaragua where power belonged to the Sandinistas, the FMLN would be forced into surrender and capitulation to an existing government. This famous 'symmetry' between the Nicaraguan contras and the FMLN in El Salvador has always been seen as a trap by leaders of the Salvadorean armed organizations, and rightly so. Such diplomatic manoeuvres, which continued with the Tela accords, are aimed at using the regional context to force the FMLN to abandon the armed struggle (when the correlation of forces is favourable to it at the national level).

Fidel Castro has reaffirmed Cuba's support for El Salvador:

> They have all our support. Why deny it? We lend the Salvadorean patriots all the support we can. If it is a case of peace, we support peace. But for as long as there is not a peaceful solution, and for as long as the Salvadorean revolutionaries struggle, they will be entitled to all the support we are able to give them. ... We can all learn from the Salvadoreans. How has such a small country, a country of barely 20,000 square kilometres, been able to resist the genocidal armies backed by the United States for eight years? We have learnt military tactics. At the beginning it was we who were teaching them. But today it is we who are learning from them. ... If an end were put to all military support, to all direct or indirect participation in Central America, I think we would be in total agreement with a halt in all forms of military activity.[20] In the case of El Salvador, there is no

doubt that, without US aid, the FMLN would not be long in organizing the final offensive, given its support and the balance of forces.

The PCC's relations with revolutionary organizations in the continent vary from country to country. Following the shock of the Cuban and Nicaraguan revolutions and then the coming to power of Gorbachev, the crisis of the Latin American communist parties is deep. From El Salvador to the Argentinian Communist Party (formerly a bastion of Stalinism under the leadership of Victorio Codovilla), self-criticism has grown under the influence of Salvadorean Communist Party leader, Shafik Handal. In 1981 he made a critical assessment of the communist parties' policy of class collaboration, and this had significant repercussions throughout Latin America. The Argentinian Communist Party has criticized the support it gave to the 'democratic wing of the military dictatorship' between 1976 and 1983.[21] The PCC's links with these parties vary greatly, depending on the country and its type of government. The Uruguayan Communist Party and its general secretary, Rodney Arismendy, have often enjoyed preferential treatment, and quite recently, the latter was presented in an interview published in *Granma* as a 'symbol of revolutionary firmness'.[22] According to Arismendy, the question facing Latin America was not to 'choose between socialist revolution and existing democracies. Socialism will not come in the short term; it is fascism that could return and that is why democracy must be consolidated.' All one can say is that there is not much self-criticism in the air as far as Arismendy is concerned. He is one of the oldest Stalinists in the continent (at the time of the OLAS conference in 1967, he played a key role in avoiding the break between the communist parties and the Castroite organizations) and will be able to slip into the mould of Gorbachev-style politics without any difficulty. The interview was all the more significant because the general secretary of the Uruguayan Communist Party referred to the Broad Front (*Frente Amplio*) as the only opposition force in Uruguay. Such a claim rather overlooked the National Liberation Movement (MLN-Tupamaros), whose entry to the Front he had rejected at the time.

His words were clearly echoed at the conference of communist party central committee secretaries in Havana in 1988. Apparently limited to communist parties from Eastern Europe alone, the meeting's impact was weak. And in the absence of every Latin American communist party, the resolution adopted expressed concern 'in the face of destabilization efforts which threaten the processes taking place' and confirmed its solidarity 'with the peoples of the continent who are struggling for democracy, national sovereignty and territorial integrity'.

There have been considerable problems as far as relations with armed revolutionary organizations are concerned. While relations with Cuba are maintained, they are strained by the eclecticism of the PCC leadership. The leaderships of the continent's revolutionary movements are more autonomous and critical. On the whole such organizations and currents criticize the concept of the single party and its democratic shortcomings. They occasionally come up against diplomatic manoeuvres and confusion over class interests in Cuba's relations with the ruling classes in their countries. And finally, their view of current developments in Eastern Europe is often the opposite of that of the Cuban party. They supported Solidarność in Poland (this was the case with the Brazilian Workers' Party, PT, including its Castroite wing), and several condemned the invasion of Afghanistan. Unlike Fidel Castro, they spoke out unanimously against repression in China.

The revolutionary movement is in the midst of recomposition. Faced with economic and social changes in the subcontinent, as well as developments in the politics of leadership and its international effects, the movement is carrying out an overall analysis and examination of revolutionary strategy. Given the record of 'actually existing socialism', questions on the transition to socialism have made it even more necessary for all revolutionary forces, both East and West, to confront each other. The Brazilian PT's invitation of Charter 77 activist, Peter Uhl, from Czechoslovakia, to its congress was a first step in this direction. For Latin American revolutionary forces, the keystone is the situation in Central America. The consolidation of the Nicaraguan Revolution and the progress of the revolutionary movement in El Salvador, which put US–Soviet manoeuvres in check, were an important element in the reorganization of the revolutionary movement in the subcontinent.

Havana no longer acts as a continental centre as it did in the past. The revolution's influence has weakened under the dual impact of the ambiguities of Cuban diplomacy and the criticisms sparked by restrictions on democratic rights in Cuba. While recognizing the breadth of social gains, the Latin American avant-gardes are more sensitive to the lack of freedom than before and less prepared to accept Fidel Castro's *caudillismo*. Twenty years after the OLAS, no stable organization exists for the co-ordination of revolution, at least for the time being. Meanwhile the bourgeoisie has equipped itself with relatively efficient and permanent tools of liaison and exchange. This relative isolation has had a number of effects, particularly on how the defence of the revolution is conceived.

A New Version of Peaceful Co-existence: Third World Revolution as the Victim of Perestroika

Picking up from where Khrushchev left off, Gorbachev is renewing peaceful coexistence. 'In the context of the nuclear era', he has said, 'we are absolutely right to refuse to see the latter as a particular form of class struggle. Coexistence based on the principles of non-aggression, respect for sovereignty and independence and non-interference in the internal affairs of others, cannot be identified with the class struggle. The struggle between two opposing systems is no longer the determinant tendency of the modern age.'[23] It is only left for the working classes of the imperialist countries to confine revolutionary mass struggles to the museum of labour history, and for oppressed peoples to put their arms back in the cupboard. This message was confirmed by an article by G. Mirski:[24] Third World development is and will remain capitalist for a long time, and the Soviet Union and national liberation movements must operate within that framework. For the revolutionaries in Central America, this amounts to a condemnation of their own struggle; and for Cuba, it represents the danger of suffocation. As well as the dispute over economic policy, this explains why Fidel Castro has given a negative verdict on perestroika.

It is true that the situation in Central America probably provides most evidence for the counter-revolutionary nature of such suggestions. As a US journalist wrote: 'The Marxists appear to move closer to consolidating power in Nicaragua. Guerrillas and death squads eat away the center in El Salvador. Armies shrivel the realm of elected government in Honduras and Guatemala. Democratic Costa Rica trembles. A drug lord in Panama scoffs at Washington's efforts to curb him.'[25] Inquiring as to why such a situation had come about, the journalist asserted that 'neither a conservative nor a liberal US administration has a workable security policy beyond improvising local containment and hoping that Mikhail Gorbachev will somehow help out'. A clearer definition of what a 'US–Soviet condominium'[26] means for US imperialism could not have been given.

The idea that such a condominium could provide a solution for underdevelopment and hunger in the world is Utopian. But above all, it would involve a complete revision of the mechanics governing capitalism and imperialism at the very time it is becoming more and more difficult to conceal the real reasons for the pillage and poverty of the dominated countries.

In such circumstances, the advocacy of 'national reconciliation' and the formation of coalition governments to end so-called 'regional' conflicts is mere window-dressing, aimed at masking the refusal to change the existing order and at giving special priority to Soviet economic recovery and interests. In order to maintain the 'dialogue' with the United States – in other words, work towards technological and commercial aid – the Soviet Union has yielded to US conditions and agreed to place regional conflicts in the negotiations basket.

Things appear differently from the point of view of the diplomatic interests of the Cuban state. Cuba's intervention in the Third World has been made possible by the means provided by the Soviet Union (arms, transport, etc.). Without this aid, Cuba's influence with the Non-Aligned Movement would be compromised, its international role (as well as its commercial trade) limited, and its room for manoeuvre restricted. Its criticisms of Gorbachev's foreign policy are therefore an expression of its different state interests. With the exception of Central America, however, Cuba's approach is perhaps not as oppositional as it seems. While making the quite legitimate proposal of a united anti-imperialist front to fight unequal terms of trade and protectionism, Fidel Castro also declared that:

> Social change is important, but right now the vital thing is to create the minimum conditions for this development, because a country, if it is building a revolution, requires a minimum of conditions in order to develop. ... I had proposed a policy of unity between all forces to solve this great economic crisis, and gave this priority over social changes, which, sooner or later, will have to come about. This does not mean changing my ideas, but making a realistic analysis of the situation we are in.[27]

The idea that there can be a preliminary form of development without a change in social relations is perhaps a simple diplomatic manoeuvre for the consumption of the Latin American bourgeoisie. But it is reminiscent of Khrushchev's concept of the non-capitalist path of development for Third World countries; a concept that Fidel Castro now seems to have taken up in a different international context, while Gorbachev is no longer troubled by such fictions. Apart from different geopolitical interests, that is perhaps about as far as the differences go. Nevertheless, the practical consequences of such differences could be highly significant.

As elsewhere, the new Soviet policy will lead to a different hand of cards being dealt in Latin America, both at the diplomatic level and in terms of the ranks of the traditional left and the revolutionary movements. Its consequences cannot yet be foreseen. But as far as the Third World is concerned, the first settlements in the 'regional conflicts' can only give cause for concern. The compromise reached in Southern Africa for the withdrawal of Cuban troops from Angola, aimed at clearing the path to Namibian independence, did not involve any halt whatsoever in US aid to Savimbi's National Union for the Total Independence of

Namibia (Unita).[28] This left Namibia under the control of South Africa. After several years of struggle, that clearly could not be regarded a victory.

Angola: Disengagement

The Cuban leadership has denounced the false symmetry established between Angola, Central America, Afghanistan, South Africa, Cambodia and other cases. The presence of Cuban troops in Angola has nothing in common with the invasion of Afghanistan by Soviet troops. The nationalist government in Angola is involved in a legitimate struggle against a pro-imperialist organization seeking to overthrow it with the decisive support of South Africa (which thus intends to cut off the African National Congress, the ANC, from its rear bases). It is an indisputable fact that it was the Popular Movement for the Liberation of Angola (MPLA) which, besieged in Luanda, appealed in 1975 for Cuban support to resist the attacks of South African troops. When the first Cuban troops arrived, 'artillery was already bombing the suburbs of Luanda and South African units had penetrated the south of the country from Namibia'.[29]

All commentators have confirmed that Cuba did not act on the orders of Moscow: 'It would be a mistake to assume that Cuba will act as told by the Soviet leadership, even though Havana is kept afloat on Soviet aid. Cuba has, on occasions, been more willing to take risks in combat than the Soviet Union would like and there have been reports of disagreement on tactics against South African incursions.'[30] Such an intervention, of course, could never have taken place without Soviet arms and logistical support, with the Angolans providing food and lodgings for the Cuban soldiers whose wages were paid in pesos in Cuba. The latest figures available since the negotiations put the number of Cuban soldiers in Angola at around 50,000. Approximately 300,000 Cubans have taken part in the war over twelve years. Contact was first made with the MPLA in 1962, with military collaboration and the training of the first Angolan guerrilla units beginning in 1965, following Che's trip to Africa.[31] At a more general level, links have also been made since the triumph of the Cuban Revolution with African revolutionary movements, such as Amilcar Cabral and the African Party for the Independence of Guinea and Cape Verde (PAIGC). And Che's presence was officially recognized in the Congo etc. According to the Angolan ambassador in Havana, 'We called on Cuba without consulting anyone, and they accepted without consultation. The withdrawal of the troops will be sorted out by Cuba and Angola, and nobody else.'[32]

Such efforts by Cuba towards the Third World are a 'way of

responding to attempts to isolate us. We have tried to broaden our relations'.[33] They have also enabled Cuba to gain military experience in this kind of conflict, as well as, in the face of an opponent like South Africa, to gain access to ultra-modern equipment that it would undoubtedly not have been able to obtain otherwise. It was thus an investment 'seen as Cuba's military contribution to the CMEA',[34] a way of paying back its debts.

Thus, just as it would be a mistake to see Cuba's initial intervention as a Soviet decision, likewise it would also be a mistake to see the cease-fire merely as a result of new Soviet policy, in spite of the latter's decisive effect. There was a coincidence of interests. For its part, Cuba needed to negotiate because of tensions within Angola and Cuba itself. It would seem that disagreements had arisen in Angola between the Angolan and Cuban governments over policy towards Unita. A number of successful military offensives, launched jointly with fighters from the South West African People's Organization (Swapo), apparently did not receive the approval of the Angolan leadership. Problems had arisen between Cuban troops and the local army as a result of exhaustion from the war. An article in *El País* reported the following conversation between a Cuban and an Angolan officer before the departure of some of the Cuban troops. The Cuban: 'See you soon, friends, we'll all soon be back at home. The Angolans already can't afford to pay us next year.' The Angolan: 'We don't need them any more. They're no longer in the combat zones. A lot of Cubans died before, but it's our people who are dying and being mutilated now. The Cubans will always have something to eat. Our soldiers have nothing but rice and dried fish.'[35]

The claim that the Cubans were no longer in the combat zones was denied. It was precisely the number of victims and disabled that was beginning to present problems for Cuba. The exact number of victims and disabled is still not known. The figure of 10,000 dead given by the deserter general, del Pino, was flatly denied by Jorge Risquet, the PCC secretary for foreign relations and Cuba's top representative at the negotiations, who estimated around 1,000 dead. Del Pino's claim that there were 56,000 deserters seems highly unlikely. But that does not alter the fact that the war had become very unpopular and a source of weariness among the population, given the seriousness of current economic difficulties. Recruitment among youth was also becoming increasingly difficult. And the Cuban leadership felt that developments in the Angolan regime no longer justified such a large effort. The difficulty of repatriating soldiers remains, and given the current situation in the country, providing jobs and social reintegration will be a major problem.

In spite of the victory of the Cuban troops over the South African army at Cuito Cuanavale, the political agreements being enforced in

Africa do not constitute a success. The satisfaction displayed by Washington appeared to confirm the verdict of the editor of *Le Monde* that 'South Africa has easily won the fight in the region and this constitutes a bitter blow for the Soviet Union'.[36]

The Castro leadership had no choice, given the international context. Cuban resentment was to express itself on a number of occasions, notably during Gorbachev's visit in April 1989. Fidel Castro had always linked the departure of Cuban troops from Angola to the end of apartheid, while the South African and US governments made Namibian independence conditional on the withdrawal of Castro's troops. In spite of disagreeing with this concept of linkage, the Cuban leader had to give way to Gorbachev's arguments. Cuba did not have the means to pursue a war of this scale without Soviet arms, even though the success in battle at Cuito Cuanavale might have led one to believe otherwise. As the commander-in-chief of the armed forces was to confirm in a speech on 5 December 1988: 'Cuban forces and logistics were not sufficient to settle the issue.'

The tripartite accord, signed in December 1988, between Angola, Cuba and South Africa, fell well short of the Castro leadership's hopes. The presence of UN forces, intended to safeguard the conditions leading to Namibian independence, would not prevent the massacre of several hundred Swapo fighters returning to their country. South Africa has made every effort to integrate the militia it had previously created into the national army of the future independent state. The weakening of Swapo has thus been a major concern, and the economic dependency of the future state on South Africa is enormous.

According to the Cahama (Angola) Accords signed on 19 May 1989, Swapo's armed units were to be 'confined to their bases north of the sixteenth parallel', with Angola and Cuba in charge of monitoring the process. 'According to Resolution 435, the Namibian police was to continue to assume its vital role, which is to guarantee the maintenance of order' and to make every effort to 'uncover arms caches left in Namibia'[37] by Swapo resistance fighters driven back towards Angola.

Thus, here was a country which was finally achieving independence after seventy-five years of South African occupation, but whose national liberation fighters were forced to return unarmed into their own country, subject to the diktats of the colonial power.

As an example of the settlement of a regional conflict and of 'national reconciliation', Namibia will make revolutionary movements fighting for liberation think. Though a signatory of the accords, the Cuban government strongly criticized the decision of the five members of the Security Council (including the Soviet Union) to make a 40 per cent cut in the UN forces that were to guarantee the implementation of Resolution 435 and

Namibia's achievement of independence. The Cuban press had highlighted the role of Pretoria's army and police, as well as Swapo's fears that massive repression would be used to prevent the movement from obtaining the two-thirds majority needed in the elections to abolish the discriminatory laws inherited from South African colonial domination. Such fears were confirmed.

All these grievances clearly explain the extreme ferocity with which the Cuban leader attacked the members of the Security Council (including the Soviet Union) in February 1989. '[They] have acted in unity of the narrowest kind, a group which enjoys the privilege of veto', he said, reminding the permanent members of 'the great responsibility incumbent upon them if the racists manage to prevent the self-determination and free choice of the Namibian people'.[38]

The warning was repeated during Gorbachev's visit that April. While Gorbachev was to declare his opposition to 'any theory or doctrine tending to justify the export of revolution or counter-revolution and [to] all forms of foreign interference in the affairs of states'[39] – such a reference to the export of revolution could only exasperate his interlocutors in a continent where there has been no end of counter-revolution to crush home-grown revolutions – Fidel Castro made the first move to counter-attack, thus provoking the departure of the US representative from the National Assembly of People's Power. Quoting the case of Afghanistan (where 'the United States reserves the right to carry on supplying arms to the Afghan opposition and counter-revolutionary forces', in spite of the withdrawal of Soviet troops), that of South West Africa (where 'the United States reserves the right to supply arms to Unita'), that of Nicaragua (where 'the United States reserves the right to support the counter-revolution organized from Honduran territory as a tool to pressure the government and people of Nicaragua'),[40] he responded to the letter to the false symmetry created in Gorbachev's speech between revolution and counter-revolution. It was necessary, he declared, 'to demand the abolition of this theory and this doctrine [the very terms used by the Soviet leader] by which the United States assumes the right to aid irregular forces against constituted governments by supplying them with arms' – a completely different approach to the settlement of 'regional conflicts'.

Under such circumstances, it is understandable that the parallel drawn by the Soviet ambassador in Cuba between the negotiated settlement reached in Southern Africa and the one needed in Central America should be so worrying. Indeed, Yuri Petrov had declared: 'The same approach as in Southern Africa should be used to resolve the conflict in Central America. Just as we collaborated with the United States over Angola and Namibia, likewise the two countries should act as mediators in the case of Nicaragua and El Salvador.'[41] But not only is the nature of the states different; there are also profound differences between the organizations concerned. How can nationalist organizations like the MPLA or Swapo be bracketed together with revolutionary organizations claiming to be Marxist like the FSLN and the FMLN? Nor can the balance of forces on the ground be compared, hence the indignation that such an absurd parallel has managed to provoke.

The US government has clearly defined the conditions for a solution to the Central American crisis. The Soviet Union, it claims, has no strategic interest in the region and should therefore respect the zones of influence once established by the Monroe Doctrine. The issue is therefore not one of a bilateral halt in military intervention in the region, as proposed by Gorbachev, but of a unilateral halt. According to Washington, the suspension of arms deliveries to Nicaragua by the Soviet Union 'is not enough'. As President Oscar Arias of Costa Rica declared in Washington, echoing the repeated declarations of James Baker, the issue was to stop Cuban arms deliveries to El Salvador,[42] and, indeed, even to pressure the Soviet Union to reduce its aid to Cuba.[43]

For the time being such demands have met with blunt refusal from the Cuban authorities. The editor of *Granma Weekly*, Gabriel Molina, claimed that Oscar Arias's initiatives on El Salvador were unrealistic in that demands for democratization in Nicaragua were not being made with the same vigour in the case of El Salvador (referring to the Salvadorean government's rejection of the FMLN's proposal that the March 1989 presidential elections be postponed to ensure that they would be democratic). Indeed, the Costa Rican president pronounced himself 'in favour of [the revolutionary movement's] surrender'.[44] For its part, the Soviet government unambiguously denounced the FMLN's offensive in El Salvador in November 1989 in the same way that it had condemned the continuation of armed struggle in South Africa.

For Cuba, 'peace is a coin with two complementary sides: the reduction of the global nuclear threat and the just settlement of regional conflicts'.[45] As well as having a different approach over peaceful coexistence, the Soviet Union and Cuba have very different national interests as far as Central America is concerned. What is merely a problem of secondary importance for the Soviet Union represents a major concern for the Cuban Revolution, which is going through a very dangerous period. In a context of economic and political crisis, witnessed by allegations of corruption at the highest level and sackings in the apparatus, pressure is being applied from all sides: from the Soviet Union; from the United States, which makes a change of direction in the region a condition for the lifting of the economic blockade; from the Latin American bourgeoisies; from the European bourgeoisies which demand economic and political concessions for a renegotiation of the debt within the framework of the Paris Club. The regional balance of forces is decisive in this wrestling match; and the outcome of the conflicts in Central America will have a crucial influence on the development of the internal situation in Cuba.

The Pentagon and its stooges in Latin America have never hidden the fact that any attempt to seize power in El Salvador would be met with all-out retaliation against those countries suspected of providing military support to the FMLN. And following the start of the Salvadorean revolutionaries' offensive in November 1989, Colonel Vargas did not miss the opportunity to state that 'if SAMs [surface-to-air missiles] were to appear here I think we would have no choice but to attack the source of supply, which would be Nicaragua', [46] itself aided by Cuba.

Defence: The Return to Popular War

On 21 October 1987, under the headline 'Moscow: the Cuban Economy is not Working', *L'Unitá*, the Italian Communist Party newspaper, quoted an article by one of the commentators from *New Times*[47] magazine replying to a letter – of touching spontaneity! – from a Colombian reader. The author of the article gave a highly critical account of Cuban economic management. The Colombian 'reader' had stated that, for fifteen years since Cuba's entry into Comecon, the oldest members of the socialist community had been trying to bring the island up to their own level of development [*sic*], but that he had been given to understand that the aim had not been achieved. In his reply, Chirkov emphasized that labour productivity was extremely low, that a third of enterprises were working at a loss, that rationing was still in force, and that the government was unable to honour its international financial commitments. Chirkov implied that one of the reasons for such a state of affairs might be that the Cubans devoted an excessive share of the budget to defence, and that this was not necessarily justified. While the socialist camp bought sugar, nickel and citrus fruits from Cuba at prices higher than on the world market, Cuba's overall debt with the socialist countries (mainly the Soviet Union and the German Democratic Republic, its privileged partners) was high, and this aid, commented Chirkov ironically, was felt by the Cubans to be a 'moral weight'. A month later, no doubt to get rid of this burden, Fidel Castro demanded that the socialist countries cancel the debt 'on grounds of principle'.[48] Chirkov's article ended with an appeal for a Cuban perestroika, mainly along the lines of the mixed enterprises advocated by the CMEA.

The choice of author for the Cuban reply was not left to chance. It was

Carlos Rafael Rodríguez – Politburo member, former PSP leader and Cuba's representative to the Cuban–Soviet inter-governmental bilateral commission – who was given responsibility. The gist of his reply was that only the comparable should be compared, giving as an example the productivity of the Soviet Union compared with that of the developed countries (Sweden, the Federal Republic of Germany or Japan); that particular Cuban problems were due to delays in external supplies and their poor quality; that prices for sugar and other goods should be compared with the much higher prices paid by the EEC or the United States in the framework of fixed quota markets. On defence, Carlos Rafael Rodríguez took refuge behind the views of other Soviet and Eastern European 'specialists'.[49] Given that they had responded to the Cuban government's military demands, he felt they shared its point of view.

Chirkov had not only challenged the costs incurred in the creation of national militias, but the very conception of Cuban defence and the changes made in this area. And he had had no hesitation in stating: 'As to the question whether the United States would attempt to attack Cuba ... there are several possible responses.' However sybilline, such a choice of words was seen as a provocation. US threats multiplied after the victory of the revolution in Nicaragua and the development of the revolutionary process in El Salvador. The aim is to 'strike a blow to the head' or 'extirpate the evil at its root'; a war of liberation would have to be 'launched against Cuba if propaganda is not enough',[50] proclaimed the Santa Fe document in May 1980.

Contrary to those who believe that the Cuban Revolution is now out of danger, such a hypothesis is not at all fantastic. In 1981 Secretary of State Haig asked the Pentagon to examine the possibility of a 'blockade of Nicaragua and various military actions against Cuba, including a display of air strength, naval exercises, quarantining arms shipments to the island, a naval blockade and even the possibility of an invasion'.[51] If the Cuban masses were demobilized, the revolution would be destroyed – that is the bitter lesson of Grenada. As Fidel Castro has rightly said, the Yankee intervention was able to take place because the revolution 'was no longer anything but a corpse'. Such is the analysis of the Castro leadership, unlike that of the bureaucrats imported from Moscow.

In 1981 Colombia and Jamaica broke off relations with Cuba. The favourable international climate created by the military defeat of the United States in Vietnam – prophetically foreseen by Che in his address to the Tricontinental – was coming to an end. It had favoured the explosion of revolutionary processes in Iran and Nicaragua and enabled Cuba to intervene in Angola. Under Reagan, the US government retook the initiative and recovered its interventionist capability with a subtle campaign combining the ideological battle over 'human rights' and 'low intensity' wars. As aid to the contras has proved, it would be risky to believe that the United States, faced with the spread of revolution in Central America, would not attempt to intervene in one form or another if it got the chance. The most effective form of deterrence since the Vietnam War is still arming the people.

What are the other 'possible responses' referred to by Chirkov? Nuclear deterrence is obviously not one of them since the missile crisis. Diplomatic manoeuvres, negotiations and Soviet protection have become uncertain in the light of the new directions being taken in foreign policy. As Fidel Castro never stops saying, Cuba is not ninety miles away from the Soviet border, but ninety miles away from Miami. And in response to the partisans of dialogue and the 'peaceful resolution of conflicts', the Salvadorean delegate at the international meeting held in Moscow in 1987 (for the anniversary of the October Revolution) said that one should not believe in the 'irreversible nature of detente', as the US was still 'thirsty for the blood of revolutionaries'.[52]

This claim has been confirmed by the development of the conflicts in the Central American isthmus. There are only two acceptable outcomes for Washington: either straightforward military suppression and organized terror, or strangulation by the knot attached to 'democracy'. Having once exhausted the mobilization of the masses through a military and economic war of attrition, pseudo-democratic elections are then intended to lead to the victory of candidates from the bourgeoisie. Nicaragua is being used as a laboratory to test this hypothesis.

Reconsideration of the way the defence system is conceived does not date from the Gorbachev era, but from the victory of the Nicaraguan Revolution, which broke Cuba's isolation for the first time. With the election of Reagan in 1980, the Soviet Union bogged down in Afghanistan, and the Polish crisis, the Castro leadership was led to reconsider the island's defences. The invasion of Grenada would have been decisive in this rethink. The head of the Cuban detachment, Colonel Tortolo, had fled along with his officers. Cuban workers had fought longer, but 'left without a leader ... they surrendered'.[53] In a 'ceremony' which was filmed and broadcast in barracks, the colonel was degraded along with thirty officers who were sent to Angola.

Such a surrender alarmed the Castro leadership and discredited Fidel Castro's warlike proclamations. A general review began. The Cuban army, with its Soviet training and associated military concepts, was not adapted to the defence of the island. The Salvadorean revolutionaries had shown that imperialism could be resisted in an area of land no bigger than a pocket handkerchief. Popular war was the only possible form of resistance in the event of an intervention. 'Cuba's defence cannot depend on the commitments made by other states or on agreements that exist with other states. The defence of our country is the responsibility of our people. A country is independent when it can defend itself by itself,'[54] declared Fidel Castro. The quote speaks for itself. Such a drastic review was simultaneously the result of national and international factors. At a domestic level, tension continued under the impact of the war in Angola. And within the military hierarchy itself, there were differences and conflicts between officers trained in the Soviet Union at the Frunze military academy and those trained in Cuba itself at the Maceo interservice academy or who were Sierra Maestra veterans.[55]

This reorientation explains the creation of the national militias (MTTs), composed of civilian volunteers who train regularly. There are about one and a half million people in the MTTs, equipped with light arms, but also with access to heavy arms and armoured cars. Soldiers returning from Angola are members. 'Every plot of land has been studied ... a mission has been assigned to every province, town and corner of the country. ... Eighteen thousand men and 3,500 machines are permanently employed in the preparation of the terrain for defence; and to this end we use 15 per cent of the reinforced concrete produced in the country, which gives some idea of the efforts made.'[56]

According to estimates of the National Bank of Cuba, the defence budget rose by 23.9 per cent in 1985.[57] This amounted to 18 per cent of the total budget (Azicri claims);[58] and if the National Bank of Cuba[59] is to be believed, the figures for 1986 and 1987 were 10.9 per cent and 11.1 per cent respectively. The cost of the MTTs is high, with training and wages during exercise periods (as well as the concomitant falls in production) all adding to the military bill proper.

The regular armed forces (approximately 300,000 men) no longer have the sole responsibility for the defence of the island. The Cubans have been to Vietnam and El Salvador to study their experiences first-hand: 'A weapon and shelter for each citizen.' Vietnamese officers have arrived to advise their Cuban counterparts. This is one of the few cases where the Cubans are not taking the advice of Soviet officers.

The testimony of former general Rafael del Pino who fled to the United States is credible, claiming as he does that relations between Cuban officers and their Soviet colleagues are either indifferent or hostile. 'The advisers who go to Cuba are more intent on spending three years on holiday than at work ... and, dividing their time between fishing and hunting snails, they do not have the slightest influence on Cuban decisions.'[60]

To complete the overall plan of action, a National Defence Council was created. Neither the constitution nor the party statutes provided for this body and its precise role in relation to officer staff is not known. It is one of the many parallel bodies that Fidel Castro often creates and which allow him to short-circuit statutory bodies. He is the Council's president and thus oversees the MTTs and the army, as well as the forces from the Ministry of the Interior whose number is not officially known.

Since then, 'defence is conceived as a task for which not just the armed forces, but the whole people are responsible'.[61] Popular struggle has become one of the principles of Cuban military doctrine.

Relations between the PCC and the army have not always been harmonious. According to W. Leogrande, 'The party in the revolutionary armed forces (FAR) concentrated its energies on supportive activities (e.g. combat readiness, military manoeuvres, troop morale, etc.) rather than on party control activities (political education, criticism and self-criticism, etc.). Even this limited role, however, continued to provoke criticism and resistance from some military officers.'[62]

Has it been the wish of the Castro leadership to limit excessive Soviet influence with the FAR? Indeed, top cadres of the Cuban army have had a long training in the Soviet Union in the use of modern arms. Reinforcing the role of the party is part of redefining defence.

The trauma caused by the defeatist conduct of Cuban officers in Grenada and, secondarily, by the desertion of General del Pino and other security officials, has led to a review of training of FAR cadres, training methods and the role of the party. Speakers at an anti-aircraft defence meeting emphasized the poor preparation of particular units. This was due, they said, 'to the lack of work by their officers ... as well as to the weak influence and lack of control by rank-and-file bodies of the party'.[63] According to the FAR journal *Bastión*, a study of 150 party cells revealed inadequate methods in the training of cadres, recommending that party training should include practical activities and not just seminars and lectures. The survey also highlighted the lack of discipline and the unpopular behaviour of certain officers; expected to set an example, trainers were called to order.

These problems were aired at the first meeting of officers in March 1988, chaired by Raúl Castro and attended by 350 to 400 officers of military units, political officials and young trainee soldiers. Ninety-three per cent of the participants were members of the PCC or the Young Communists. Significantly, one of the chiefs of staff, Major General Rosales del Toro, insisted that revolutionaries do not surrender and emphasized the need for young officer cadets to be prepared for the difficulties of military life: 'Perhaps there will be less of them, but they will be better.'[64]

In other words, the specialization and professionalization of the army during its modernization had led to a bureaucratization of the military hierarchy. Technical qualification had come to be seen as the decisive factor, and had gradually relativized the importance of revolutionary motivation. The profession of officer had also become the passport to social advancement and a status that is particularly valued in Cuba; it was not just the end-result of a conviction or a vocation. This attitude has also existed among young people, some of whom grumbled about leaving for Angola to fulfil their 'internationalist duty' and even today are resistant to the idea of doing their military service. All these signs have converged to produce the current 'rectification', reaffirming the primacy of the leading role of the PCC and of ideological motivation – 'politics grows out of the barrel of a gun'.

Should this shift (which implies a more independent approach to the island's defence) be seen as the Castro leadership's fear of the armed forces becoming increasingly autonomous? Are the tensions that have arisen between the party leadership and a section of the military hierarchy an expression of this? Is the Ochoa affair part of the same picture?[65] Do the Soviet military advisers[66] have sufficient influence to become an alternative counterweight to the Castro leadership? One can still only speculate. Until further notice, the commander-in-chief faces little challenge in this area, unlike economic policy where jokes are readily made on the sly about his (in)competence.

It is true that, even in 1986, one could still come across strange phrases flowing from the pens of certain ideologues and 'doctors of Marxist-Leninist philosophy'. For example: 'The rich experience of the Soviet Union, the events in Hungary in 1956, Czechoslovakia in 1968 and Poland in the 1980s have demonstrated that the army is an indispensable need of the socialist state.'[67] That is not an official point of view but is that of an article which appeared in 1986 in *Revista de Ciencias Sociales*. This journal publishes articles – clearly inspired by the most retrograde Soviet publications – on historical or ideological issues. This reference to the army as an instrument of repression is not part of the Cuban tradition, if only for geopolitical reasons. Internal tensions of such gravity would involve the threat of US intervention, and, in such circumstances, the survival of the revolution could not be guaranteed.

The insistence on reinforcing the party's role and changing the criteria for the training of cadres (attaching greater importance to personal dedication and political mobilization) are more a reflection of the need to re-establish a certain independence from the Soviet Union, given the verdict on the current course of Soviet politics. Indeed, it is at the military level that contacts with the Soviet Union have been the closest. The importance of arms (delivered free), the scope of military operations abroad, the need to modernize and professionalize the military apparatus, the continuous training of cadres in Moscow, as well as the permanent presence in Cuba of officials from the Soviet officer staff, have not been without their consequences. Today, the situation is changing. The withdrawal of 50,000 soldiers and officers from Angola must be dealt with. Moreover, the end of missions abroad and the Soviet government's repeated 'advice' that arms deliveries and arms expenditure be cut, will affect both the role and internal structure of the Cuban armed forces.

The Angolan Trauma

There can be no doubt that the war in Angola is at the heart of current difficulties. The start of the war coincided with the period of institutionalization during the 1970s under the guidance of the Soviet Union. And confrontation with South African troops very quickly led to significant changes in Cuban military traditions. For the first time, notes J.-P. Clerc, 'the title of general was to appear before the grade itself was introduced in 1976, following Angola. Raúl was then to become the only army general.' Much later, on 14 June 1989, the Minister of the Armed Forces was to outline the difficulties that had been met in a speech at the twenty-eighth anniversary of the western army:

> This army command has put all its energy into dealing with the critical situation it went through in 1986, reflected among other things by the deficient use and maintenance of equipment, the low level of combat training, as well as the generally unsatisfactory results of checks and inspections carried out – so many things that noticeably reduced the fighting spirit. I am obviously not unaware of the tensions during those years: the departure of 8,000 officers on an internationalist mission and the rotation system caused difficulties in the cohesion and consolidation of the command.

As the situation deteriorated, the last years of the war had a serious effect on the troops' morale. The number of losses and wounded, the latent conflict with Angolan officials, corruption, as well as the spread of drugs and Aids were just some of the factors which played a role in the Cuban leadership's acceptance of the tripartite compromise. The 1989 scandals involving prestigious military leaders like General Ochoa were the reflection of a long-standing crisis. The internationalist fighters have not returned unscathed from a war that has lasted over ten years.

As the Cuban writer, Angel Santistebán Prats – who was given a mention of honour by the jury of the Juan Rulfo Prize[68] for his novel *Midsummer Night's Dream (Memoirs of a Cuban Returning from Angola)* – has written, describing the state of mind of young Cuban soldiers battling with Unita rebels:

> How can you forget? ... Every day that goes by, you get the clearest of images

> coming back. You even remember the smell of those starving cattle as you were crossing the bush, turned into a desert by the lack of rain. And then, suddenly, those endless downpours which transformed continents of dust into oceans of mud. Dead cows scattered here and there, swollen with all that water they had waited so long for. ... Vultures rejoice everywhere, devouring a carcass bristling with sated cobras, ripping out its eyes, setting free a mass of crawling grubs which spread over the rest of the body. A hyena prowls. ... In spite of exhaustion, sleep does not come quickly, as you toss and turn on the mattress, trying to make a hole where you can blot yourself out. Someone shrieks, sobbing like a child who has had a nightmare. In this hell, nightmares are reality. Some cry out for their mothers or for our lieutenant who has been here for a long time and been through it all before. That reassures us a bit when we come to fight. They are frightened of not coming out alive. And you, you think you have more luck than the rest; but you daren't say so.

Those who have been there will not easily forget the war in Angola.

The Angola affair has shown that Cuban international policy is 'out of proportion' with the country's size and status. It stems from a dual need: to fight isolation and the US blockade, and to use this international 'presence' as a means with which to increase its room for manoeuvre with the Soviet Union. It has been a kind of tithe – dearly paid – to repay the debt.

The Castro leadership is now haunted by the idea that peace and detente between the Soviet Union and the United States might mean the elimination of the revolutionary movements in Central America,[69] and reduce its scope for diplomatic manoeuvre. This is perhaps the most serious area of disagreement with Gorbachev. Najibullah's visit to Cuba in 1988 and the signing of a Cuban–Afghan treaty reflected the will of the poorest members of the 'socialist camp' to defend themselves against the aims of their powerful allies. This visit could certainly not be interpreted as an act of allegiance to Moscow in the current situation! The exact terms of the friendship and co-operation treaty are not known, but whatever they were, the general mood of the visit was one of 'fidelity'.[70]

Relations with the Eastern countries are conducted through CMEA and its occasional meetings. Events in Poland have led the Castro leadership to think long and hard, but the official version of events has hardly changed. It is a case of 'destabilization'[71] fomented by the West, aimed at 'bankrupting the country and dismembering the socialist community'.[72]

The repression of the popular uprising in Peking did not provoke any form of condemnation. Hiding behind the 'principle' of non-interference in the internal affairs of fraternal parties, Fidel Castro did not condemn the repression. The heavy silence of the first few weeks retrospectively highlighted the irony of the comments of the first secretary of the Cuban party on the insufficiently critical nature of the Cuban press. The weekly international edition of *Granma* devoted a mere half page to the events, and then only on 18 June. One of the articles limited itself to reproducing Deng Xiaoping's speech, while the other was a report on the visit of Chinese Foreign Minister Qian Quichen who was honoured with the title of 'distinguished guest of the town'. This visit took on particular significance in that it was the first time that a leader of such importance had visited Cuba in twenty-eight years. The recent development of commercial trade, in particular the purchase of large quantities of sugar by China, is not unrelated to the stance taken by Cuba. But this time, the Cuban government cannot justify its position in terms of Soviet pressure; a position that cannot fail to spark a hostile reaction among Cuban youth, not to mention the condemnation it has already provoked throughout Latin America, particularly in Mexico where the entire left has protested.

The position of the PCC leadership is very clear. An official delegation, led by Lionel Soto, the secretary of the Central Committee, visited China in October 1989. The trip's aim was to prepare for the visit of Fidel Castro, a 'visit enthusiastically awaited'. According to *Granma*, the secretary of the Chinese Communist Party, Jiang Zemin, explained the reasons for 'counter-revolutionary sedition' at the meeting. For his part, Lionel Soto conveyed the 'warm message of President Castro and of the Cuban people and party to the Chinese Communist Party and the Chinese people on the occasion of the fortieth anniversary of the creation of the People's Republic'.[73]

In assessing the crisis of the official international communist movement, Fidel Castro has spoken in favour of pluralism, as well as respecting the independence of each party and differences of opinion. He has done so on the grounds of the diversity of the specific circumstances of each country, and it is unfortunate that he does not apply the same conclusions to Cuba. 'At the time, there was only one centre, the Soviet Union. Today, there is no other choice but to respect the right of each party and each country to interpret doctrine and apply it to the specific conditions of each country.'

Such a conversion to polycentrism, as well as to the rejection of hegemonism and 'doctrinaire zeal', even benefits Yugoslavia, which has long been the *bête noire* of Cuba and whose experience of self-management is now being studied. But in the current international context, polycentrism is not a solution for the isolation suffered by the Cuban Revolution.

Cuban foreign policy is aimed at reducing inequality in relations with the Soviet Union and at introducing an 'element of interdependence'. This would provide the Cuban state with a lever with which to consolidate its cause in the Third World and secure its own political space. But such political, diplomatic, and occasionally, economic gains are not enough to break the grip of the contradictions in which it is caught.

Notes

1. Irving Louis Horowitz, *El comunismo cubano*.
2. Fidel Castro, in *Granma*, 15 November 1987.
3. Ibid.
4. Ricardo Acciaris, 'Les relations économiques de Cuba avec l'Amérique latine et les Caraïbes', in *Courrier des pays de l'Est*, Documentation française, November 1983.
5. *El País*, 1 February 1989.
6. *Caribbean Report*, 18 June 1987.
7. Interview granted during the meeting of women at the magazine *Tercer Mundo*, 1985.
8. *Granma*, 13 March 1988.
9. *Veja*, 18 March 1987.
10. Che Guevara, Algiers speech (1965), *Ecrits d'un révolutionnaire*.
11. *Veja*, 18 March 1987.
12. *Perspectiva Mundial*, July/August 1988.
13. *Nouvelle Revue internationale (Problèmes de la paix et du socialisme)*, July 1989.
14. *Veja*, 18 March 1988.
15. Interview with Maria Schriver for NBC, 13 March 1988.
16. *Latin American Weekly Report*, 14 July 1988.
17. *Caribbean Regional Report*, 20 January 1984.
18. *Pravda*, 13 August 1987.
19. *Pravda*, 10 October 1987.
20. Interview with Maria Schriver for NBC, 13 March 1988.
21. On the crisis of the Argentinian Communist Party, see the articles by H. Tarcus in *Inprecor*, no. 232, 15 December 1986.
22. *Granma*, 17 April 1988.
23. *Le Monde*, 29 July 1988.
24. Quoted by Ernest Mandel, in *Inprecor*, 4 July 1988.
25. *Herald Tribune* and *Washington Post*, 21 June 1988.
26. J. Amalric, in *Le Monde*, 13 April 1988.
27. Gianni Miná, *Un encuentro con Fidel*.
28. 'Angola: l'accord tripartite', in *Inprecor*, no. 282, 20 February 1989.
29. *Granma*, 2 May 1976.
30. *Financial Times*, 1988.
31. *Granma*, 12 November 1989.
32. *Sunday Times*, 19 June 1989.
33. Fidel Castro, in *Granma*, 24 February 1985.
34. *Problèmes d'Amérique latine*, Documentation française, second quarter, 1982.
35. *El País*, 15 September 1987.
36. André Fontaine, in *Le Trimestre du Monde*, second quarter, 1989.
37. *Le Monde*, 21–22 May 1989.
38. *Granma*, 12 February 1989.
39. *Granma*, 16 April 1989.
40. *Granma*, 16 April 1989.
41. *Le Monde*, 7 April 1989.
42. *El País*, 6 April 1989.
43. *Newsweek*, 5 December 1988.
44. *Granma*, 30 April 1989.

45. *Granma*, 26 February 1989.
46. *Financial Times*, 20 November 1989.
47. *New Times*, no. 33, August 1987.
48. *El País*, 25 September 1987.
49. *New Times*, no. 41, October 1987.
50. J.-P. Clerc, *Fidel de Cuba*.
51. *Cuadernos semestrales*, no. 12, Mexico 1982.
52. *Le Monde*, 7 November 1987.
53. J.-P. Clerc, *Fidel de Cuba*.
54. Interview with journalists from the *Washington Post*, in *Granma*, 11 February 1985.
55. Irving Louis Horowitz, *El comunismo cubano*.
56. Fidel Castro, in *Granma*, 26 September 1984.
57. Report of the National Bank of Cuba, 1984.
58. Azicri, *Cuba*.
59. Report of the National Bank of Cuba, March 1986.
60. *Del Pino Speaks*, Cuban American Foundation, 1987.
61. Azicri, *Cuba*.
62. Leogrande, *Arms and Politics*.
63. *Quarterly Report*, United States Information Agency, Radio Martí program, Washington DC, first quarter 1988, p. 6.
64. Ibid.
65. *Globe*, November 1989.
66. J.-P. Clerc, *Fidel de Cuba*.
67. *Revista de Ciencias Sociales*, no. 12, Havana.
68. *Le Monde diplomatique*, November 1989.
69. M. Schriver, in *Granma*, March 1988.
70. *Bohemia*, 20 May 1988.
71. Raúl Castro, in *Granma*, 23 January 1983.
72. *Bohemia*, 20 May 1988.
73. *Granma*, 22 October 1989.

6

The Cuban Revolution on a Knife-Edge

> This is a country where we carried out the revolution with our own resources. No one did it for us. We did it ourselves. We did not know a single person from the Soviet Union when this revolution started. We did not know a single person from the Soviet Union when this revolution triumphed. Our country has always had highly independent views, and has consistently followed the policy of learning from all the useful experiences of other revolutionary countries.[1]

That is the strength of the Cuban Revolution, and everything else follows from it, 'only ninety miles from home',[2] as the flabbergasted North Americans used to say. The first free territory in America was born right under their nose. Everything that happened during the decade 1960–70 was only possible because the Cuban Revolution did not owe anything to anyone. Soviet aid, of course, was not long in arriving in response to the blows dealt by imperialism; and the political and strategic benefit to the Soviet Union was huge. It is all too often forgotten that the context of the revolution's victory was marked by the rise of revolution in the colonies, the Sino–Soviet conflict and the considerable prestige of China at that time in the Third World. It would also not be excessive to say that the prestige of the Cuban Revolution rubbed off onto the Soviet bureaucracy and boosted its fortunes, and took the shine off Maoism. This is worth remembering today, as bureaucrats in the Eastern bloc smugly recall the 'aid provided by the socialist camp'.

Such autonomy was a considerable trump card, allowing the revolution to forge ahead, in spite of the enormous economic difficulties caused by the US blockade. It led to the consolidation of the popular masses' support, especially when their social gains were without precedent in Latin America. The egalitarian social democracy of those years enabled

Cuba to achieve impressive results in the area of the right to work, education and health care that no one would dream of denying. Infant mortality, for example, came down to the level of 13.6 per 1,000, equivalent to the rate of the industrialized countries.

Latin Americans are well aware of this. According to a UN report on slavery (quoting the conclusions of the Federation of Human Rights), for example, there are more than 30 million abandoned children in Brazil, many of whom become prostitutes or are sold into forced labour.[3] This is a judgement in itself on the 'Brazilian miracle' and puts in their place sarcastic comments about the 'Castromania' of people who can no longer bear the spread of poverty, violence and hunger on the streets.[4]

Such social gains have deepened popular support for the revolution and enhanced its prestige in the Third World and Latin America. The enthusiastic support enjoyed by Cuba in the 1960s, as well as the renewal of revolutionary communism personified by the immense symbol of Che, strengthened the room for manoeuvre of the Castro leadership, faced with pressures aimed at ending its support for the subcontinent's revolutionary movements.

While there has always been a difference between the two, 'Castroism' and 'Guevarism' were seen as a new international reference point during this initial phase, at least until 1968. The non-institutionalization of the revolution appeared as a guarantee against bureaucratization, in spite of the disorganization involved. It was only in the following decade that Cuba's double identity – simultaneously 'bird and mammal'[5] through the mix between Soviet-style institutions and the 'institution of Fidel' – was to be born.

Dependency

'We have done everything we can to ensure the revolution's survival', Fidel Castro was to say. Comecon membership in 1972; the First Congress of the PCC in 1975; adoption of the new constitution in 1976; introduction of the new system of economic management between 1975 and 1980: so many dates marking the influence of the Soviet Union. Economic development was conceived in the long term as part of the international division of labour within the CMEA.

The record is a sombre one:[6] dependence on sugar; dependence on the Soviet Union; and a debt in foreign currency that must be paid by increasing exports when there is a distressing level of productive efficiency (or rather inefficiency). The diversification of foreign trade, particularly with Latin America, which ought to be the natural outlet for the Cuban economy, is still extremely limited because of the US embargo.

Moreover, since 1975, Cuba has been submitting its plans to the member countries of the CMEA, or more precisely the Soviet Union, as part of joint co-ordination. From 1972 management and planning bodies were reorganized under the guidance of specialists from those countries, and only recently have readjustments been made. It is therefore surprising that such tightly controlled collaboration has ended up making the island a 'recipient of economic aid', to use the characteristic language of Soviet managers who find the slightest excuse to stress the need to end the 'economic disasters' represented by countries like Cuba or Vietnam.

This has led to strong pressures on the latter countries, and the Vietnamese have had particular experience of this. According to Truong Chinh, secretary of the Vietnamese Communist Party (VCP), aid from the Soviet Union and other socialist countries 'is in danger of being lost bit by bit'[7] without a reorganization of the economy. Nineteen eighty-six was a watershed year, as the Sixth VCP Congress came out in favour of deep reforms, and changes in the leadership led to the promotion of 'reformers'. Satisfied with the outcome, Ligachev, the CPSU representative, announced an increase in aid for the 1986–1990 period, and this increase has since been confirmed.[8] In effect, aid more than doubled, thus emphasizing the importance attached by the Soviet Union to Vietnam as part of its policy towards Asia.

As to Cuba, the effects of long-term Soviet aid on economic development must be examined. And in this respect, the studies carried out have become increasingly critical. Firstly, as Turits has underlined, because the 'circuitous methods [by which the Soviet Union provides assistance] obscure the extent of Soviet dependence and aid, and also render problematic ... any rigourous estimate of them'.[9] Secondly, because the emphasis on the development of sugar production in CMEA countries – with 12 million tonnes planned for 1990 and aimed at replacing the less profitable cultivation of beet – is being challenged as a result of the uncertainty surrounding future outlets. As W. Jampel has emphasized, this is especially the case when the share sold on the open market has fallen from 32 per cent in 1975 to 22 per cent in 1986, 'hence the growing deficit in trade with the Western countries and significant indebtedness. ... It very much seems that imbalance in foreign trade is linked to the composition of exports, more than 80 per cent of which consist of food products.'[10]

Jampel's conclusion reinforces that of Turits:

> The aid and credits provided by the Soviet Union and CMEA countries are not high enough to lead to a rapid improvement in the population's lot and to

> stabilize the growth of the economy. ... Moreover, since 1972, Cuba has had to pay for credits granted by the Soviet Union through increased sugar deliveries. Increased sugar, nickel, citrus fruit and tobacco deliveries ... to the Soviet Union and its CMEA partners have prevented Cuba from having any chance of settling its bill with the Western developed countries, thus making it impossible to obtain the new consumer and industrial goods needed for the development of its industry.[11]

In other words, Cuba has not been able to take full advantage of the significant rise in nickel prices on the world market since 1977, for example. A clearer explanation for Fidel Castro's insistent demand for the debt with the Soviet Union to be cancelled could not be found!

It is on the basis of these factors that the idea that Cuba has gone from dependence on the United States to dependence on the Soviet Union is often refloated. Beyond the differences between the social regimes of the United States and the Soviet Union, it remains to be seen whether 'the economic surplus obtained through the mechanisms of Soviet trade can generate self-sustained development or will delimit a structural dependence'.[12] Cuba's development is still subject to the conditional aid of the Soviet Union.

It is of course undeniable that at the beginning of the Cuban Revolution, Soviet aid made a crucial contribution to its survival and improved the standard of living of the masses. Such economic and social gains enabled the new regime to resist the US blockade victoriously and to enjoy considerable popular support. With the exception of the bourgeois and petty-bourgeois strata, all sectors of the population gained in one way or another, in spite of rationing, from new social benefits in the areas of health, education and employment (as well as housing in the early years with the drastic cut in rents). And thanks to the agrarian reform, there was a radical change in the situation of peasants.

While it was necessary to introduce rationing, this led to an adequate and egalitarian distribution of basic goods which ended the poverty that had existed among the most dispossessed groups. Due to the speed and size of Soviet aid, such a relatively favourable situation has always been recalled by the Castro leadership which credited Nikita Khrushchev with the decision.

As a gauge of this support for social needs following the takeover, one only has to compare it with the situation of Nicaragua ten years later. The plan to destroy the Sandinista revolution through a combination of military attacks and economic strangulation, thus sapping popular support for the regime, has not been countered by the Soviet Union, which does not even grant Nicaragua as large a proportion of aid as Cuba.[13]

Other than playing the Soviet card, did Cuba have any other available choice? Clearly not. The circumstances under which power was seized in

1959, the balance of forces in Latin America, and the omnipotence of US imperialism forced the Cuban leadership to turn to the Soviet Union. However, this has not prevented Fidel Castro from emphasizing, in recent interviews, that with more experience and less haste, the rhythm of expropriations would have perhaps been slower, in order to neutralize the reaction of the US government.[14] Such reflections are not unrelated to the decisions taken in Nicaragua following the victory. It would very much seem that, at the time, the Castro leadership strongly advised the Sandinistas not to concentrate most of their trade with the Eastern European countries and to maintain a certain room for manoeuvre with European and Latin American governments. But twenty-three years later the international situation was very different and it is not clear that the greater flexibility of the Sandinistas and their efforts to escape the iron collar of the Soviet Union led to a more favourable situation. Besides, one can only reserve judgement on the validity of such comparisons.

Just before he left Cuba, Che analysed relations with the Soviet Union from a theoretical and political perspective, particularly in his Algiers speech at the second economics seminar of Afro–Asian solidarity. Starting from the premise that any anti-capitalist revolution can only reinforce the countries where such a revolution has already taken place (which is not the premise of the Soviet leadership), Che highlighted the workings of unequal exchange, the exchange of raw materials at falling prices for increasingly expensive manufactured goods:

> How can one speak of 'mutual benefit' when raw materials, obtained through the sweat and endless suffering of workers in the backward countries, are sold at world market prices in order to buy machines, produced in the huge automated factories of modern times, at world market prices? If we establish that form of relations between these two groups of nations, we must acknowledge that the socialist countries are in some way accomplices of imperialist exploitation.[15]

This point of view is today expressed by Carlos Tablada, the author of a book which won the Casa de las Americas prize in 1987.

In his work, Tablada quotes freely from Che's speeches (which had been unobtainable for a period) and takes up the quotes he used from Marx to back up his arguments: 'Two nations can proceed, according to the law of profit, to trade with each other in such a way that both benefit, even though one exploits and constantly robs the other.'[16]

> The more developed socialist countries can thus contribute to the development of the dependent countries; but if the norm is maintained whereby foreign trade is carried out on the basis of market mechanisms and the law of value,

> they can also participate, to a greater or lesser degree, in their exploitation. The most backward country can benefit from trade with a developed socialist country; and yet part of its wealth can be transferred to the socialist country without any similar reciprocal reward.[17]

Added to the economic effects of unequal exchange have been the social effects of bureaucratization. The Soviet model wrought havoc, as bureaucratic disorganization was grafted onto an already hypertrophied state apparatus characterized by underdevelopment. The specific nature of the Cuban crisis thus stems from this bureaucratization in the context of dependency.

Carrot or Stick?

The work of specialized researchers studying Cuban–Soviet trade,[18] as well as the information that the National Bank of Cuba is obliged to provide to the Paris Club as part of the renegotiation of the debt, enable an appraisal to be made of thirty years of Soviet aid and of Cuba's CMEA membership. Such studies also allow one to appreciate how aid has fallen in the 1980s, as well as the price paid for the enforced adaptation of the Cuban economy to the requirements of 'socialist integration', reflected by the emphasis on sugar and citrus fruit production, nickel exploitation and fishing.

In 1986, the price paid for sugar by the Soviet Union fell by 10.9 per cent. And in the case of nickel, Cuba suffered heavy losses due to the existence of long-term contracts: the value of exports did not change, in spite of a considerable increase in nickel prices on the world market. In 1979 and 1980 Cuba had already lost between $32 million and $37 million on nickel sales to the Soviet Union. In 1986 Cuba paid 113 per cent more for cement than Mongolia (in 1978 the Soviet Union had already sold cars to Cuba at a price 32 per cent dearer than to other CMEA countries, and cement at a price 21 per cent higher for the same years).

As Brezinski has stressed, 'these examples demonstrate the difficulty of estimating Soviet subsidies accurately'; he nevertheless put the commercial deficit with the Soviet Union for 1987 at 1,628 million pesos, a figure he claimed was unprecedented. In terms of oil, re-exports of which represented 500 million pesos between 1983 and 1985, revenues were merely 248 million pesos in 1986 and 370 million pesos in 1987. Moreover, interest rates for credits granted were higher than in the past.

The terms of the last agreement signed between the Soviet Union and Cuba for the 1986–90 period were less advantageous than previously.

Sugar was to be bought at 850 roubles a tonne instead of the 915 roubles a tonne at the start of the decade. It should be remembered that comparisons should not be made with prices on the world market (or the 'sugar dustbin', to use Fidel Castro's expression), but with prices paid on the quota markets which represent a considerable share of transactions. Outside the Eastern countries, such markets relate to sugar exports from the African, Caribbean and Pacific countries (ACP) to the European Community, and those from the countries of Latin America and Asia to the United States. The preferential prices granted are higher than those on the world market and often as high or higher than those paid by the Soviet Union to Cuba. But the method used to set them can never be guaranteed and the import quotas granted by the United States, in particular, have fallen significantly in recent years, thus causing exporting countries an often dramatic loss of revenue. Cuba, on the other hand, has hitherto benefited from the guarantees provided by long-term agreements with the Soviet Union.

The situation with other CMEA countries is much more negative. Hungary has withdrawn its credits, as have Poland and Romania. The greatest co-operation is with the German Democratic Republic, Czechoslovakia and Bulgaria.

Since 1976, Cuba has participated in the co-ordination of the five-year plans and in the introduction of the CMEA's long-term plans. Notwithstanding the major changes linked to the upheavals now taking place, its specialization in agriculture and the production of raw materials has been maintained. The planned target for the sugar harvest is 12 million tonnes for 1990, and citrus fruit production must reach 2.6 million tonnes by the same date (1.4 million tonnes in 1985).[19]

As far as long-term agreements are concerned, Cuba participates in some scientific and technological development plans in information technology, electronics and biotechnology. There have been impressive achievements[20] – in the field of health, for example: the development of an advanced biomedical sector is aimed at the export of chemical and pharmaceutical products to Latin America, and Cuba is seeking to play a vanguard role in preventive health care and sophisticated surgery.

But looking at the CMEA's technological development plan to the year 2000 (comprising 93 units and 930 sub-units), Cuba will only participate in 52 sub-units in the field of nuclear energy, electronics and biotechnology. According to Brezinski, Cuba's participation is extremely limited, in spite of official assertions that the island, like the other less-developed CMEA countries, will benefit from privileged treatment. The forty-fourth CMEA session in June 1988 and the Prague conference in April of the same year suggested that Cuba could enjoy preferential tariffs until the end of the current five-year period. Soviet economists, however, spoke out against 'subsidizing' Cuba in the 1990s on the grounds that it would not lead to an 'improvement in the performance of the Cuban economy'.[21] Whatever the case, one fact is clear: Cuba remains largely confined to its role as a producer and exporter of raw materials and will continue to do so in the long term.

Beyond the fluctuations in aid and the difficulty of assessing its exact size, another remark is in order. The Soviet Union is Cuba's main supplier. But not only are the financial terms of particular imports not always advantageous; the quality of capital goods and of products from the Soviet Union is often in question and it is not uncommon to hear Cuban officials express the view that Cuba 'benefits' from the worst Soviet goods. In any case, it is undeniable that the Cuban government, whenever it has the financial opportunity to choose its suppliers,[22] prefers to pay in foreign exchange and buy from market-economy countries, in spite of the limits of Western credits. While not an official view, a harsh judgement is made of Soviet aid which, in addition to its conditional nature, is seen as ill-suited to the island's economic development.

Cuban criticisms can be summarized as follows: deliveries are based on Soviet priorities rather than Cuban needs; equipment and machinery are often obsolete and delivered with considerable delay (huge transport problems in autumn 1988 were put down to delays in the delivery of spare parts for the maintenance of buses by factories in Eastern Europe);[23] it is public knowledge that the Soviet Union's failure to honour its commitments has led to a halt in nickel production and an estimated ten-year delay;[24] certain pieces of equipment promised have never been delivered (in 1979 the Soviet Union failed to deliver 40 per cent of the 500,000 tonnes of wood promised); products are sometimes replaced with others which are useless; commitments are broken without prior warning, thus forcing last-minute purchases in foreign exchange at the full price; and given their efficiency, the cost of particular services is high (it is particularly shocking that 80 per cent of the salaries of Soviet technicians are paid in hard currency, without counting free housing, transport and medical care and access to the special shops).

An evaluation of aid must take all these factors into account. Recorded figures are impossible to assess with any precision: while the Soviet Union has claimed its annual aid is as high as $2,700 million, Western estimates have given $4,000 million, and the US State Department's latest figure, for 1986, was $6,800 million. Of this, $4,700 million took the form of subsidized sugar and nickel purchases in return for oil, $600 million was earmarked for specific projects, and $1,500 million was for military aid (traditionally provided free by the Soviet Union).

The final factor to be taken into account is one that is independent of the will of Cuba's partners, namely the exorbitant transport costs involved by the distance between Cuba and the Soviet Union. The distance travelled by Soviet oil tankers (at least one every two days) is approximately 12,000 kilometres and represents 7 per cent of the total cost of oil imports from the Soviet Union.[25] Agreements have been reached for delivery from Venezuela, but only limited quantities are involved. During a trip to Cuba, US cereal producers estimated that the United States could deliver cereals 30 per cent cheaper than the Soviet Union.

The latter points clearly raise the problem of the US embargo and the benefits Cuba would gain from its possible elimination: that was one of the suggestions made by Gorbachev during his visit; and it is part of the summit talks, as well as a potential issue in the bargaining over Central America.

The Aftermath of Gorbachev's Visit

The signing of a twenty-five-year friendship and co-operation treaty between Cuba and the Soviet Union during Gorbachev's visit in April 1989 was above all symbolic: given the speculation over the possibility of a break, it was a way of confirming that privileged relations would be maintained between the two countries. But while the treaty reaffirmed the need to 'restructure international economic relations on a just and democratic basis, so as to eliminate unequal exchange and all forms of discriminatory practice in world trade ... to exclude economic coercion for political ends from relations between states ... to settle the problem of foreign debt which is crushing the overwhelming majority of Third World countries',[26] the Cuban debt was not cancelled. This decision was particularly significant. Given that repayment of the debt was more or less discounted anyway, the occasion could have been the opportunity for a low-cost public relations exercise, boosting the prestige of the Soviet Union in its search for an economic rapprochement with Latin America. The likelihood of such a decision had even led to a front-page headline on 4 April in the Italian Communist Party daily, *L'Unitá*, which took literally Gorbachev's UN speech of 7 December 1988 in which he announced that the Soviet Union was 'ready to introduce a lengthy moratorium of up to 100 years in the debt servicing of the least developed countries, and in some cases, to cancel the debt altogether'.[27] There can be no doubt that the decision not to cancel the debt had been given considerable thought, and was probably based on two factors: on the one hand, a de-emphasis on the Third World in Soviet foreign policy, and the need not to destabilize or hinder Western governments in the renegotiation of the debt; and on the other, its usefulness as a lever with which to gently pressure Cuba into changing its economic policy, or at least into searching for 'the most efficient forms as part of bilateral interaction', co-operation over economic matters and trade, and 'economic and socialist integration, in accordance with resolutions of the CMEA'.[28] The decision also went hand in hand with a rejection by the Soviet government of the preferential agreements favouring the developing countries demanded by the Group of 77 and the 'new international economic order' advocated by Fidel Castro. Instead, the Soviet government gave a commitment to eliminate trade barriers, while turning down demands by the developing countries for 0.7 per cent of the Soviet budget to be devoted to them.[29]

According to the protocol on commercial trade between Cuba and the Soviet Union for 1989 (signed in Moscow on 26 March),[30] the Soviet Union would deliver fuel, raw materials, and various pieces of machinery and equipment to Cuba, while Cuba would supply the Soviet Union with more than 4 million tonnes of sugar, fresh or tinned citrus fruit, nickel, and also items of new equipment for the electronics industry, in line with Cuba's specialization within the CMEA (investment having been earmarked for the manufacture of computer keyboards and electronic circuits). But while an increase in trade between the two countries was planned, Soviet officials made it clear that the current level and forms of aid could not continue as they had done in the past. As the elliptical commentary of the *Granma* correspondent in the Soviet Union pointed out, 'negotiations on the protocol of agreement have taken place in the context of the process of restructuring and reorganization of the central bodies of administration of the state and enterprises in the Soviet Union, and they have required a lot of work, persistent effort and great flexibility'.[31]

Everything points to the Soviet Union using the opportunities provided by the new rules of the game to apply pressure indirectly. It should be remembered that since 1 April 1989, Soviet firms have had the right to plan and organize their external relations as they see fit, and to co-operate freely with other foreign firms and countries. As the Soviet Deputy Minister for Trade Relations, Alexander Kachanov, stated, this measure 'is going to change Soviet foreign trade radically'.[32] How can Cuba not be affected? The same official also made it clear that co-operation with Cuba should adapt itself to this new reality: 'The forms of this collaboration must be changed so that its efficiency can be increased.'[33] The nineteenth session of the intergovernmental Cuban–Soviet Commission of Economic, Scientific and Technological Collaboration has apparently been engaged in the overall reorganization of economic relations. Chaired by Carlos Rafael Rodríguez, the Vice-President of the Cuban Council of Ministers, and Vladimir Kamentsev, a Vice-Chairman of the Soviet government, the commission has adopted measures to ensure that agreements on mutual trade in goods and the increased efficiency of economic projects financed with Soviet aid should be carried out. According to Carlos Rafael Rodríguez, this restructuring is the result of both perestroika and the current rectification process in Cuba.[34] But it would appear to have been accepted that deliveries of oil – which are vital for Cuba and cannot be left to the mercy of the interests of Soviet enterprises – will be the subject of specific agreements and state guarantees, though it is not known for how long they will last. As far as everything else is concerned, the Cubans have begun to experience the new system. According to a document quoted by the *Miami Herald* (corroborated by the information given by the deserter Pérez Cott, a former official of the State Committee for Technology), Soviet enterprises already give priority to Western clients paying in foreign exchange, to the detriment of Cuba and in spite of the agreements reached between the two states.

The message is quite clear. Cuba is of course 'free' to determine its economic policy; but if the country does not engage with the need for economic profitability and efficiency, it will have to face the consequences: namely, isolation and unprecedented difficulties in terms of its experience to date. The 'irresistible force of perestroika' of which Gorbachev has spoken will not tolerate exceptions. That, then, is the basic framework for relations between the two countries.

In terms of trade, particularly sugar, Kachanov also stated that current deliveries of four million tonnes a year 'represent an optimum level with maybe a slight increase in the future'.[35] A somewhat veiled statement, it was unclear whether it questioned the prospects anticipated by the CMEA or whether it was related to the will of the Soviets to diversify their imports, including those from other Latin American producers. Indeed, this has begun in the case of Honduras and the Dominican Republic, where the Soviet Union has signed contracts for the supply of sugar at prices lower than it pays to Cuba.[36]

Among the new forms of co-operation advocated by the Soviet Union, there is one that is inspired by a current example from Mexico and the United States – the assembly plants [*maquiladoras*] which have sprung up along the border between the two countries. Under the new system, the Soviet Union would send processed raw materials to Cuba for the manufacture of clothes and shoes, which would then be re-dispatched for sale to Soviet consumers.[37] The aim would be to encourage Cuban enterprises to establish direct relations with their Soviet counterparts (on which they would depend), thus improving their efficiency through the use of cheaper labour. The distribution of consumer goods, disrupted by the crisis raging in the Soviet Union in the enterprises subjected to the first doses of reform, would also improve.

It is clear that this type of collaboration would make the operation of Cuban enterprises highly dependent on Soviet management and would reduce the Castro leadership's scope for opposition to perestroika. Or at least that was the discreetly expressed wish of the Soviet officials accompanying Gorbachev on his last visit.[38]

Soviet policy also has another aim: to use Cuba to penetrate the Latin American market and distribute Soviet products, thus breaking the cultural and linguistic barriers to trade with the subcontinent.[39] Such an enterprise would require a shift in Cuban diplomacy – one which is now well underway – to back it up, and on this Castro and Gorbachev are agreed. The specialization in electronics, biotechnology and advanced medical technology is part of this general approach.

But this new role in store for Cuba involves significant changes and is faced with major obstacles. As Brezinski emphasizes, prices for agricultural goods and raw materials are still prone to considerable fluctuation and 'will not rise as fast as the prices for industrial goods' – and to the extent that 'Cuba's economic structure continues to be dependent on Soviet technology, a shift towards Western technology remains extremely difficult, if not impossible'. Once again, the problem of the US blockade rears its head. And all evidence suggests that Bush will only normalize relations with Cuba in return for a complete halt in aid to Central America in terms of support for Nicaragua and El Salvador, and for the isolation of the revolution: a very high price for the Castro leadership.

For their part, C. Mesa-Lago and F. Gil consider that 'the low level of world sugar and oil prices will certainly not favour exports, while restrictions on imports of certain goods may create bottlenecks and lead to a fall in production'. That was the trend of the 1987 results. Moreover, if the current policy of reducing imports, increasing exports and improving productivity do not produce the expected results, pressures on the Cuban economy are likely to be severe. And the recent agreements reached with Moscow do not reverse previous trends. Cuba's whole record of economic development (and economic integration within the CMEA) is in question.

To develop an industrial infrastructure, Cuba was able, thanks to high sugar prices in the early 1970s, to import Western products and make use of Western technology. Then re-exports of Soviet oil took over. Following the fall in sugar prices and oil revenues, the government tried to maintain the same level of imports through Western loans. All these resources have now dropped considerably. Negotiations with the Paris Club in May 1989 produced no result, and debt repayments are sucking up available foreign exchange: between June 1987 and June 1988, the debt with the imperialist countries went up by 15.5 per cent, rising from \$6,400 million[40] in 1988 to \$6,800 million in 1989.

In spite of these constraints, Cuba did achieve a certain level of industrialization in the 1970s, although interpretations vary as to its significance. A. Zimbalist stresses the considerable progress made in the mechanization of sugar harvesting, as well as in the processing of sugar derivatives. Cuba, he claims, has transformed its industrial base since the 1960s. Imports of manufactured goods went down from 58.9 per cent in 1970 to 44.7 per cent in 1983. The construction of a nuclear power station (which is due to begin operation in 1995) should reduce oil imports in the next decade, although Cuba will continue to depend on the Soviet Union for deliveries of enriched uranium. Zimbalist also highlights the technological progress made in health and the possibility of exporting sophisticated pharmaceutical products.

Brezinksi, on the other hand, points out that sugar still accounted for 77.2 per cent of exports in 1986, in spite of these advances in industrialization, and challenges 'a strategy relying on growth based on the export of the economy's traditional goods, while import substitution has not achieved the success anticipated'. He notes that foreign trade was still characterized in 1988 'by the typical model of trade between industrialized countries and developing countries'; and that such a structure of foreign trade has been made worse by the lack of foreign exchange that would enable Cuba to buy more from the West. He concludes that Cuba's international competitiveness 'has fallen since joining the CMEA'. Such a verdict matches that of C. Mesa-Lago and F. Gil who judge that Soviet aid has contributed to the maintenance of long-term imbalances and distortions in the economy.

While the development of particular high-tech sectors is recognized, doubts are expressed – on the one hand, over Cuba's reliability as a supplier 'when the workers that produce these quality products have to spend much of their time waiting for a bus or standing in a queue for tomatoes'; and on the other, over the prospects for exports, since 'It is one thing to produce interferons, it is another to sell them to the rest of the world.'[41]

Cuba's autonomous economic development would thus appear to be hindered by external dependency, the prevailing chaos in enterprises and the organization of production, the effects of the division of labour within the CMEA and, above all, by the uncertainties looming over the future development of economic relations with the Soviet Union as a result of the current reforms. Contrary to superficial analyses, neither Gorbachev's visit nor the agreements signed have dispelled the worries hanging over the evolution of the Cuban economy. Quite the opposite.

Perestroika at the Door?

After three years, the initial aims of rectification proclaimed by Fidel Castro appear to be getting blurred. The leadership is trying, above all, to gain time.

Gorbachev's visit gave Fidel Castro the opportunity to move to the front of the stage and to reaffirm, in the name of the principle of non-interference, 'the right of each country to apply its own formulae in the construction of socialism'. And setting the cat among the pigeons, he declared: 'If a socialist country wants to build capitalism, we cannot intervene, just as we demand that no one interferes in the sovereign decision of any capitalist or semi-capitalist country from the developed or developing world to build socialism.'[42] Beyond the rhetoric, the two speakers expressed different views on peace, the debt, defence and the construction of socialism. Fidel Castro's speeches against the 'methods of capitalism', however, have given way to the harsh reality of agreements with European or Japanese firms (in the form of mixed enterprises, not only in tourism but also in textiles, the food industry, and sugar derivatives). In some cases these foreign firms can determine recruitment and dismissal procedures and wage levels, and occasionally have the right to repatriate profits.[43] As a columnist has said: 'Perestroika is at the door but no one dares say so.' Adapting to national idiosyncracies, the president of the Cuban Chamber of Commerce, Julio G. Oliveras, has dubbed this 'cha-cha socialism',[44] since the socialist dancer needs a partner.

The reality is highly contradictory and fraught with tensions. In sectors where the labour force needed is poorly qualified and badly paid (agriculture and construction) there is a different approach. Financial incentives are limited – given the low qualifications required – and barely effective. Indeed, popular savings bank deposits rose by 45 per cent between 1984 and 1988,[45] as the shortage of consumer goods worsened. Increasing the distribution of income is therefore not a solution if demand remains unsatisfied. The head of the governmental Market Research Institute, Eugenio Balari, favours increasing imports to avoid problems, particularly among youth, but the shortage of foreign exchange is a constraint. This is why the recourse to voluntary work – compulsory for young people in many schools, who study part time and take part in the citrus fruit harvest – is the subject of an intense ideological campaign. Youth, unions and the army are used to solve specific labour-power problems, hence the development of micro-brigades and the use of 'internationalists' returning from Angola.

A move is thus being made towards the coexistence of economic sectors which are managed in very different ways. This was precisely what Fidel Castro had denounced at the beginning of the rectification process as a source of divisions and inequalities.

This pragmatism is partly the result of constraints outside the Castro leadership's control. But it also reflects the absence of an overall conception of the relation between socio-economic democracy and political democracy in an economy in transition in an underdeveloped country. The contrast between the widespread confusion in the overall organization of the economy and the development of particular high-tech sectors provides a good illustration of the incoherence and chaotic nature of the policies carried out. For example, one might question the need in a small country like Cuba for extremely costly investment in the area of organ transplants, cancer research or immunology. Some blame the megalomania of Fidel Castro who, they allege, is set on catching up with the most advanced imperialist countries, even though such publicity projects are being carried out at the expense of more immediate needs. At the heart of the economic dislocations is 'the inability of the political structure to respond adequately to the severe economic strains and planning failures'.[46]

The decisive control of Fidel Castro and his henchmen over major economic decisions, combined with the Communist Party's monopoly of power, have the effect of hiding responsibilities, concealing incompetence and corruption and of favouring bureaucratic complicity. Effective organizational and political devices to correct dysfunctions do not exist; mechanisms of control are devoid of any power; mass organizations are mere echo chambers; and the political influence of the organs of people's power, which had aroused so much hope, is non-existent, even though their administrative activities are real. The idea that bureaucratic paralysis could be fought by voluntarism alone – and what is more, by an elitist voluntarism limited to a few people – has been crumbling, even though the regime, unlike the Soviet Union, can still count on the selflessness and commitment of certain sectors. Only the confrontation of ideas and policies, the transparency of responsibilities and decisions, the introduction of mechanisms of control, and the freedom to criticize could be effective against the impenetrable nature of the system. Unlike Castro, Gorbachev has fully understood the role of glasnost in economic restructuring; and according to the editor of *Moscow News*, Yegor Yakovlev, the main lesson of the Chinese crisis is that priority must be given to political reforms.

It is already clear that the 'rectification of errors' has been unable to correct the system's flaws. The Cuban people have shown ironical scepticism towards a process they have nicknamed the 'rectification of horrors'. The effects of a rhetoric combining verbal radicalism with appeals for effort – 'We must work hard, we must work a lot',[47] repeats

Fidel Castro – may be to increase cynicism, if there is no other change. A section of youth is already pinning its hopes on very uncertain possibilities of social advancement. Opportunities do not always correspond to qualifications attained; and responsible positions in every area are already filled – in the best of cases, by veterans of the revolutionary war or eleventh-hour supporters who do not always seem invested with an authentic legitimacy, or, in the worst of cases, by people involved in corruption.

Ideological development, the ability to maintain the mobilization of the new generation and its support for Castroism are vital to the future of the revolution. Yet it has to be said that the revolutionary motivation of a section of youth is wavering. This demobilization is nourished by the absence of debate and political democracy, by irresponsible muddles in the economy, and by the loss of credibility of anti-imperialist discourse as a direct result of the diplomatic opening in Latin America.

This latter policy is a source of contradictions in itself. It reinforces the need for a political opening up inside the country which, in spite of a few recent concessions and the development of cultural exchanges with the subcontinent, is not always forthcoming. In terms of information, it is already coming up against the existence of a radio station in Miami which gives Cubans all the information that their press does not provide (the events in China, for example, were barely mentioned in the first few weeks). And it would seem that a television channel is also about to broadcast from Florida.

On the diplomatic and commercial level, the search for support in Latin America runs the risk of compromising the traditional support of revolutionary organizations for Castroism, as has been shown by the stirs caused by Fidel Castro's visits to Mexico and Venezuela. As one of the main leaders of the Mexican opposition, Cuauhtémoc Cárdenas, declared: 'They [Castro and Ortega] have their reasons for going [to the inauguration ceremony of Salinas de Gortari, the new president of Mexico].[48] But they will pay a price.'[49] Following the riots in Venezuela and Argentina, the development of stable commercial trade has been unpredictable.

In short, Fidel Castro is in danger of building up contradictions and losing on several fronts: at home, by not taking the initiative over a democratization that is inevitable; and abroad, by losing precious support for no tangible reward.

The Theory and Practice of Rectification

The need to improve economic efficiency and raise labour productivity is at the centre of debates. For some Cuban economists, workers' participation in the planning process, as currently carried out, is problematical, for it leads to incoherent bargaining between different institutions, enterprises, mass organizations, local organs of power and branches of ministries.

Even though the participation of the masses is real, in so far as the decisions are not based on an overall plan, the overall result is muddled and, indeed, contradictory. Final decisions are made by the party leadership and the central planning bodies, in this case the 'central group'. For their part, the workers, having given their opinion, do not see the end result of the choices made, and the sum total of all these local interests does not come to define an overall approach. There can even be friction when workers of an enterprise come to realize that their proposals have not been respected, but without really knowing why.

Many opponents of the rectification process are also opposed to the ideas of self-management which are regarded as Utopian and idealistic. They see market reforms, encouraging the workers' 'economic awareness', as the only way of correcting the system's flaws. If the problems are structural, the solutions should be so as well. Vertical bureaucratic pressures should be replaced by 'horizontal'[50] market pressures, transferring decision-making power from state institutions (and the PCC) to enterprises and, more precisely, to managers.

Decentralization, however, comes up against the major obstacle of underdevelopment. Shortages 'force priorities to be ordered centrally and greater control to be exercised over investments. The idea is to decentralize management, to give greater autonomy to grassroots units, it is said in Havana. But when imports fall by a half, it is the central group which must decide where our available raw materials should go.'[51] G. White echoes similar comments: underdevelopment in a small country means structural imbalances and the international dependence of Cuba makes central controls even more necessary. Such controls are also an indispensable tool with which to correct inequalities between regions and sectors.

How efficient could market reforms in agriculture be? It should not be forgotten that 80 per cent of land suitable for cultivation is in the state sector – 'Cuba is a laboratory for studying the role and implications of state management of agriculture in the Third World', [52] according to C. Feuer. As Fidel Castro once again recalled on 26 July 1988, Cuban agrarian reform did not 'divide landed properties. ... The large units were kept as they were and only the plots occupied by the various groups of tenant farmers, sharecroppers, farmers etc. ... were returned.'[53] It was the small peasants who were encouraged to form the agricultural co-operatives. Today, two-thirds of private land is formed into co-operatives instead of 11 per cent in 1980.[54] Only the remainder belongs to private farmers, in spite of their greater productivity. The problems are thus completely different from those in the Eastern bloc. Among other problems, the free markets contributed greatly to the fall in sugar-cane production. As well as economic and administrative reasons – raw material shortages, the poor use of resources, inefficient management, etc. – it would seem that the effect of the free markets had been to stimulate the production of alternative crops that were more profitable when sold at speculative prices on the free market (but which nevertheless failed to resolve supply problems, except for particular sectors of the population). The legalization of the free market bore a strong resemblance to a legalization of the black market. Banning them, however, was not in itself a solution, given the inadequate agricultural production of the state sector.

One of the most difficult problems faced is the division between the urban and rural populations. Out of a population of 10,356,201 inhabitants, 72.3 per cent live in urban areas.[55] In a country which still remains highly dependent on agricultural production, this imbalance must obviously be resolved. The government faces major problems. It was forced to put an unprecedented mobilization scheme into action (involving 232,000 workers to carry out non-mechanized sowing and planting work in the cane fields). And by bringing in workers from enterprises, this has produced dislocation in the factories. Moreover, the results achieved have not been satisfactory,[56] all the more so because there is also a shortage of labour power required to do other agricultural work not linked to sugar-cane.

In principle Che's economic and theoretical writings are central to rectification. 'The hands of the clock have gone as far back in time as the mid-1960s. ... It is an implicit admission that one of the reasons why Che then left Cuba was that he had been beaten in the debate of the 1960s', concludes the columnist of the *Financial Times*.[57] The Cuban leadership is involved in a reflection on the problems surrounding the transition to socialism; and for the first time this is being done in an autonomous fashion, on the basis of the classical texts and the most diverse experiences – from China to Yugoslavia and North Korea. Fidel Castro is engaged in an indictment of the 'technocrats, second-rate capitalists, [and] bureaucrats who hinder the construction of socialism'.[58] In response to those who think that man is a donkey which only moves as a result of carrot and stick, he has reasserted that only an appeal to awareness will enable socialism to be built.

> Capitalists criticize us and try to have everyone believe that Cuban revolutionaries are not realistic. ... We will see what we are capable of, even with this lame old nag, covered with sores which we smear with iodine, an old nag we stuff with medicine, cover with splints and bandages and try to get back on the road. ... We have to stick with our old nag, for we know its vices and dangers,

> the kicks it can give and how to pull on the reins. We must do everything we can to lead it along our road, instead of letting it drag us off to wherever it wants to go.

To achieve these aims 'a rider, a party cadre, an administrative cadre, armed with Che's ideas'[59] is needed.

The rectification process has entered a new stage. Initial speeches, viciously criticizing market economic reforms and capitalist mechanisms, have been replaced by a phase in which work is being reorganized and rationalized. The Cuban leadership is searching for a middle way to avoid the pitfalls of bureaucratic planning, on the one hand, and the damaging effects of market reforms, on the other. Emphasis is being placed on economic development, particularly industrial development: 'This is not the time for thinking about consumption. What needs thinking about is development which will provide for consumption on a more secure and solid foundation later on.'[60]

Absolute priority is being given to investment, particularly investment that brings in or saves foreign exchange. While the political tendencies underlying rectification are still not completely clear, important signs already exist.

First, rectification has led to a reduction of the material incentives introduced with the System of Economic Management and Planning (SDPE), in an attempt to make up for the plan having been overtaken: enterprise managers had fixed work norms at an artificial level and bonuses were often higher than wages, but without a corresponding increase in production. It is not surprising that ever since 'perhaps one of the most difficult aspects of rectification has been to convince the workers to give up the excessively high wages stemming from the implementation of outdated norms or erroneous criteria', as a commentator from *Granma* pointed out.[61]

Secondly, the workforce has been rationalized and reorganized. The number of managers has been revised downwards in public services and enterprises, but the reduction of the number of workers employed has been more widespread, possibly by as much as 30–40 per cent.

Surplus workers are being re-employed elsewhere, possibly in the microbrigades, provided they accept the jobs they are offered. Reallocation to new jobs has not been smooth, particularly in the case of young people whose qualifications are often higher than those required by the jobs they are offered.[62]

Thirdly, smaller working teams have been introduced to fight absenteeism and the lack of discipline at work, as well as instability and the excessive mobility of workers. They are provided with machines and raw materials. With the microbrigades, or rather the contingents, the control of productivity has been easier. It is exercised by the workers who organize production themselves, drawing up their work plan and managing their own accounts and wages. Economies in resources and increases in productivity occasionally provide large bonuses, except for those workers who have not 'deserved' them.

Fourthly, planning devices are to be simplified and a certain economic decentralization is being studied. Intermediate administrative structures between production and distribution should be eliminated or changed. The Cuban Ministry of Basic Industry, on which major sectors of production depend, has announced reforms aimed at 'de-bureaucratizing' its structure. The administrative staff in central offices has been reduced by 60 per cent. The bulk of management of production has been transferred from bureaucratic ministerial bodies to the hands of enterprise managers.

Fifthly, the reform of the CMEA could mean that the autonomy of certain enterprises will be strengthened. At its forty-third extraordinary session in October 1987, the CMEA outlined a number of special projects concerning co-operation between the body's European members, and Vietnam and Cuba. Economic relations could now take place at three levels: between states, between sectors and between enterprises themselves: 'Direct economic links between enterprises must become the principal lever, thus ensuring the success of specialization and co-production.'

It is difficult to believe that all this will not affect the Cuban economy. Having criticized mixed enterprises, Fidel Castro has now just confirmed that they will be developed, not just in industry, but also in export-oriented sectors, the aim being to take advantage of the technology, raw materials and outlets provided by investors. Where has this change come from? Has it been due to the influence of his collaborators, some of whom 'have been converted to the benefits of capitalism and the market economy'? These measures and their effects on wages, in terms of increased differentials, are in danger of being at odds with the egalitarian themes of Castro's recent speeches. For example, contracts signed with Spanish businessmen for the construction and management of hotels and restaurants authorize the hiring and firing of workers according to their work performance.[63] Does rectification thus boil down to a kind of ideological radicalism at the political level, combined with a reinforced pragmatism at the economic level?[64]

According to this hypothesis, the Castro leadership would combine an economic approach that is more compatible with the Soviet Union's perspective than would first appear, albeit allowing for the differences in the level of development of the two countries. Appeals for voluntary work and references to Che would therefore be – at least as far as part of the apparatus is concerned – a way of getting workers to swallow the pill of austerity, without challenging the 'colossal bureaucratic incompetence' (to use García Márquez's phrase) which is one of the principal causes of the current crisis.

From now on, the problems of daily life and the deterioration of working conditions and transport (as a result of the fall in imports, of spare parts in particular) cannot fail to have an effect on the mobilization of the masses, and there are visible signs of discontent. Official statements themselves echo the difficulties affecting the distribution of essential goods.

Queues form outside shops from dawn. The suppression of the free farmers' markets may have curbed the quick enrichment of private farmers, but it has not solved the supplies problem. Transport has again deteriorated, with repairs becoming more difficult to get done and breakdowns increasing. Speculation has increased and police operations and raids – widely reported by the Cuban press – have taken place against speculators.

In a more worrying development, displays of 'indiscipline' at work have increased. The introduction of economic reform in 1975, and its implementation over the next ten years, had been intended to raise workers' motivation and discipline. But the number of court cases for lack of discipline at work – covering all kinds of offences, including joint arrangements between managers, middlemen and workers over wages, standards and working conditions – rose from 9,988 in 1979 to 25,572 in 1985.

The launch of the rectification process in 1986 was aimed at amending this situation, for which the SDPE and its trail of inequalities and corruption were held responsible. If the PCC Politburo is to be believed, however, 'groups of exemplary workers are carrying out veritable feats of production', even though 'signs of indiscipline at the work and social levels persist, anti-social elements are trying to challenge order and discipline'. Moreover, on 11 December 1988 Fidel Castro again dwelled on 'social indiscipline and delinquency, negative signs that reached a worrying level in recent months'.

The crisis point was reached in December 1988 following an unprecedented incident: a fire at the main telephone exchange in Havana on 13 November had paralysed the capital's telephone system. *Granma* claimed that it had been a case of sabotage by an operator who had deliberately set fire to the installations 'to harm the management of the enterprise which had twice reprimanded her for desertion of her post'.[65] The seriousness of such events was highlighted by the fact that they were mentioned in the international edition of the newspaper. Social unrest and the worries of workers in the face of growing difficulties at work and in daily life have thus become apparent. It was certainly not coincidental that two months after this incident, on the thirtieth anniversary of the revolution, the Minister of Labour and Social Security decided to rehabilitate workers who had disciplinary measures on record against them (sanctions for indiscipline at work ranging from a reprimand to dismissal), but who had subsequently displayed a positive attitude at work. This decision was certainly linked to the sabotage of the telephone exchange; and though a limited measure, it reflected the authorities' concern not to step up disciplinary measures against the popular masses during this period of 'austerity'.

The social contradictions inherent in the current ambiguities of rectification have been highlighted since the third meeting of production and services enterprises in Havana in mid-1988. Chaired by Fidel Castro, it focused the discussion of the rectification process on the problem of costs, enterprise profitability, the organization of work, and the system of wages: in other words, the need to increase labour productivity.

For the first time, the Cuban government has recognized an unemployment rate of 6 per cent instead of 3.4 per cent in 1981. The Castro leadership obviously does not hide the extent of the economic crisis and its lasting nature, as was confirmed in the last session of the National Assembly of People's Power: 'The situation in 1986 did not improve in 1987, but got worse. And it deteriorated even further in 1988. In the years to come absolute priority must be given to economic investment, particularly investment that enables convertible currency to be saved or earned.'

How are the masses going to react? Who is going to pay for the costs of the crisis? What is the social target of the rectification process? So many questions are still left open. The mobilization capacity of the Cuban masses is perhaps still sufficient to stand up to shortages and the grind of daily life at the same time – provided, of course, that the sacrifices are equally shared. And this involves a reduction of privileges, a genuine struggle against bureaucracy and the democratization of political life, not just for the benefit of the ruling group, but for the workers and youth.

Having started out as a campaign against 'the technocrats and the new capitalists', rectification's future is unknown. It alternates with measures to increase labour productivity; no one is clear about the next stages. As a Cuban journalist has pointed out, the rectification process 'has its supporters and its enemies. Some hold it back and others would like to push it further. ... Cubans have the habit of laying responsibility for every mistake at the door of managers of enterprises, directors of organizations and cadres. It's easier to see a mote in your neighbour's eye than the beam in your own.' This comment means just what it says. Conceived as a 'strategic counter-offensive', the policy of rectification conceals conflicting social interests. Managers are in favour of a greater autonomy for enterprises and would be the first to benefit. The workers, on the other hand, press for the power of managers to be reduced. It is clear that a quiet battle is taking place in ruling circles to strip Castro's discourse of its initial content; and in order to get draconian measures aimed at increasing productivity introduced, voluntarism, moral incentives, appeals to revolutionary consciousness and ideological motivation are all being put to cynical use.

The Impasse of Castroism

In asserting that 'the secret of productivity is in discipline, technology ... the rational and efficient use of materials and labour power', as well as that it is possible 'to do more than the capitalists if one is capable of leading men – and this is the secret – with revolutionary methods',[66] Fidel Castro is in danger of awarding both himself and the team surrounding him with a certificate of incompetence. That is, unless he makes an effort to challenge the non-revolutionary methods of those in charge of the operating controls of the economy and the state apparatus and distances himself from them. In attacking either the masses or the apparatus, according to circumstances, Fidel Castro still retains his role as an arbiter. But his tight-rope act is threatened by the weight of the bureaucracy, the growing scepticism of the masses and international constraints, in particular Gorbachev's policies.

Indeed, the economic and political practices of recent years have led to a stratification of an apparatus which is not just numerically larger than before, but also more structured and thus more difficult to control. Fidel Castro's descriptions speak for themselves. Abuses of power, corruption, the introduction of sanctions into the Penal Code against those using their position for personal ends, are illuminating. Yet just as clear is the powerlessness of the workers to gain redress, and this forms part of the active campaign that *Trabajadores* is leading against privileges. In a survey on the personal use of official cars, barely half of enterprise managements replied to the questionnaires, and the answers that were given, the journal noted, were highly unconvincing:[67] 'In other words, measures are not taken', the writer of the article concluded. A campaign to ration and save oil is now in full swing. Popular intervention has led to incompetent or corrupt managers being relieved of their duties. But these are isolated cases; and dismissal occasionally amounts to nothing more than a transfer, due to the privilege – which is more important than the material benefits – of having 'connections' in the state apparatus and enjoying the reciprocal protection that those belonging to it grant each other.

This is what the people call *sociolismo* (the socialist old boys' network) – the reign of the *socios* where 'tacit associates are engaged in equally tacit deals'.[68] Paternalist appeals for mobilization have, at best, had a temporary effect against this network of complicity and mutual aid. But with their increased power, the bureaucratic strata have not been its only holders. It is quite conceivable that the rectification campaign was initially an attempt to limit their prerogatives, but in favour of Fidel Castro taking the situation back in hand.

This form of government and paternalistic leadership, based on the prestige of the leader (a key concept in Fidel Castro's thought),[69] is now beginning to go into crisis. For the first time a gap can be sensed between Castro's discourse and the needs of particular groups. This stems from the overall rise in the level of education, as well as the assessment that young people and officials at several levels have made of the policy shifts in recent years. Cuban intellectuals ask the reasons why Cuban ideology was led to borrow from Soviet rhetoric for between ten and fifteen years. How were education, history and economic and social sciences allowed to serve as a vehicle for the most hackneyed dogma? Why are Soviet manuals now being dumped in the bin, and why did no one listen to the people who had been criticizing them for years? Is Soviet pressure enough to explain this, and if so, why today rather than yesterday?

There is no unilateral answer to these questions. And to understand why, one must go back to Cuba's underdevelopment at the time of the seizure of power. It was not just a question of illiteracy; the rapid and profound radicalization of the revolution, as well as the expropriation of firms owned by foreign capital and the national bourgeoisie, led to the massive departure of managers and technicians, albeit limited in number, on which the country relied. Che often complained that he was lacking managers in all fields. Those forged in the struggle did not have the necessary knowledge – many soldiers from the rebel army were illiterate themselves. The situation was distressing at all levels: economic, administrative and political. Such deficiencies were progressively remedied. Internally, the 'weakness of the organic structure of the 26th of July Movement'[70] enabled the old PSP to place a number of its cadres in positions of control, and this subsequently led to several crises. The Soviet Union went on to provide, particularly during the Brezhnev era, the material infrastructure and ideological training staff that have been the model for tens of thousands of military, economic, administrative – and, to a lesser extent, political – cadres. The training of PCC cadres was carried out in Moscow and it is these generations which today occupy the different levels of the state apparatus. From now on, training will be provided in Cuba itself. But the previous 'Russification' does not explain everything. Fidel Castro's own conception and practice of power must be challenged.

All these internal contradictions have been accentuated by the sudden developments taking place in the Eastern bloc countries and by Gorbachev's policies. The Soviet head of state would like Cuba to form part of his policy of negotiation with US imperialism and to accept an economic policy based on true prices and austerity, thus enabling the Soviet Union to reduce its aid. Bush is encouraging this pressure, seeing it as a way of dividing the regime's social base. For his part, Castro is stepping up relations with Latin American governments and is trying to negotiate, along the lines of the Angola accords, a rapprochement with the United States. But such a policy once again has strings attached: respecting the rules of the game of the club one wants to join. As a US diplomat has said: 'Cuba cannot try and play football by the rules of baseball.'[71] In other words, one must show one's entry pass to become a member of the club – by halting aid to revolutionaries abroad, tightening one's belt at home and modernizing an inefficient system.

Gorbachev is saying something similar. Cuba must choose: either to act as a lone warrior and take the consequences, or to play the game with the other so-called 'socialist' countries and reform its economy.

The development of inequalities linked to the privilege of power is no less a threat to the revolution than that presented by the inequalities generated by the use of market mechanisms. For such bureaucratic privileges not only exist, but are highly resistant, as witnessed by the surveys of *Trabajadores* magazine on efforts to fight the improper use of official cars. Material privileges, particularly within the bureaucracy in charge of economic management, have been the subject of public denunciation by Fidel Castro himself. But the political privileges of power – those of the party apparatus and mass organizations – are never mentioned, and this is not by chance.

The political framework, as institutionalized, is never challenged, except by the supporters of market reforms and the pro-Gorbachev sectors. At a 'grassroots' level among youth and intellectuals it is a very different story, with the desire expressed for greater debate and less authoritarianism and paternalism: 'He treats us like children, but he is a bad father', a youth told *Juventud Rebelde*. At the Congress of the Young Communists, a speaker asked Fidel Castro to speak less and to listen to others more. Such demands, stemming from the level of educational development among youth, are new, and, for the time being, do not form part of a political project. But if Fidel Castro insists on turning a deaf ear, he will strengthen the position of the supporters of market reforms by allowing them to wave the banner of 'democracy'. He will thus make easier the task of those wishing to identify the current 'radical' discourse of the ruling group with a neo-Stalinist orientation.

Opting for ideological motivation and mobilizing the masses through appeals to revolutionary consciousness can still perhaps work in the Cuban context. But to be effective, such an option must give greater powers of control and decision to the masses. This means breaking with the PCC's monopoly of power, concentrated as it is in the hands of a single leader and his collaborators. And it means that the command, 'The best at the helm!' – applied locally in the case of the microbrigades – should also be enforced nationally, in order to put an end to the bureaucratic waste which is the main obstacle to an improvement in productivity.

In a planned economy, only if workers have a free choice between major economic options, as well as decision-making power and control, can the consciousness of the masses be stimulated, in so far as socialist planning is not just an economic mechanism but a social relationship. Workers' control, self-organization, the confrontation of different positions, and effective responsibility for decisions taken are the social and political mainsprings in the construction of socialism – a system that should allow workers' emancipation to be the task of the workers themselves. This option is on the agenda in all countries with post-capitalist economies; and it is forcing its way on to the agenda in Cuba as well.

Cuba, of course, is not the Soviet Union of the 1920s. But the aggravation of internal difficulties and the accentuation in recent years of phenomena such as bureaucratization and the uncertainty surrounding the development of Soviet policy have led to a sense of urgency. While no magic solution exists for the problems of economic development within the general context of the Third World, it is at least possible to introduce necessary changes in terms of economic and political democracy.

So far, the revolution has survived through two crucial strategies: satisfying social needs and appealing to anti-imperialist dignity. This winning back of the nation, this 'sovereignty of resistance' has had considerable impact on the Latin American subcontinent. Fidel Castro's recent visits to Ecuador and Mexico, as well as the Latin American summit in Ecuador have been a defeat for US diplomacy. Cuba's scope for diplomatic manoeuvre has increased. Even the most conservative governments have been forced to distance themselves from Washington's policy. Relations with Cuba have given their anti-imperialist credentials a boost and have also provided the Cuban government with a noteworthy commercial and political space. Nevertheless, the fate of the Cuban

Revolution is intimately linked with the new revolutionary victories. A checking of revolution in Nicaragua or El Salvador would severely weaken Cuba in the face of imperialism, increase its dependence on Soviet bureaucracy and aggravate its internal crisis.

It is this process that was set in motion following the death of Che in 1967, as defeats in Bolivia and Chile, the defeat of armed movements in Uruguay, Argentina and Brazil, the imposition of military dictatorships, and the strengthening of imperialism, all led to the growing ascendancy of Soviet influence and a deeping of the social and political crisis in Cuba. It is to be feared that, in order to check this chain of events, certain leaders, including Fidel Castro himself, will attempt to resolve internal difficulties by further centralizing power; by preventing the development of any political autonomy through repression; and by struggling against selfish interests and bureaucratic appetites through the example of the firing squad. This is an ominous prospect and would seriously underestimate the social processes at work on the island.

Notes

1. Interview with Maria Schriver for NBC, 13 March 1988.
2. The title of a book by Warren Miller, published in the United States in 1960.
3. *Le Monde*, 7–8 August 1988.
4. Ch. Vanhecke, in *Le Monde*, January 1987.
5. *Problèmes d'Amérique latine*, Documentation française, second quarter 1982.
6. G. White, 'Cuban Planning in the Mid-1980s: Centralization, decentralization and participation', in *World Development*, vol. 15, no. 1, 1987.
7. *Problèmes d'Amérique latine*, Documentation française, 8 July 1987.
8. Brezinski, 'Cuba's economic ties with the Soviet Union and the CMEA in the mid-eighties'.
9. R. Turits. 'Trade, Debt and the Cuban Economy', in *World Development*, vol. 15, no. 1, 1987.
10. W. Jampel, in *Courrier des pays de l'Est*, Documentation française, November 1987.
11. Ibid.
12. Turits. 'Trade, Debt and the Cuban Economy'.
13. Daniel Ortega, in *Granma*, 27 June 1988.
14. Interview with Maria Schriver for NBC, 13 March 1988.
15. Che Guevara, Algiers speech (1965), *Ecrits d'un révolutionnaire*.
16. Carlos Tablada Pérez, *El pensamiento económico de Ernesto Che Guevara*.
17. Ibid.
18. Turits. 'Trade, Debt and the Cuban Economy'; Brezinski, 'Cuba's economic ties with the Soviet Union and the CMEA in the mid-eighties'; Mesa-Lago and F. Gil, 'Vingt ans de relations économiques entre l'URSS et Cuba', in *Courrier des pays de l'Est*, Documentation française, December 1988.
19. Credits, some in foreign exchange, have been granted so that the necessary investments can be made.
20. *Financial Times*, 17 February 1989.
21. Brezinski, 'Cuba's economic ties with the Soviet Union and the CMEA in the mid-eighties'.
22. Mesa-Lago and F. Gil, 'Vingt ans de relations économiques entre l'URSS et Cuba'.

23. *Le Monde diplomatique*, April 1989.
24. Robert Graham, in the *Financial Times*, 17 February 1989.
25. Mesa-Lago and F. Gil, 'Vingt ans de relations économiques entre l'URSS et Cuba'.
26. *Granma*, 16 April 1989.
27. *Problèmes politiques et sociaux*, Documentation française, 31 March 1989.
28. Friendship Treaty, articles 2 and 4.
29. Mesa-Lago and F. Gil, 'Vingt ans de relations économiques entre l'URSS et Cuba'.
30. *Granma*, 2 April 1989.
31. Ibid.
32. *El País*, 3 April 1989.
33. Ibid.
34. *Granma*, 28 May 1989.
35. *Financial Times*, 12 April 1989.
36. *The Economist*, 27 August 1988.
37. *Miami Herald*, 23 April 1989; *Latin America Monitor*, May 1989.
38. *Miami Herald*, 23 April 1989.
39. *Financial Times*, 12 April 1989.
40. *Financial Times*, 17 February 1989.
41. Ibid.
42. *Granma*, 16 April 1989.
43. *Herald Tribune*, 12 January 1989.
44. *Newsweek*, 5 June 1989.
45. Ibid.
46. *Financial Times*, 17 February 1989.
47. Fidel Castro, in *Granma*, 26 July 1988.
48. Salinas de Gortari was elected president of Mexico as a result of massive fraud; see *Inprecor*, no. 271, 5 September 1988.
49. *Nacla, Report on the Americas*, New York, March 1989.
50. G. White, 'Cuban Planning in the Mid-1980s'.
51. *Le Monde diplomatique*, December 1987.
52. C. Feuer, 'The Performance of the Cuban Sugar Industry', in *World Development*, vol. 15, no. 1, 1987.
53. *Granma*, 26 July 1988.
54. *World Development*, vol. 15, no. 1, 1987.
55. *Juventud Rebelde*, 20 June 1988.
56. *Trabajadores*, 1 June 1988.
57. *Financial Times*, 27 September 1988.
58. Speech made on the occasion of the twentieth anniversary of Che's death, in *Granma*, 18 October 1987.
59. *Granma*, 18 October 1987.
60. Fidel Castro, in *Granma*, 11 December 1988.
61. *Granma*, 18 September 1988.
62. Suárez Vega, in *Die Zeit*, 28 October 1988.
63. *Herald Tribune*, 12 January 1989.
64. Brezinski, 'Cuba's economic ties with the Soviet Union and the CMEA in the mid-eighties'.
65. *Granma*, 13 November 1988.
66. Fidel Castro, in *Granma*, 29 January 1989.
67. *Trabajadores*, 28 June 1988.
68. Ariel Hidalgo, 'Cuba, l'Etat marxiste et la nouvelle classe'.
69. Gianni Miná, *Un encuentro con Fidel*.
70. Ernesto Che Guevara, 'El cuadro, columna vertebral de la revolución', *Obras revolucionarias*, Havana, September 1962.
71. *El País*, 1988.

7

Executed as an Example

> What does history prove? That men have possessed power and that they have abused power. Even in revolutionary processes, certain men have had extraordinary power, above all during this stage, in the initial years. When revolutionary processes become institutionalized, when there is a party, when there are established norms, when these norms practically become the community's culture, then there is no longer any danger.[1]

'Someone once said that revolution was like Saturn who devoured his own children. ... This revolution has not devoured and will never devour its own children.'[2] Is this prediction of Fidel Castro's no longer valid? In July and August 1989 a general who was a hero of the republic and three officers were executed; and four ministers, including Minister of the Interior José Abrantes, a member of the PCC Central Committee, were dismissed. In June, Abrantes had enjoyed the public support of Fidel Castro who reaffirmed his confidence in him. Yet he was sentenced to twenty years' imprisonment just a few weeks after the execution of Arnaldo Ochoa. His arrest was also followed by that of other officials from his ministry, as well as the demotion and retirement of several others. In addition to Abrantes, Major General Pascual Martínez Gil was sentenced to fifteen years' imprisonment, Brigadier General Roberto González Caso to thirteen years, Lieutenant-Colonel Manuel Gil Castellanos to eight years, and Lieutenant-Colonel Rolando Castaneda Izquierdo to ten years. Two other officials from the Ministry of the Interior, Oscar Carreño Gómez, the former head of Customs, and Héctor Carbonell Méndez, the head of commercial enterprises, were sentenced to thirteen and twelve years' imprisonment respectively. Among the five generals downgraded to the rank of colonel or sent into retirement, General Arsenio Franco Villanueva had been Deputy Minister of the Interior, General

Valdés González had been in charge of the border guards, generals Véliz Hernández and Suárez Alvárez had been officials of the political leadership and General Bermejo Labrada had been Chief of Staff of the border guards. For his part, Colonel Alvárez Cueto, the head of financial management of the ministry, committed suicide 'out of despondency and shame at the situation that the institution is going through'.[3]

It amounted to a complete dismantling of the ministry. Never had historic representatives of the regime been so harshly condemned since the seizure of power. This time it was not a case of old communist officials being accused of sectarianism or complicity with Moscow; most were longstanding Castroites. That is why this has been the most serious leadership crisis that the Cuban Revolution has ever known. The trafficking of foreign currency and ivory in Angola by 'internationalist' fighters, the embezzlement of funds in Panama by Cuban chargés d'affaires, fraudulent activities and drug trafficking – those are the issues that prompted the accusations of 'negligence in the fulfilment of duty, corruption, the irregular use of resources and the illegal appropriation of state funds for expenses unrelated to the Ministry of the Interior ... weakness of character and nepotism which have led to grave problems at the ministry and to the creation of unauthorized enterprises engaged in activities linked to foreign trade'.[4] The cross-examination of the defendants[5] (by Padrón, in particular) and the closing speech of the prosecutor, Escalona, the Minister of Justice, as well as Fidel Castro's speech to the Council of State,[6] highlighted the extent of the corruption and the degree to which regulations and laws had been violated by the very people entrusted with their enforcement.

How should the scope given to the trial and the gravity of the punishments be analysed? The legal and democratic aspects must be examined (the veracity of the facts, the circumstances of the verdict, the rights of defence) and questions must be asked as to responsibilities at all levels. But several questions will remain unanswered. And the political significance of these events, some years after the beginning of rectification, must be at the centre of the analysis.

The 'Cuban Connection'

> Cuba has been offered fabulous sums of money on occasions to co-operate in drug trafficking and, in spite of being a country subjected to a US blockade, we have never accepted a single trade activity linked with drugs. I must therefore declare that it is absolutely scandalous to try and implicate Cuba in drug trafficking. I can state categorically that not a cent has entered this

> country from drug-trafficking. And in twenty-six years of revolution I do not know a single official who has participated in such trafficking. ... Our record in this area is the best in the continent.[7]

On 4 July 1987, the director of the Drug Enforcement Agency had declared: 'Cuba is deeply involved in drug trafficking in this hemisphere. The Cuban government or certain individuals belonging to the government of that country are using Cuba to facilitate drug trafficking in this hemisphere.'[8] Two years later, in a climate of extreme tension, the Ochoa scandal broke in Havana.

There would seem to be no doubt that drug trafficking actually took place. But one cannot see what advantage the Cuban leadership could have gained from the publicity of an affair that does it a profound disservice and which is at odds with the principles and ethical values claimed by the revolution. The charges had the effect of an earthquake in Havana. But the trial's progress, having failed to clarify either the scope of responsibilities, the aim of the drug trafficking, or the motivations of those sentenced to death and the other accused, did not manage to dispel a profound sense of disquiet.

To say that the accused were part of the revolutionary clique is an understatement, at least in the case of Ochoa, the La Guardia brothers or Abrantes. They were above all part of the 'hard core' of Castroites at the heart of the state apparatus, those to whom the most difficult and delicate missions were entrusted: Ochoa was responsible for the military mission in Angola; the La Guardia brothers had the highly secret and dangerous task of creating a body in the Ministry of the Interior – the 'MC' department – in charge of overcoming the US blockade. At the time of the Chilean military coup, the La Guardia twins, Patricio and Antonio, were in Santiago alongside President Allende[9] in the La Moneda presidential palace. It was they who wrapped Allende in the Chilean flag when he was murdered. No one knows how they managed to leave Chile and return to Cuba. Along with Ochoa, they were also the first to enter Somoza's bunker in Managua during the triumph of the Sandinistas. Ochoa was adviser to the revolutionary movement in Venezuela, crushed by Carlos Andrés Pérez, who was then Minister of the Interior and is now President of the Republic. How did Ochoa avoid being taken prisoner? No one knows how he managed, alone and without support, to get out of Venezuela and finally reach Havana. As recalled by the 18 September 1989 edition of the Mexican magazine, *Proceso*, these are just some of the feats of men whose lives were dedicated to revolution.

With such a background and responsibilities, they deserved other than a summary procedure and special courts. And as far as the death sentence was concerned, it was not justified.

As usual,[10] the defence contented itself with seeking admissions by the defendants of their treachery. Indeed, officially appointed barristers were used. Given Cuban traditions, this should not have been surprising. But shortly afterwards the notorious dissident, Elizardo Sánchez – the leader of a human rights organization, arrested with two others on 6 August 1989 for calling the execution of four Cuban officers 'murder' – was authorized by the Minister of Justice to choose his own barrister to defend himself at his trial.[11] Although Ochoa and the other defendants were accused of treason, one can only be surprised at the difference in the way an opponent of the regime and a former hero of the republic were treated.

While Ochoa displayed his usual humour throughout the trial, he did not really co-operate with the court, particularly in terms of clarifying what the money was used for. On the contrary, the former general claimed he intended to spend the money obtained for military, rather than personal, purposes. And to a question from the prosecutor concerning the money deposited in Panama, and from which his aide-de-camp Martínez allegedly gained, he replied: 'But no, Martínez was not going to take that money for himself and nor was I, of course. What would I have done with two hundred thousand dollars?' And replying to the prosecutor who again asked him what the final destination of the money brought back from Angola was, he declared: 'As I have said before, we were going to use the money I sent back to Panama for the army.'[12] He then repeated: 'The dealing that took place in Angola was aimed at building airports,[13] not at improving living conditions. ... I repeat: in an irresponsible way I said: "If there's a bit of money left, send it to me, I'll need it for the army."'[14] In all of his interventions, Ochoa accepted responsibility for the activities carried out ('I have said from the start that I am the person responsible for this affair') but denied embezzling funds for personal ends, justifying them on the grounds of military needs. While this did not in any way change the seriousness of the deeds, it did mean that the 'motive for the crime' could not be ignored. But his barrister said nothing about this; and the prosecutor focused his accusation on Ochoa's betrayal, thus leaving the chain of events unclear. As Ochoa himself said, several witnesses cross-examined by the court had not been present at the summary trial conducted by the special court martial, and several pieces of information to which he had referred had not been published in *Granma* nor recalled by the defence.

Ochoa also did not fail to emphasize that the transactions on the black market in Angola (dealing sugar for diamonds or ivory) in order to raise foreign exchange and Angolan money to build an airport were part of a trade 'that has always existed in Angola. ... The two issues have been mixed up before the court, but that is not fair. The building of the airport was separate, and the Finance Department was in charge of it. When Estupiñan [one of the accused] made a trip to Cuba to ask for the 90 million kwanzas [the Angolan currency] and didn't get them, at that point I simply decided: some of these things can be sold and the airport can be built in any case. ... That's how everything began.' In other words, the various bartering activities were carried out under the auspices of the State Committee for Finance and the Ministry of the Interior (the head of which committed suicide in July 1989); and such trading operations were almost routine, even though the new element was the trafficking of drugs.

The disparate and fragmentary nature of the pieces of information mean that there can be no certainty as to what actually happened. From Ochoa's intentions it can be deduced that there was an urgent need to build airports to allow planes from Cuba to land in preparation for the battle of Cuito Cuanavale. On 5 December 1988, Fidel Castro had already indicated that, in the light of the critical situation at Cuito Cuanavale, the staff of the FAR had met on 15 November 1987 and had decided to use all necessary means to prevent the South African army from decimating the Angolan and Cuban troops, including sending the most experienced pilots to save the town. And he had extolled 'the feats of building, for in a few weeks an airport for our fighters – a real airbase – had been created, allowing our planes to gain more than two hundred kilometres and seriously threaten South African troops situated in key locations. There was no improvisation or adventurism on our part. The enemy realized that it was confronted not just with very powerful forces, but highly experienced forces.'

If Ochoa's intentions are correctly understood, Havana did not provide enough funds and he had to get by with what he had. The seriousness of the situation should not be forgotten. According to Fidel Castro, it was due to military errors for which he implicitly blamed the Soviet Union – which had apparently not provided the means needed to get out of the impasse.

> The political situation was complex. President Gorbachev was due to meet President Reagan in Washington on 7 December 1987 to discuss important issues relating to world peace [to sign an intermediate nuclear weapons reduction treaty] and action by Cuba might have been considered inconvenient [*sic*]. It was the worst moment for taking a decision of that kind. But the issue was either to take the decision or to accept the consequences entailed by allowing the South Africans to act with impunity and thus decide the military outcome of the Angolan conflict.[15]

This explains the tensions at the time and Havana's decision to send, on its own and in record time, massive reinforcements.

But without Soviet aid, could Cuba afford such a costly policy? Were not such actions out of proportion to the country's resources? How could such an effort be financed when the Soviet government was advocating disengagement? According to Alberto Sendic, these were the questions that Ochoa and his colleagues had to resolve.[16]

This is not a case of turning Ochoa into an innocent victim. According to the statements of Raúl Castro to the Council of State, Ochoa had had three young Cuban soldiers executed in Angola. They had been guilty of serious crimes (the rape of Angolan women[17]): Ochoa himself was probably hoist by his own petard. Nevertheless, he enjoyed a certain degree of popularity during his trial (as was recognized by the *Granma* editorial of 10 September 1989, which referred to the 'public sympathy for the main defendant'). This was no doubt due to his prestige and the fact that he appeared to have been motivated by 'professional' concern. It was a different matter with José Abrantes, for whom a twenty-year prison sentence was felt, by comparison, to be insufficient, undoubtedly because of the little sympathy felt by public opinion for the Ministry of the Interior. Ochoa's more political speech highlighted the autonomy of the high-ranking leaders and their almost limitless powers, as well as the personal degradation of former revolutionary activists who had become disillusioned and cynical leaders. The old saying that absolute power corrupts absolutely was thus confirmed.

In answer to the prosecutor who asked him whether he was entitled to take decisions of that nature, Ochoa replied naturally: 'I have done many things without authorization. And in this particular case, I don't think it was in any way illogical to do so.' Habits had been formed and methods of operation had been created; and it was clear in Angola that Cuban soldiers, outside of any control, were not careful about the means they used: 'The justice of the causes they were defending left other implications in the dark and produced other, less exalting approaches.'[18] The many tensions with the Angolans bear witness to this.[19]

The aim of the Ministry of the Interior's activities in Panama was to circumvent the US blockade by setting up firms as a front, using all financial and commercial means to carry out 'fraudulent' operations for Cuba's benefit – legitimate operations, given the thirty-year-old embargo which, in spite of optimistic predictions, has not been relaxed at all since the election of George Bush. In a significant development, the US Treasury Department, using the trade blockade as a cover, has prevented the US television station ABC from buying exclusive broadcasting rights for the Pan-American Games to be held in Havana in 1991 (and for which it had offered $9 million).

Cuba's right to defend itself, both economically and commercially, is therefore not in question. But in this line of business, it is true that commercial promiscuity is not particularly virtuous. The environment in which agents from the Ministry of the Interior were moving was one of gangsters. The almost limitless material resources at the disposal of the 'MC' department created a state within a state. No one was in control of its officials; and they were not in control of the people under their orders. This special department had a logic of its own. The owners of the boats employed to break the US blockade, and the businessmen acting as intermediaries, were traffickers who made no distinction whatsoever between drugs and the rest of their activities. As Martínez, one of the defendants, declared, one was seen 'as a person who was involved in illicit business dealings' of which cocaine trafficking was just one aspect. The need of the commercial firms created abroad to bring in foreign exchange must also be mentioned. At the beginning, when there was a dramatic need for foreign exchange in the Cuban economy, they were in deficit, and that represented an additional pressure. There was thus a kind of chain-reaction in operation, based on the tasks assigned by the department and the practices and contacts that these would involve; a chain-reaction that was facilitated by the scope of the powers enjoyed by the ministry, by the absence of any control and by pervasive corruption.

'Did you have a system for controlling your officers' activities?' asked the prosecutor. And like Ochoa, La Guardia replied: 'I couldn't. I was alone. I couldn't control them. ... The officers had become detached pieces. I couldn't manage everything. ... The operations would have required direct intervention to keep control. ... I was sure that the officers would return the money to me.' It was not just a question of increasing receipts, but of then laundering the money and passing it off as earnings from commercial activities. For some, the personal fraud would come quickly. There were other reasons which explain why drug trafficking became commonplace, and Ochoa invoked 'the countries that live off that, forced into it by the nature of their economy'. But such operations represented considerable political risks for Cuba, and in Ochoa's case it is difficult to explain how he could have taken them by himself. The transport of six tonnes of cocaine was carried out on Cuban land and in Cuban shipping space by Colombian pilots and also *marielitos* (the name given to the Cuban exiles who left the country in 1980 via the port of Mariel en route to Miami), whose dollars were exchanged on the black market for pesos intended for their families. But some of them were obviously linked to the CIA. The meeting of Ochoa's aide-de-camp with Pablo Escobar, one of the Medellín cartel tycoons – responsible for the massacre in March 1988 of scores of Colombian peasants, and for the murder by one of his commandos of killers (in collusion with the armed forces) of agricultural workers suspected of links with the guerrillas – was, regardless of any other consideration, extremely compromising and risky for the Cuban state. It is also one of the arguments which give a certain credibility to Fidel Castro when he claims to have been unaware of what was going on.

Were irresponsibility, cynicism and personal corruption the basic motivations for such dealings? Other hypotheses have been formulated. There has been considerable speculation over the arms purchases made by the Ministry of the Interior (called into question by Fidel Castro in his speech to the Council of State), with some seeing them as a sign of an attempted military plot.[20] Given the current state of information, this supposition cannot be backed up and the idea, circulated in Miami, that such a conspiracy could have been successfully carried out against the two Castro brothers seems totally unrealistic. Moreover, the ministry was entitled to purchase arms destined for other countries (Angola and Nicaragua were mentioned during the trial), although purely speculative purchases had been made.

Whatever the case, several grey areas still exist and a number of questions remain unanswered. It cannot be discounted that the accused were put in the hot seat for reasons that were not just limited to drug trafficking. But even if these are mere hypotheses, the very fact that such a crisis exploded at the top of the armed forces and the Ministry of the Interior, calling into question the leadership of the party and the state, revealed the depths to which the ruling group had been shaken and ruptured.

How had this situation come about? The accused, mainly Ochoa, gave a few elliptical clues:

> Firstly, I think I had reached the point where I had strayed from my route, from the objectives of the revolution; I think that that is how it happened. ... What right did I have to fiddle money – something I had never done in my life? I had never been a man greedy for money; I had never had money; I had absolutely no need for it, far from it. But I can also tell you that I had reached a point in my military life where I felt tired. That is to say that, objectively speaking, I am no longer the man that the prosecutor spoke of – the man who has fought here, who has commanded there; I felt exhausted. When I was in Angola, I found myself in difficult, extremely difficult, extremely complex situations. And combined with having spent so many years, how should I put it, working alone, I took the wrong path; I somehow lost my sense of reality. Besides, people have often said that I didn't do any work. That's not true. I made a huge effort to fulfil my duty, perhaps not all my duty, but a lot of people think I mainly devoted myself to business affairs. But that wasn't the case either. I sent other people to look after the affairs, but I personally didn't spend all my time on them. ... I think we could spend a lot of time thinking and reflecting; I can't even explain it myself; I don't know why I did it; there's no reason.[21]

He also made these comments: 'You groan when you receive an order and the moment comes when you end up thinking that any order that we get from the superior command is a bad one. Once on that slope, you assume an independent mode of thought and end up thinking that you are right.' Saverio Tutino, the former correspondent of *L'Unitá* (the Italian Communist Party newspaper) asked: 'Ochoa: Dr Jekyll or Mr Hyde?' Probably neither, but exhaustion, solitude, demoralization and scepticism instead. Ochoa's declarations did at least have the merit of highlighting the way in which the functioning of the ruling group can grind down the best people. That is what stands out above all else.

In this infernal machine that is the Castroite staff, watch out for failure: as in war, leaders are either heroes or traitors, paragons of virtue or scapegoats. What a lesson! No wonder the ruling circles play musical chairs over who is responsible; and who alone could withstand such ordeals, save the commander-in-chief?

Paradoxically, the trial has inevitably led to a questioning of Fidel Castro that he had undoubtedly not foreseen himself. For if the declarations of the accused are true, if the commander-in-chief was unaware of the situation in such a centralized, hierarchical and 'verticalist' regime, then it is a terrible indictment of that style of leadership and changes must be made. Such secrecy is intolerable and, as experience has shown, it can only have grave consequences.

And if the affair has now come to light, is this not also because these are precisely the questions that some people have been raising? The 'national prophylaxis' proposed by Raúl Castro is officially justified on the grounds of the extent of corruption and the need to fight it, beginning at the top. This statement has already been backed up by several measures and cannot be placed in doubt. But why today? As Fidel Castro has rightly recalled, the problems are not recent and there have been plenty of warnings, particularly in relation to the Ministry of the Interior. As early as the Second PCC Congress in 1980, the First Secretary declared in his opening speech: 'As far as the Ministry of the Interior is concerned, it has been noted that, in some areas, efficiency and the exemplary attitude that had always been displayed by cadres in the years of extraordinary and heroic struggles have slackened. ... There have been occasional signs of bureaucracy and of discipline and requirements being slackened.' And he added, prophetically: 'The trees will not hide the wood from us, but we want our Ministry of the Interior to continue being a wood where cuts will not be necessary.'[22] The desertion of army officers and of the Minister of the Interior in 1987 was an alarm signal. Nine years after the Second Congress and three years after the beginning of the rectification process, not only had 'cuts' been necessary, but as the street sellers of

Granma pointed out, 'the Ministry of the Interior has been cleared out!'[23]

'A Caste above All Others'

In his report to the Third PCC Congress in 1986, Fidel Castro had again insisted on the need 'for the combatant at the Ministry of the Interior to have irreproachable conduct, to be incorruptible and of outstanding purity. For in the eyes of citizens everywhere, he is the very symbol of authority, law and morality'. He had mentioned the fact that 'the health, sport and leisure facilities built during the course of the five-year period' for the private use of officials from the Ministry of the Interior had been given over to the organs of people's power and placed at the disposal of the workers. In 1989, the party secretary again denounced all kinds of abuses of power, embezzlements and perks: clinics, restaurants and exclusive entertainment places. Televisions, videos, tape recorders, not to mention cars and even yachts – these were just some of the Cuban nomenklatura's most notorious privileges as described by Fidel Castro. That is undoubtedly a serious matter in a country where the breadth of the revolution's social base of support is particularly due to a rejection of corruption under both the Batista dictatorship and the parliamentary regime of Prío Socarrás (overthrown in Batista's 1952 coup). It should not be forgotten that the leader of the Ortodoxo Party, Eduardo Chibás, a resolute supporter of 'administrative honesty', had committed suicide in 1951 during a radio programme, in protest at the rotten nature of the regime. This had also been one of the central themes of the 26th of July Movement during the revolutionary struggle.

With daily sacrifices demanded from the people, the Castro leadership could not remain passive in the face of the ruling circles' growing moral degradation. The process of rectification is a warning that has followed many others. But the gravity of the current crisis is in a completely different league. As the editorial in *Granma* of 10 September 1989 declared, 'the problems that have been faced by the country this summer go well beyond the fate of a handful of corrupt and disloyal men'. And stressing that this was a much more far-reaching stage of rectification, the leader writer (often Fidel Castro himself) went on:

> It is necessary to state quite clearly that, in everything that has happened, there has been a series of errors encompassing every institution of the revolution in one way or another. ... One of the main features of the situation we have been through ... is that we have not been dealing with the activity of enemy agents, but with people from our own ranks. We have not had to settle a conflict

> between revolution and counter-revolution. The serious, hard lesson to be drawn from these events is that, without going over to the enemy, men who have fought for our cause can do us more harm than any counter-revolutionary; and that, in practice, they can serve the aims of imperialism which has not given up on destroying us. ... In this sense, the first and foremost lesson of this trial [is that] respect for the law applies to every citizen, whatever their position in the political hierarchy or the state. ... The higher the political or state responsibility with which a citizen has been entrusted, the more they are obliged to act with dignity and honesty, both in the public domain and in their private life.

But the most significant part of the editorial was the following:

> What kind of a revolutionary is someone who does not respect either the law or morals, and purports to act as if he belonged to a caste above everything else and all others? What socialism and what revolution can one speak of when one has not had the sensitivity to realize that privileges, arbitrariness, abuses and alienation from the masses are the main reasons for the difficulties now convulsing the socialist system – a system whose vocation was precisely to do away with all such calamities of capitalism?

The statement was startling in more than one respect. First, because the causes of the difficulties of the 'socialist system' were attributed to the existence of a privileged and corrupt bureaucracy. The emphasis had usually been placed on the subjective errors of leaders and the damaging effects of market reforms, with opponents seen as counter-revolutionaries in the pay of imperialism. This time the enemy was within. The statement left no ambiguity. The Ochoa trial was not about the work of 'enemy agents' nor a settling of a 'conflict between revolution and counter-revolution'. And this made it all the more serious because the people involved were 'from our own ranks' and could do the revolution more harm than any counter-revolutionary. The diagnosis, then, was clear and the target selected: at the height of the rectification process, unscrupulous elements, intoxicated with power, had taken advantage of their positions and responsibilities, and had violated the revolution's ethics and standards.[24]

There would have to be exemplary punishment and even the party would not be exempted; it would have to be, not just the subject, but also 'the object of rectification'[25] in so far as negative tendencies 'have not, as a general rule, been discovered by means of the party'. As to the PCC, the first measures were not long in coming: a campaign to confirm membership cards (a self-purge) was carried out. More than 400,000 members had an interview with representatives of higher bodies or with comrades from their cell. More than 6,000 were sanctioned and some

12,000 others were expelled from the party. These sanctions were mainly imposed for the infringement of party statutes (around 40 per cent), but also because of negligence and lack of discipline at work (31 per cent).[26]

Such moves have not just concerned the party. As part of the preparations for the Sixteenth CTC Congress to take place in January 1990, rank-and-file workers' assemblies have debated the draft plan of the main report. This has taken a stand 'against the repugnant and damaging phenomena of illicit enrichment, corruption and other signs of delinquency detected in enterprises and certain units of production',[27] and has admitted the 'responsibility of the CTC and the trade unions in terms of the mistakes and deviations they had both either made, or failed to denounce with the necessary energy at the right time'. Such statements thus lead one to expect a significant renewal of trade union cadres.[28]

The purge has not just hit the Ministry of the Interior, but several other ministerial departments as well. As a Cuban official has stated, in so far as *sociolismo* is very widespread in administration, 'gentle therapies cannot be used, and the scalpel must be applied to all affected organs'.[29] This wide-ranging campaign in the wake of the trial has not only affected ministries, but also mixed enterprises where Cuban officials have been challenged for leading a life of luxury. The Ministry of Foreign Trade has closed the offices of thirty-two mixed enterprises, twelve of them Spanish, officially on the grounds of their 'insufficient volume of trade'.[30] The managements of the enterprises concerned are now responsible for appointing non-Cuban officials who must deal directly with state bodies without intermediaries. According to *Granma*,[31] hundreds of Cubans have been arrested for black market activities; emissaries of Fidel Castro have burst into the best Havana restaurants where high-level cadres were accustomed to dining; and official cars parking outside cabaret bars or near beaches have been booked. The top dignitaries have made no mistake about the situation: 'The restaurants full of customers whose official cars used to wait outside the door are empty. ... You no longer see a single official on Varadero beach or at Havana's most famous cabarets. They can all feel the blade of the guillotine on their necks, and they don't take any initiative out of fear of making a move in the wrong direction.'[32]

While Cuban leaders have all replaced the Ochoa trial and its aftermath by the rectification process, there can be no doubt that the latter has speeded up remarkably, in spite of its numerous ambiguous features at the economic level. This speeding up can only be understood in the context of the intensified conflict running through the state apparatus, with the Castroite ruling core and its supporters facing the new generation of technocrats and officials, often influenced by Moscow, who are increasingly challenging the 'out of date' and 'voluntaristic' (to use the expression of a top official) leadership of the Castro team. The backdrop of this friction, of course, is the economic and social difficulties that we have analysed at length; difficulties that are further exacerbated by Gorbachev's policies. But they are also the specific product of the political power structure in Cuba, of the duality of prerogatives and powers, of the diarchy that exists at the top of the state apparatus, arising from history and the revolutionary process. Any analysis which does not take this factor into account – which identifies the evolution of the Cuban leadership with that of the bureaucratic dictatorships of the Eastern bloc countries, for example – cannot enable current developments to be understood. As Pierre de Charentenay stated in an article published in the magazine *Etudes*, founded by the fathers of the Society of Jesus: 'Cuba is a unique system and one must be careful not to slap down any ready-made analysis about it.'[33]

In different words – indeed, different approaches – all analysts who are aware of the Cuban situation make a similar assessment: the Castroite group (mainly Fidel Castro, but also encompassing the faithful veterans of the Sierra Maestra) is not the product of a bureaucratic apparatus; and while its style of working has favoured the emergence of such an apparatus, its origins, concerns and forms of action are highly distinct. The ruling group plays on this difference, with the PCC Politburo frequently denouncing in official statements 'the effect that the incompetence or inadequacy of state administration has on socio-economic reality, directly affecting the living conditions and welfare of the population and giving rise to states of opinion which reflect worry, concern, a lack of understanding, and irritation'.[34] This approach has been particularly explicit since rectification. For F. Martínez Heredia, 'Fidel is a collective pseudonym',[35] and he opposes the legitimacy of the revolutionary leadership, the personification of revolutionary consciousness and popular power, to state institutions and their representatives. Far from embodying a kind of Latin American *caudillo*, he claims, Fidel Castro is the expression 'of the cohesion and unity' of the revolutionaries, an element of clarification and 'conscientization', whose moral authority allows him to highlight the 'shortcomings of men and the system' with the aid, it is true, of the party, which is the decisive element in the 'balancing of power with state institutions'. Fidel Castro is thus an institution all by himself, exempt from any responsibility: was it not Castro himself who initiated the process of rectification of errors, considered by Martínez Heredia to be a 'revolution within the revolution'?

Beyond such apologistic examples, this analysis is present in several foreign studies, even though they start from different viewpoints and might lead to separate conclusions. Carlos Franqui, for instance, who can hardly be suspected of sympathy towards the regime, confirms this analysis in his own way. He claims that 'Castroism is a military camp supported by a Soviet-style political apparatus ... a strange union between nationalist and revolutionary *caudillismo* and the Soviet model, from whence is born not the new man, but the new monster'.[36] Hugh Thomas draws a similar conclusion, considering that while political institutions and infrastructure are directly copied from the Soviet Union, the Cuban political system has no equivalent in the Soviet Union or Eastern Europe. Backed by a relatively limited group (only three out of the sixteen members on the PCC Politburo are not former guerrillas from the Sierra Maestra), Fidel Castro's charismatic authoritarianism sanctions the 'political-military pre-eminence of an elite at the centre of the system',[37] with the latter traditionally based on mass organization and mobilization, whose dynamic (unlike that of the Eastern bloc countries) continues to be anti-imperialism and the defence of the revolution's social gains. But, as Hugh Thomas emphasizes, the power of this ruling elite has been eroded by the effects of the institutionalization of the 1970s and by the fact that

> a new generation of Cubans has emerged since 1959. A younger generation of managers, bureaucrats and technocrats is reaching high levels of authority. This new generation differs in many ways from the small guerrilla elite that has ruled for over twenty-five years. As technocrats, their priorities are likely to be somewhat different from those who participated in the revolution. With a greater technical training and less of a guerrilla and siege mentality, it is conceivable that they might place a lower value on political priorities and a greater one on economic development. What this portends for Cuba's future economic performance is not yet clear and in any event is some time away.[38]

The differences in approach between the old guard and the apparatchiks *de nuevo cuño* (of the new generation) were confirmed by the dismissal of Humbero Pérez and the subsequent debate over economic reform and the record of the SDPE. While the differences should not be reduced to splits between economic officials on the one hand, and the political apparatus on the other (for they also run through the latter), there can be no doubt that the market reforms led to a certain weakening of central controls; and in so far as the hypercentralization of the Cuban economy is the counterpart of the centralization of political power, it was predictable that Fidel Castro would not go along with such a development without reacting. Along with this one should also mention Castroite style and methods which simultaneously combine an 'institutionalized anti-institutionalism'[39] – the source of economic disorganization – with the reflexes of a guerrilla given to bouts of impulsiveness. This state of mind still persists, as shown by a poster reproduced in *Bohemia* magazine of 25 August 1989 in which Fidel Castro appears brandishing his gun with the following caption: '"Twelve thousand men were enough to make the revolution," says the man who believed in other men in the most difficult moments. ... History is a wise old woman who teaches what believing means.' Such warlike style and voluntarism are typical. As Jésus Díaz pertinently notes in a study of Cuban cinema, it is 'a device which consists of using violence against reality whatever the price, a feature of Cuban voluntaristic bureaucracy and responsible for many shortcomings in our production'.[40]

This productivist socialism, founded on moral demands, clashes with the extent of privilege and corruption. It leads to repeated denunciations from Fidel Castro, and rectification would merely be another episode of this if the socio-political situation were the same as it was. But on this occasion the changed international situation has given new vigour to a destabilized apparatus that had been doomed to Castroite condemnation, but whose perestroika is bound to encourage the hints of opposition shared by a section of the intelligentsia. The iconoclastic behaviour of young Cuban painters from the Higher Institute of the Arts led to the withdrawal of several paintings from an exhibition in Havana in September 1989: one of them had depicted Fidel Castro speaking to himself in *Plaza de la Revolución* (Revolution Square), multiplied as if in a mirror by thousands of faces.[41]

The banning in August 1989, just a few months after the GDR, of *Moscow News* and *Sputnik* – an unprecedented measure in the history of Cuban–Soviet relations – was as much due to internal tensions as it was to differences with Moscow. It was a warning to anyone who might be tempted to infringe the Castroite credo: 'A single leader – him; a single discipline – his' and 'an unlimited confidence in his actions and words'.[42] Paradoxically, a month earlier, Monsignor Carlos Manuel de Céspedes confirmed in an interview in *Granma* that the Pope would visit Cuba in 1991.[43] He also announced that the government had authorized the Church to reopen a printing house to publish specific publications, catechistic texts and other general teaching pamphlets. In view of its cost, 'the publishing house would probably be financed by the Catholic Church or other institutions from the Federal Republic of Germany and perhaps other countries'. The publications controlled by the Catholic hierarchy and financed by capitalist countries are therefore more favourably looked upon than those of the Soviet 'sister party'.

A statement of the party leadership (published in the international edition of *Granma* on 13 August 1989) justified the ban on ideological and political grounds: the two journals, it claimed, were an apology for bourgeois democracy as a superior form of popular participation; were fascinated by the American way of life; denied the existence of imperialism; valued foreign investment and private property; and questioned internationalism. The statement also noted that such interpretations had found an echo among some ill-informed young people, including certain people pressed to justify their mimicry of the Soviet Union. In order to fight this influence (which was indeed undeniable, for *Moscow News* was disappearing from newsstands instead of rotting there as in the past), the PCC leadership decided to resort to censorship and even recognized that it had had to 'repeatedly dissuade journalists, cadres and specialists who had offered to polemicize with this or that Soviet article or to engage in such a confrontation'. A more explicit recognition could not have been given of the fact that even though the PCC monopolizes the right to expression, it prefers the absence of any debate – even one that is under its control.

What is the correlation of forces within the state apparatus, the key administrative and economic posts, the army and the secret services in this multifaceted conflict? Fidel Castro, of course, controls the political leadership; but Carlos Franqui – in spite of his obsessions and the personal hostility which often blights his analyses – was on target in 1988 with his assertion that 'when the apparatus was not so strong, when Fidel was more popular, he could have challenged the apparatus' and come out on top. Today, however, 'the apparatus is more powerful than Fidel', even though the latter 'who is not an apparatus man, only believes in the revolution and believes that he is the revolution'.[44] This was precisely what Ariel Hidalgo said when he compared Fidel Castro with a madman trying to control the boats out at sea from the coast.[45] Perhaps for the first time he has not accurately gauged the correlation of forces. Following the executions in July 1989 and the eviction of some of the faithful from among his faithful followers, a sword of Damocles clearly hangs over potential opponents wherever they are. But his power has emerged weakened from such an ordeal and the revolution's prestige has been tarnished. Writing in the magazine of the Tupamaros, Alberto Sendic claimed: 'As in other countries, the trial has sown confusion and shaken the left in Uruguay. The Cuban model, the myth of Fidel, have been shattered for a whole generation of activists. Part of our lives and hopes has been buried.'[46] The death sentence, that barbaric punishment, now discredits the regimes which resort to it.

If the Ochoa trial and the banning of *Moscow News* have a common meaning, it is as a warning to all those who might be tempted to believe, as the US administration does,[47] that the 'post-Fidel situation' is already on the agenda, given his age (he is 64). Indeed, it would very much seem that a battle for power has already begun and that some people believe, given the international situation, that they can prepare the succession. The official nomination of Raúl Castro as Second Secretary of the PCC at the Third Party Congress was aimed precisely at keeping leadership problems 'bolted'. Even if there is nothing to confirm that Ochoa or Abrantes had been involved in a political struggle, their condemnation has led to everyone being aware that in a short period of time any leader can be sent back to the ranks, and, indeed, even imprisoned or executed. The conflict does not necessarily set two ideologically identifiable factions against each other, but rather all those who, rightly or wrongly, question Fidel Castro's embodiment of revolutionary legitimacy – that machine which sometimes crushes the government's opponents just as coldly as it does its most faithful collaborators.[48]

So why should a distinction be made between Fidel Castro and a Ceausescu-style despot, for example? One can bear in mind, of course, that Ceausescu, as a pure product of bureaucracy, has never been anywhere near leading a victorious revolution. That is the main difference, but it is not the only one. There is a Robespierrist dimension to Fidel Castro that might seem anachronistic, but which has been noticed by Herbert Matthews, one of the first chroniclers of Castroism.[49] Indeed, the pertinence of the comparison lies in the huge significance of the contradictions involved in such a radical revolutionary process in an underdeveloped country having had to combine the completion of its formation as a nation with its economic and social emancipation. The Castroite slogan of year one of the revolution – 'Neither freedom without bread, nor bread without freedom!' – thus provides an explanation for André Malraux's comment: 'In every case where the revolution was not carried out by the proletariat but by the people, the lessons of the French Revolution ... retain a prestige that is at least equal to that of Marxism.'[50]

Fidel Castro has always been a great admirer of 'the Incorruptible' and his prison letters were surprisingly premonitory:

> Robespierre was an idealist and honest right up to his death. With the revolution in peril, the borders surrounded everywhere by enemies, traitors ready to attack from behind, and waverers blocking advance, it was necessary to be harsh, inflexible and severe. It is better to sin out of excess than by default, for it is the latter that can lead to defeat. A few months of terror were needed to end a terror that had lasted for centuries. Cuba needs many Robespierres.[51]

That was five years before the seizure of power. In 1989, the press highlighted the particular significance of the Bicentenary – with its emblem of the Phrygian cap – for Cuba. Several books have been published in homage to the French Jacobins, first and foremost *Robespierre* by G. Walter. Even though the historical analogies are inevitably limited, one can only be struck by the similarity of the concerns. The besieged fortress syndrome is a key one. Can this be dismissed with a wave of the hand as some observers, including Soviet observers, do? While the danger of armed intervention is highly unlikely in the immediate future, the embargo reinforced by Reagan is as rigid as ever; economic retaliation measures are still just as severe; and the US threat remains latent.

For the first time in thirty years, regular deliveries from the Soviet Union are no longer assured. In envisaging, on 26 July 1989, the hypothesis of a complete isolation of Cuba, was Fidel Castro engaging in a simple manoeuvre aimed at stirring up national sentiment among the population? Yes and no. Yes, in the sense that recourse to anti-imperialist mobilization and the defence of sovereignty are the Cuban leader's best trump cards in an extremely difficult situation, and he has always used them to get out of a tight corner. No, if one looks, from the perspective of the Third World countries in general and Cuba in particular, at the dangers incurred by a policy in which two superpowers are involved in negotiating peace 'while continuing the war against the small progressive countries'.[52] When Fidel Castro dreads, in the light of the difficulties – indeed, collapse – of the Soviet regime, that the US administration and the Soviets might decide that the time has come to 'make Cuba pay the price for thirty years of revolution'; when he comments on Bush's triumphant visit to Poland – in which Bush was greeted with placards proclaiming that 'the best communist is a dead communist' – he is without doubt right to fear that 'such euphoria might increase the aggressiveness and hostility of imperialism towards Cuba'.[53]

As the PCI leader Gerardo Chiaromonte points out.

> Fidel Castro's positions also show desperation. It is not just a question of his person and the regime he has created. The Cuban leader remains the man who, a few years ago, raised the problem of the Third World countries' (unpayable) debt. There have been recent attempts to raise the issue in new terms, but such efforts have merely been sporadic. The imbalance between North and South has grown and become more dramatic. The Third and Fourth Worlds feel even more isolated, and view the new peace and disarmament situation with mistrust. Is this attitude fair? I do not think so. But it is shared by other countries, not just Cuba.[54]

The Shadow of Saturn

The revolution's survival, however, also depends on the struggle against the bureaucratic monster which has revealed all its flaws. The strength of the latter's inertia demonstrates that, in order to be shaken, it will need more than the *máximo líder* making threats, placing people under surveillance and, indeed, punishing them – measures that, in the long run, weaken his power and might lead to his downfall. Like his model, Fidel Castro only recognizes two groups: 'the one containing good citizens, and the one containing bad';[55] those who are models of austerity and dedication, who lead a modest life and are devoted to him, and the rest – 'the malignant cells that must be eliminated'. To paraphrase Trotsky's judgement of Robespierre: Fidel Castro would like a republic of reason and virtue as part of bureaucratic domination; he would like to sustain the peak of revoluionary élan by instituting the state of siege; and he would like equality while retaining his monopoly of power. He is thus 'seated on the cutting edge of a huge contradiction and calls to his aid the blade of the guillotine'.[56]

Voluntaristic subjectivity sanctions ignorance of the conditions under which social relations could be truly transformed in the transition to socialism. As with the Jacobins, purge is a key word of Fidel Castro, who should nevertheless remember that the Thermidorians' success was facilitated by the growing isolation of the Robespierrists from the masses. Instead of letting differences express themselves (allowing the masses to learn from experience and educate themselves in order to mobilize) and thus relying on the support of the only social force capable of disarticulating the nomenklatura, the commander-in-chief has made a clean sweep. Instead of stopping, the purge has continued. The Vice-Chairman of the State Committee for Finance, the Deputy Minister of Agriculture, the Deputy Minister of Basic Industry and the Minister of Construction have been dismissed for inefficiency or incompetence.[57] The train and air disasters in the summer of 1989 led to new expulsions: the general manager of the Union of Cuban Railways, two regional managers and several other officials from the Ministry of Transport were sanctioned, while a train driver and some other workers were taken to court.[58] Once again, instead of encouraging the control of working and safety conditions by the workers themselves, the opposite path was chosen – that of repression from above, the inefficiency of which no longer needs demonstrating.

Moscow News bothered the Cuban leader for several reasons. What would Cuban workers have thought on reading the June 1989 issue? This carried a report on a meeting in Moscow of groups of workers discussing the creation of an independent trade union, with one delegate criticizing the official trade union. 'Who proposes the candidacy of the trade union leader? – generally, the party secretary. Who does the president of the regional council of trade unions consult on the most important issues? – the regional committee of the party.' Cuban workers would have thought that their situation was not very different. Indeed, like an echo, the preparatory text of the Sixteenth CTC Congress stated that 'several administrative managers did not attach the necessary importance to workers' participation during the discussion of plans in the production assemblies, pay little attention to workers' proposals'[59] and see to it that the machinery provided for workers' participation in the preparation, control and execution of economic plans is merely formal.

The spokesman of equality and the prophet of virtue is now faced with radical choices. But can he break with his own history and renounce the traditions that he himself has put in place? His recent international decisions, however provisional they may be – for his pragmatism can lead him to change his mind from one day to the next – do not give cause for optimism. Although the GDR was a privileged commercial ally, how does one account for Fidel Castro rallying round an anti-Gorbachev campaign at Honecker's side before the popular upsurge and the crisis? Whatever his disagreements, he is usually more prudent. Was he banking on Gorbachev's fall, or at least on a setback in his current policy that would force him to change direction? Does he think it is in his interests, internationally, to bolster the opposition camp as a means of retaliating against the acts of aggression suffered by Cuba? His attacks on Poland and Hungary have not been gratuitous. The dispute with the latter country has become publicly embittered[60] after Hungarian enterprises unilaterally changed the terms of their commercial trade with Cuba and increased prices by 20 per cent from one year to the next. Such moves have led the Cuban government to fear a breakdown of the agreements reached within the CMEA framework.

Fidel Castro's public recognition of arms deliveries to Nicaragua[61] following Moscow's commitment to suspend its own deliveries[62] was a provocation to Soviet diplomacy and a challenge to Gorbachev. The latter cannot disregard Cuba's clout and influence, mainly in the Third World, but also with other communist parties (take, for example, the repercussions on opponents of the French Communist Party like A. Moroni, who circulated important extracts of Fidel Castro's 26 July 1989 speech). But while the Castro leadership was prone to such gestures in the past (it delivered military equipment to the Algerian FLN when it was struggling for independence, even though Soviet arms were supposed to remain under the control of the Soviet Union), it cannot afford such adventures in an international context characterized 'by the improvement of international peace'.[63] This was what the Soviet Foreign Minister, Eduard Shevardnadze, opportunely reminded Havana during a brief stop after talks with the US Secretary of State, James Baker. The latter had insisted on the Soviet Union fulfilling its commitments in Central America and ensuring that its allies did the same.[64] And Soviet diplomacy has made no bones about doing this.

Events in the GDR – one of his most trusted allies – in October 1989, however, should lead Fidel Castro to reflect on the irreversible development of bureaucratized societies; all the more so because the Socialist Unity Party (SED) could not be suspected of heterodoxy in the eyes of the Cubans. The commander-in-chief cannot fail to have asked himself whether the exacerbation of tensions could lead, if not to demonstrations in Cuba, at least to the emergence of confrontation along similar lines.

As we have said, there can be no doubt that the Ochoa trial and the current purges are a sword of Damocles hanging over the heads of possible 'troublemakers'. For the time being, only the top levels of the hierarchy have been affected by the purge, and that is why analogies with the repression that took place during the Cultural Revolution in China are misplaced. Such a development in the island is difficult to imagine after the precedent of Grenada and when a million Cubans live in 'Little Havana' (the nickname given to Cuban Miami by the exiles). Fidel Castro has frequently repeated: 'If one day the revolution was to no longer enjoy the majority support of the population, it would not be able to survive. This revolution cannot be maintained by force.'[65]

A Cuban version of the Terror, then, could only lead to a tragic repetition of Thermidor in 1789. Fidel Castro is undoubtedly haunted by this danger; and, on a more subjective level, he cannot be unaware of the tragic fate of Latin American *caudillos*. Yet the path to which he is committed is leading him up a cul-de-sac. Apart from voluntary work, microbrigades and the struggle for a hypothetical better future, something else is now needed to mobilize young people who represent half the population. With the withdrawal of troops from Angola and Ethiopia, overseas battles no longer represent an outlet that occasionally provided a distraction from cultural anaesthesia and political immobility. The stagnation of revolutionary processes in Latin America – even if it is only temporary – limits the revolutionary engagement of days gone by. The time of Briones Montotos (the name of a young Cuban who fell at the time of Cuban arms deliveries to the Venezuelan guerrilla war in 1967) would seem to be in the past. The anti-imperialist discourse of yesteryear echoes in a void.

Of course, the Castroite leadership has no hand in this, except by overestimating the mistakes committed at the time of *foquismo*. Without minimizing the effects of this, they cannot be held responsible for current difficulties, the impact of which is being heavily felt by the Cuban Revolution. This continental exhaustion is suffocating the revolution. Young people are suffering the consequences head on; and if those in power cannot even offer alternatives, there is absolutely no point in blaming the substitutes for rebellion when youth ridicule the symbolic values of the regime, or in attacking 'anti-social elements'. In a country like Cuba, which proclaims its intention to build socialism, to resist and survive in an environment that will be unfavourable for at least a few years to come, such a project cannot be granted or imposed without something in return. For the new generations and their rebellious potential to blossom, the old methods and schema, as well as the material and political privileges of the caste denounced by the PCC leadership, must be abolished. If he wishes to avoid sinking, the old leader must not delay any longer in taking advantage of rectification to rectify his own power before it is too late; a power that is becoming sclerotic, for 'the upheavals caused by the Ochoa trial show, if it needed showing, that the political project and collective aspirations no longer coincide'.[66]

Notes

1. Fidel Castro, *Central Report to the First PCC Congress*.
2. Ibid. This reference was also used by Osmany Cienfuegos during the session of the Council of State which ratified the death sentence for Ochoa and the three officials from the Ministry of the Interior (*Granma*, 23 July 1989, p. 5).
3. *Le Monde*, 8 August 1989.
4. *Le Monde*, 2 August 1989.
5. *Granma*, 16 July 1989.
6. *Granma*, 23 July 1989.
7. Fidel Castro, in an interview with a US academic and a US congressman in 1985, Editora Política, Havana, quoted by Juan Marrero, in *Cuba Socialista*, March/April 1988.
8. *Cuba Socialista*, March/April 1988.
9. Provided by the Mexican magazine, *Proceso*, such information has been verbally challenged by Chilean exiles in Paris.
10. An understanding of, and self-criticism for, the mistakes committed were part of the attenuating circumstances recognized. See in this regard, Jorge Valls, *Mon ennemi, mon frère*.
11. *Le Monde*, 20–21 August 1989.
12. *Granma*, 16 July 1989.
13. He was referring to the airports built as an emergency to prepare for the Cuito Cuanavale offensive and the reinforcement of air forces, whose decisive role against the South African army had been recognized by Fidel Castro.
14. *Granma*, 16 July 1989.
15. *Granma*, 5 December 1988.
16. *Mate Amargo*, journal of the Tupamaros, 2 August 1989.
17. *Granma*, 23 July 1989.
18. Alberto Sendic, in *Mate Amargo*, 2 August 1989.
19. *El País*, 15 September 1987.
20. *Globe*, November 1989.
21. *Granma*, 16 July 1989.
22. *Central Report to the Second PCC Congress*.
23. *El País*, 1 August 1989.
24. Pedro Miret, 'Statement to the Council of State', in *Granma*, 23 July 1989.
25. *Granma*, 10 September 1989.
26. *Nouvelle Revue internationale (Problèmes de la paix et du socialisme)*, September 1989.
27. *Granma*, 8 October 1989.
28. Since this chapter was written, the CTC Congress has taken place. Former general

secretary, Roberto Veiga, was replaced by a newcomer, Pedro Ross, before the congress had even taken place.

29. *El País*, 3 August 1989.
30. *El País*, 1 August 1989.
31. *Herald Tribune*, 2 October 1989.
32. *El País*, 12 July 1989.
33. P. de Charentenay, 'Eglise et Etat à Cuba', in *Etudes*, December 1988.
34. *Granma*, 2 October 1988.
35. Martínez Heredia, *Desafíos del socialismo cubano.*
36. Carlos Franqui, *Vie, aventures et désastres d'un certain Fidel Castro.*
37. Hugh Thomas, Georges A. Fauriol, Juan Carlos Weiss, *La revolución cubana 25 años después.*
38. Ibid.
39. Hugh Thomas, Georges A. Fauriol, Juan Carlos Weiss, *La revolución cubana 25 años después.*
40. Jésus Díaz, *Les défits de la contemporaneité: notes sur le cinéma de fiction cubain*, forthcoming.
41. *Le Soir*, 24 September 1989.
42. Carlos Franqui, *Vie, aventures et désastres d'un certain Fidel Castro.*
43. *Granma*, of July 1989. This visit has since been postponed indefinitely.
44. Carlos Franqui, *Vie, aventures et désastres d'un certain Fidel Castro.*
45. Ariel Hidalgo, 'Cuba, l'Etat marxiste et la nouvelle classe', 1984, mimeograph.
46. Alberto Sendic, in *Mate Amargo*, 2 August 1989.
47. Philip Brenner, 'Cuba after Fidel' in *Nacla Report on the Americas*, New York, March/April 1989.
48. J. Valls. *Mon ennemi, mon frère.*
49. Herbert Matthews, *Fidel Castro.*
50. André Malraux, *L'Anti-mémoires.*
51. Fidel Castro, from the prison of the Isle of Pines, 23 March 1954, quoted by C. Franqui, *Journal de la révolution cubaine.*
52. Fidel Castro, in *Granma*, 26 July 1989.
53. Ibid.
54. Gerardo Chiaromonte, in *L'Unità*, 17 August 1989.
55. Speech of Maximilien Robespierre on the 8 Thermidor, quoted by Trotsky, *Nos tâches politiques.*
56. Trotsky, 'Non pas jacobin et social-démocrate, mais jacobin ou social-démocrate', *Nos tâches politiques.*
57. *Granma*, 20 August 1989.
58. *Granma*, 17 September 1989.
59. *Granma*, 8 October 1989.
60. 'Disgraceful path', in *Granma*, 1 October 1989.
61. *Le Monde*, 5 October 1989.
62. *Le Monde*, 6 October 1989. National Bank of Cuba, February 1985.
63. *Granma*, 15 October 1989.
64. *Le Monde*, 5 October 1989.
65. Interview given to Jeffrey Elliot, professor of the University of North Carolina, and Mervin Dymally, member of the US Congress, March 1985, Havana.
66. I. Ramonet, in *Le Monde diplomatique*, September 1989.

8

The Interrupted Debate

Marxists had certainly not anticipated that the first socialist revolution in the Western Hemisphere would take place on a small island with ten million inhabitants and an underdeveloped and dependent economy. If the Russian Revolution was already a paradox – its survival seen as being linked to the development of other revolutionary processes in the more developed countries of Europe – what can be said of Cuba?

After thirty years, there have been considerable gains. Cuba is recognized as the 'most advanced welfare state in the Third World'[1] in terms of living standards and the social protection of the population. And that is no mean achievement for a revolution which has taken place under the nose of the United States.

For Cuba, which was one of the last countries to break with Hispanic domination, this emancipation from the imperialist yoke was the final episode in the creation of a national entity. Frustrated by US intervention, the last war of national liberation had produced a stunted offspring, a neo-colonial republic, a sort of US protectorate. It is no coincidence that Fidel Castro has always invoked José Martí, 'the intellectual author of the 26th of July Movement', and that the Moncada generation gave itself the title of the 'Generation of the Centennial': between the death of Martí and the takeover, sixty years went by, the Sierra Maestra continued the wars of independence, and the liberation war was undertaken in order to fight what Fidel Castro would later describe in 1973 as a 'process of destruction of our nationality'.

The Cuban Revolution draws its strength from these two sources: on the one hand, the end of humiliation and the winning back of national dignity and sovereignty; and on the other, the end of poverty and the achievement of social gains – free health care and education for all, and the right to work. For the peoples of the small dependent capitalist countries of the so-called 'periphery', the Cuban experience has represented a huge symbol of hope.

Yet since the advent of Gorbachev, the future now seems more uncertain, both for reasons relating to the international situation and because the political limits of the Cuban experience are becoming much clearer.

Internationally, the revolution has survived for thirty years as a result of the popular support enjoyed by the regime, but also because of the balance of forces between the United States and the Soviet Union in the wake of the Second World War, as was illustrated by the October 1962 missile crisis. While Cuba could be struck off the map by a US intervention, as in the past, without the Soviet army intervening, the fact that the island has not been invaded since the missile crisis has sanctioned such a balance. This does not mean that US imperialism has given up on re-establishing its influence in its 'back yard', as has already been made clear by Reagan's plans following the victory of the Nicaraguan Revolution. Bush's declarations in April 1989 that the Soviet Union has no 'legitimate interests' in Latin America – unlike the United States which has 'many'; the US refusal to cease all intervention in Central America in return for a halt of all military aid, whatever its source; its insistence on emphasizing the strategic nature of the region and making it a touchstone in disarmament negotiations with the Soviet Union – are all there to remind those who might have forgotten that the Monroe Doctrine is not dead.

Central America and the Caribbean, in spite of their weak economic power, are one of the crucial features of the global horse-trading between the United States and the Soviet Union. This has been not just a question of preventing any revolutionary victory in El Salvador, but of using economic, political and military pressures to strangle the Nicaraguan Revolution. No one can predict the consequences for Cuba should it be isolated in this way.

Given such a context, comments on the 'excessively high' nature of the Cuban military budget in the light of the new international 'climate' are either incredibly naïve or irresponsibly suspect. Soviet allusions (particularly in the magazine *New Times*) display both a high-powered arrogance and a thinly veiled lack of interest. The latter is more apparent as regards Nicaragua and the 'Tom Thumb of Central America', as El Salvador is nicknamed.

The Soviet government condemned the offensive of the FMLN in November 1989 and Cuba's military aid: 'The Soviet Union has never delivered arms to the FMLN or any other rebel movement in Central America, and nor is it prepared to do so.' And it added: 'With the aim of facilitating a political settlement in the region, the Soviet Union has even stopped delivering arms to Nicaragua.'[3] Accused of exporting revolution, Fidel Castro had given a completely different response on 21 May 1967:

> They accuse us of wanting to disturb order in this continent, and indeed, we proclaim the historic need of peoples to disturb the order established by imperialism in Latin America and the rest of the world. They accuse us of advocating the revolutionary overthrow of established governments in Latin America, and indeed, we believe that all oligarchic governments – led by reactionaries with or without uniform who are the servants of imperialism and accomplices of its crimes – must be swept aside by the revolutionary struggle of peoples. They accuse us of helping the revolutionary movement, and indeed we give and will continue – as often as we are asked – to give help to revolutionary movements struggling against imperialism anywhere in the world. We will never accept the status quo that imperialism intends to impose on humanity. Nor will we accept its draconian laws or its morality of the unscrupulous pedlar. Our right is the right of peoples to emancipate themselves from exploitation and slavery, the right of humanity to rebel against the aggression and crimes of imperialism as the main bastion of reaction in the world.[4]

Apart from the different political circumstances, the difference in language is due to the respective situation of the two countries: the Soviet Union is a superpower which these days is only worried about itself; Cuba is a small 'peripheral' country, an anomaly of history that is still unacceptable to US imperialism, especially at a time when the Soviet leadership has been hailing the 'democratic' politics of the United States.

Given this context, a fundamental question is raised: can such a revolution survive without the spread of revolution? Can it survive without bureaucratic distortions? And if the latter are inevitable, how should they be fought?

Yes to Glasnost

'Human rights' violations have been the subject of repeated, and occasionally deceitful, condemnation by the Western media. In Cuba today, there is no mass terror, 'murder and systematic torture as ... in other parts of Latin America'.[5] The report of the UN Human Rights Commission exempts Cuba from the most serious allegations made by the United States in 1987 and 1988 over the number of political prisoners, executions or disappearances.[6] According to the report of the UN Human Rights Commission, the limits imposed on democratic rights may range from the loss of one's job to imprisonment, as well as systematic harassment and 'acts of repudiation' (insults, attacks on one's home) against those considered opponents of the regime, including applicants to emigrate.[7]

Since the advent of Gorbachev, the denunciation of Stalinism has highlighted the damaging effects of monolithic one-party rule on a massive scale. In Prague as in Berlin, the constitutionally recognized leading role of the party has been abrogated. The insurrection in Peking in May 1989, followed by the huge anti-bureaucratic demonstrations in the GDR and Czechoslovakia have confirmed the topicality of the struggle for socialist democracy.

In such a context, Fidel Castro is caught in the trap of his own ideas. Faced with the democratic challenge of Gorbachev, he has criticized perestroika and kept quiet over glasnost. Yet the authoritarian-charismatic exercise of power in force since 1959 is in crisis, even though criticism is sharper among the intelligentsia than among the popular masses who still attribute responsibility for errors to Fidel Castro's entourage rather than to the leader himself. But he is on the defensive, basing his response on the social gains made, and silent on the demands of the new generations. His response during Gorbachev's visit – 'If I'm Stalin, then my victims are doing well'[8] – was both dismissive and cynical given that the testimonies of former prisoners who reported ill-treatment have never been refuted.

Above all, he does not offer any prospect for the aspirations of youth and the artists and intellectuals. He does not respond to the campaigns led by the Western press, and thus makes the defence of the revolution more difficult. The tide will not be turned by invoking the ephemeral 'victories'[9] won in the UN Human Rights Commission in Geneva. Such moves against Cuba, coming from a government that has been responsible for massacres in Vietnam and has supported every dictatorship in Latin America, from Argentina to Chile and from El Salvador to arming the contras in Nicaragua, are indeed sickening. But there is no glory in Cuba availing itself of the votes of the Iraqi, Colombian, Peruvian or Mexican governments. One would have expected the denunciation of such a diplomatic farce. It would have been better not to have to bargain for the support of some and the neutrality of others.

For while political repression in Cuba has nothing at all to do with Stalinist repression, it undoubtedly exists. It consists mainly in the repression of written propaganda and the proscription of any organized group which is not in agreement with the official line. These restrictions on freedom of expression and the right to organize have even led to imprisonment, as has been shown by every inquiry and all recent testimonies. It must be pointed out, however, that there has been an improvement in the situation, as has been stressed by all commentators, and that most political prisoners have been freed over the last two years.

Nevertheless, the new tolerance enjoyed by the two human rights commissions in Havana (given that they are tiny groups, the threat is not very great), as well as the recognition of the Church as a new interlocutor are merely a substitute: socialist democracy does not form part of Castroite ideas, and this tolerance might only be temporary. The execution of Ochoa and three officers, the detention of several leaders and the arrest of opponents for spreading rumours are a bad omen.

Gorbachev's offensive has put the Castro leadership on the defensive and has produced further mistrust on the part of the international labour movement. The defence of the socialism and the Marxism-Leninism that Fidel Castro would like to embody ('Marxism-Leninism or death!', he exclaimed in 1988) can only be effective and credible in the current international situation in so far as it takes up the gauntlet thrown down by the new General Secretary of the CPSU. The condemnation of the damaging effects of market reforms, or of a conception of peace in which the latter is achieved on the backs of oppressed peoples, would gain popularity. But the example of Nicaragua – where opposition parties and press were authorized, in spite of the existence of an armed counter-revolution – is there to demonstrate that, even in an acute crisis, a certain political democracy is possible. 'No to perestroika! Yes to glasnost!' is the only response to those in the international labour movement and Cuba itself who see market reforms as the sole path to democratic salvation. This would also provide the framework for a truly internationalist offensive that would allow the Cuban Revolution to grow in prestige and break its current isolation.

In the absence of such a response, questions have been asked as to the possible links between Castro and Ligachev and the conservatives of the different communist parties. The simultaneous presence of Georges Marchais and representatives of the Czech, East German and Portuguese communist parties in Havana did indeed suggest such a possibility. But this attempt to create a common front of conservatives on an international scale has collapsed with the Berlin Wall. Though it's a phoney song, Georges Marchais is humming the tune of glasnost. And Fidel Castro is too dependent on Soviet aid. Austerity, economic restructuring, and increased efficiency and productivity – these are the needs of the moment.

The Transition to Socialism and Underdevelopment

Thirty years on, an assessment can be made of the difficulties encountered in the construction of socialism in a small underdeveloped country like Cuba. In the absence of a general theory of transition,[10] these lessons are all the more important because the liabilities of the bureaucratized societies (whose 'actually existing socialism' represents a terrifying perversion[11]), the revelation of Stalinist crimes on a massive scale, Pol Potism, the discredit surrounding Vietnam, as well as the repression of the insurrection in Peking, have all helped to sustain doubts as to the possibility of building socialism as envisaged by the founders of Marxism and invoked in the following terms by the first constitution of the Russian Soviet Federal Socialist Republic: 'To abolish the exploitation of man by man and to institute socialism in which neither class nor state will exist.'[12]

Such a society, without classes, state or market production (or a very limited market production) does not exist anywhere in the world. Indeed, it would presuppose the fulfilment of at least two conditions: that the construction of socialism be undertaken in countries that were already industrialized; and that this process, in order to survive, be extended to several other countries.

What has been proved is that the seizure of power and the overthrow of the bourgeoisie by forces claiming the support of the proletariat were possible, even in extremely difficult conditions; indeed, conditions that had not been anticipated by Marxist theorists. The geographical fatalism condemning the peoples of the dominated countries to wait for the go-ahead from revolutionary victories in the imperialist countries was halted. Such was this victory that a theory even emerged – based on the rise of colonial revolution in the 1960s – that revolutionary breakthroughs would spread 'from the periphery to the centre'.

Today, the significance of these victories is forgotten, and only the price paid in terms of economic, social and political difficulties is remembered. This price would already seem to be a deterrent for the developed countries (to the extent that, in terms of democracy, no so-called 'socialist' country has been in a position to prove its superiority – indeed, far from it). But the experience would even seem to be uncertain in the underdeveloped countries. Indeed, unlike Cuba, the human cost in Vietnam or Nicaragua has been very high and the social gains meagre. The result is in line with the goal sought by US imperialism.

What, then, are the major problems for the transition to socialism in the underdeveloped countries, as registered by the Cuban experience and the reflections of certain Nicaraguan theorists (particulary Orlando Nuñez)?

The contradiction between the victory of socialist revolution in a few countries and the survival of capitalism in the rest of the world has had a serious effect. Relations with the world market and the pressure of the capitalist environment are particularly felt in a country like Cuba, which is dependent on its foreign trade and whose economic strategy has relied from the beginning on agro-exports. As Carlos M. Vilas points out, the two development strategies for the small 'peripheral' countries – the agro-exporter option, or that based on broadening the domestic market and satisfying the basic social needs of the population – both assume

> the maintenance of a minimum import capability for the productive apparatus to function; they mean that the countries are forced to maintain the production of exportable goods, even at a loss, with the sole aim of earning foreign exchange for imports. The vulnerability of these economies to the fluctuations and instability of the international market is very high, for increasing exports to compensate for a fall in prices leads to further price falls, and thus to the need to further increase the quantity of exports. This situation points to the urgent need of these economies for an external rearticulation as a precondition for the viability of internal transformations. ... Only access to significant, flexible and cheap foreign co-operation can enable the revolutions that have taken place in the small, backward and peripheral countries to overcome this stage.[13]

Economic difficulties have been joined by social and ideological pressures. Fidel Castro has repeated that the model of consumption (if it is in fact a 'model') existing in the industrialized countries is not within the reach of the underdeveloped countries: 'Perhaps one of the tragedies of Third World countries is that they covet the consumption of the developed capitalist societies. ... It is a dream, an illusion. If you want the abundant material wealth we need and want, you have to work, you have to work hard. Labour productivity must be raised. All human and material resources must be used rationally.'[14] This realistic discourse clashes with the attraction that the consumer society exerts on the popular masses, and the Western media take advantage of their vague feeling of dissatisfaction to proclaim the 'defeat of socialism'. The US government uses the visits of Cuban exiles in Miami with consummate skill to encourage this sense of frustration. Radio Martí – broadcasting from Miami – and the project to beam television to Havana, both share the same objectives. The fact that rationing – in a context of shortages caused among other reasons by the US embargo – has enabled equal mass access to certain basic goods to be preserved is conjured away. Free access to health care and education have similarly been maintained; and in the case of the latter, the comparison with other underdeveloped countries is illuminating.

The survival of bourgeois distribution patterns and their related contradictions surely amounts to one of the most complex problems. The relation between wage policy and increasing productivity, and the role of monetary incentives, were at the centre of the great economic debate in Cuba in 1965. The articulation between individual and collective monetary incentives, the method of distributing popular consumer goods, the relation between qualifications obtained and prospects available, the system of professional promotion (seniority, work performance, voluntary work, participation in defence activities) are just some of the unresolved problems which are leading to serious social tensions.

What is the real content of the phrase ' To each according to his or her work'? How should each person's reward be decided? How should the quantity and quality of work done be defined? 'How can it be objectively determined that the "quality" of the work of a manager, a minister, an academic, a marshal or, indeed, a prima ballerina is worth ten times more than the quantity of work of a metalworker or a computer operator?'[15] This was one of Che's preoccupations, not in terms of his supposed opposition to monetary incentives (he spoke of the 'correct use' of monetary incentives), but in terms of his insistence on limiting their effects, as well as his advocacy of the development of voluntary work, particularly for leaders.

But problems of work organization, one of the central issues of Cuban rectification (and of perestroika), will not find any solution if they are approached from a bureaucratic perspective.

The irony and scepticism of many commentators towards this approach is merely because it has been deformed by history – principally Stalinist bureaucracy and Stakhanovist degeneration. When Fidel Castro today engages in apologias for this, his proclamations appear laughable in view of the huge waste and bureaucratic incompetence. Yet at the risk of appearing old-fashioned, it is worth recalling the spirit in which Lenin advocated 'Red Saturdays', communist emulation, voluntary work for communists. This moral dynamic has gone astray. But the problem of the 'driving force' of a society in transition – in other words, the motivation of the men and women who provide its impetus – is there.

Even in the Soviet Union 'experience has shown that incentive methods, used so far in a purely material form, were unable to avoid a steady sag in the growth of labour productivity'.[16] Gorbachev is also aware of this problem, claiming that 'the elements of social corrosion that have appeared in recent years have had a negative effect on the population's state of mind. ... The inevitable result has been a fall in interest in collective values, signs of indifference and scepticism, a weakening of the role of moral incentives at work.'[17]

In so far as the masses themselves will take responsibility for the debate over how society is to be built, it is conceivable that they will implement the decisions they take. Democracy will thus be able to become the instrument of economic adjustment. It will finally play its true role as a political stimulant, representing not just the sum total of civil rights, but the organization of society itself.

... No to Perestroika

Since the beginning of the rectification process, Fidel Castro has repeated *ad nauseam* that it is a major mistake to rely on 'economic mechanisms' to lead society forward towards socialism. Cuban officials have frequently recalled that Lenin only saw the New Economic Policy as a transitory expedient. Opposed to perestroika, the speeches of the years 1986 and 1987 were undoubtedly influenced at the international level by the Chinese experience (which had led to an exacerbation of social tensions), and at a national level by the implementation of market reforms which were nonetheless very limited in relation to what had been introduced in China. Yet in spite of the differences between the two countries in terms of scale, the effects of the market reforms were similar, with the emergence of inequalities, privileges and corruption. Beyond a certain threshold, basic social gains won following the takeover were challenged.

It was no coincidence that the Chinese 'May '89' began with bitter denunciations by the students: 'Down with official racketeering!', 'Down with corrupt officials!', 'Long live the people, down with official privileges!' These slogans were then taken up by the students and workers in the GDR ('*Vopos* to the factory!') and in Czechoslovakia where a purge of the top levels of the bureaucracy was demanded.

Contrary to what interested parties would have us believe, the exceptional thing about the Chinese May was not just the demand for freedom, but the combined demands for political freedoms and social equality. The subversive nature of these demands was lost on no one, whether the bureaucracies in power or the bourgeois leaderships of the capitalist countries. Such a combination, which should be embodied by a truly socialist society, has so far not existed anywhere. And that is why the dynamics of the anti-bureaucratic movement in China and the Eastern bloc countries are one of the most outstanding events of this last quarter of a century.

The political democratization at work in the bureaucratized states of the East has been accompanied by considerable illusions regarding the ability of the 'free market' to solve the economic crisis. The blind laws of the market appear even more clear-sighted than the great army of bureaucrats which is supposed to plan and manage the economy rationally!

The Chinese experience has put a spanner in the works. It has confirmed, in spite of initial positive results in agriculture, that market mechanisms combined with the scourge of bureaucracy can only lead to an impasse.[18] That is the lesson that all governments are trying to obscure. For their part, Bush and the European leaders have declared that events in China confirmed that there can be no freedom without free enterprise.

As far as Gorbachev is concerned, the Chinese experience has shown that market reforms cannot be effective without political reforms; it was the absence of the latter which was at the root of the Chinese crisis. The Soviet leadership has understood that, in order to strengthen the credibility of an economic project whose effects might question social benefits and be a source of destabilization, institutions must be given a new legitimacy by democratizing the political system. The major significance of the Chinese conflict has served as a warning and encouraged reflection and prudence.

Yet China had been a model for the advocates of 'market socialism', which was seen as being especially suited to the underdeveloped countries, particularly in the area of agriculture. The results in the wake of the Maoist experience of the Great Leap Forward had been positive enough. But this experience was already being questioned in Cuba where a negative judgement had been made on the experience of free markets – the most noteworthy of the reforms undertaken at the start of the 1980s. The attempt at market reform had been carried out even though the existence of large plantations and a waged agricultural workforce had led to the development of collective solutions in the countryside, enabled real advances to be made in productivity in certain sectors (for example, increases in egg output, improvements in cattle breeding), and contributed to a relative diversification of agriculture. Nevertheless, small private farmers still remained and they played a significant role in the production of particular food products. Pressure was put on small and medium farmers to rejoin the co-operatives, but no form of coercion was used, even though the eventual goal was their gradual decline rather than consolidation as a social group.

The initial aim of the free markets once they had been introduced was to stimulate food production and improve supplies to the towns. The experience ended up a semi-failure. This improvement merely benefited the most privileged sectors of the population who already enjoyed high incomes which enabled them to acquire foodstuffs occasionally sold at prohibitive prices. Socially, the effects were disastrous. Corrupt middlemen and speculators prospered, farmers got wealthy, and the process of integration into the co-operatives was interrupted. Social divisions threatened the alliance between the urban masses and the farmers.

The increased use of monetary incentives in a country subject to severe restrictions on imports due to a lack of foreign exchange led Cuba to an impasse. How could they provide an incentive to produce more when the consumer goods capable of satisfying the aspirations of the population were not available? Likewise, the advocacy of material rewards for enterprise managers merely exacerbated the perverse effects of bureaucratic planning, as well as the distortions in the assessment of the results achieved.

In Nicaragua the adjustment and stabilization plan introduced in 1988 was a patent failure, with the *Agencia Nueva Nicaragua* speaking of general bankruptcy and the collapse of industrial production.[19] There was enormous financial speculation, employment and wages fell dramatically, and certain gains of the revolution were under threat. Was the mixed economy in the process of becoming mixed poverty? Nicaragua was on the verge of bankruptcy. Yet the Soviet ambassador hailed the process of 'economic co-operation' with the private sector as highly positive and the Soviet Union declared its readiness to co-operate – not with the Nicaraguan state, but with the private sector 'which controls most of the country's productive apparatus ... in so far as all productive forces must take part in the struggle against inflation and to increase production'.[20] This was somewhat ironical in view of the record, with Deputy Industry Minister Gilberto Guzmán pointing out that, since 1980, private investment in industry had represented a mere $60 million, or 7 per cent of the whole of public investment!

Such decisions by the Soviet Union in the field of economic co-operation (the implicit glorification of the market economy as the means to improve economic efficiency), as well as their corollary at the political level (a halt in arms deliveries while the US Congress maintained 'humanitarian' aid to the contras) can only give rise to doubts and questions.

Socialism in Question?

The extreme difficulties of Cuba and Nicaragua, the Chinese crisis, as well as the recognition by East European leaders of the bankrupt nature of their bureaucratized societies, give credibility to the idea that there has been a 'defeat of socialism'. In Eastern Europe, 'it is the price to be paid for the transformation of the capitalist system under the sign of Stalinism following the Second World War'.[21] In the countries of the Third World where the bourgeois state was destroyed, the communist movement gained an initial legitimacy in the anti-imperialist struggle, in China, Vietnam and Cuba. And in spite of similarities, this is what distinguishes them from the bureaucratized societies in Europe. Today, however, the historical credibility of these regimes is also under attack: on the one hand, because the military background of the revolutionary-nationalist leaderships of the Third World has not favoured the flourishing of democracy in those societies; and on the other, because they have been held responsible for economic failures which are mainly not of their doing, in so far as they are the victims of the capitalist market and military aggression. Comparisons with the 'successes' of the newly industrialized countries leave out one thing: that the wealth of some has been achieved at the cost of the poverty of others. As Carlos M. Vilas correctly points out, an examination of income distribution in Latin America, for example, shows that

> between 1960 and 1980, the income of the poorest sections of the population of Brazil rose from $197 to $401 (in other words, double) while in Peru, after a decade of military reformism, it fell from $232 in 1961 to $197 in 1979. In Cuba, on the other hand, the income of this same section of the population went up fivefold: from $182 in 1960 to $865 in 1982. ... Finally, in spite of the crisis, industrial production ... which represented 32 per cent of material production in 1960, reached 46 per cent in 1981; in Latin America, during the same period, it went from 32 per cent to 35 per cent, and in Brazil from 35 per cent to 36 per cent.[22]

But the trauma of Stalinism has been so violent that its defeat now seems irrevocable and, above all, without alternative. Revealing in this respect are the comments of one of the Sandinista commanders, Víctor Tirado, who has analysed the effects of perestroika on the Third World and reflected on the relations between socialism and poverty. Starting from an acknowledgement that 'the battle between the socialist system and the capitalist camp has been temporarily lost by socialism', he believes that a period of reforms, as well as parliamentary, electoral and trade union struggles, has opened up. Armed struggle is not on the agenda. 'Historical stages cannot be jumped with impunity ... all the more so because the Soviet Union cannot afford to grant all the help needed by countries like ours.' A 'socialism of poverty'[23] cannot therefore be built. This speech reflects well the sharp contradictions facing the small so-called 'peripheral' dependent countries. While the Cuban Revolution was able to represent a credible perspective for the Latin American vanguard in the 1960s, Nicaragua would not appear to be a viable autonomous model for economic development. This is perhaps the greatest gain that imperialism has made.

What is to be done to achieve development? What is to be done in the last decade of the century? What is to be done for the masses? What can people be offered? To these questions, Tirado provides no answer; or if he does provide one, it is to beat a real retreat. Yet even in Nicaragua there are different answers. In an article titled 'Restoration or Democratic Socialism'[24] Orlando Nuñez, faced with the dilemma of 'the restoration of capitalism or bureaucratic socialism' – or 'state socialism', as he calls the latter – points to the possibility of a third way. He claims that the limits and contradictions of state socialism are due, in the first place, to the backward nature of the country where socialism has taken place, as well as to the double need for state intervention and centralization – on the one hand to promote economic development, and on the other to organize the military defence of the country in the face of foreign aggression. But he adds: 'If intervention by the state in the economy – and by the party over social classes – outstrips popular participation ... then this imbalance will end up limiting social and popular control over the state and delay the democratization of society.'

On this basis Nuñez infers the need, in a second stage,

> to encourage the autonomy of civil society vis-à-vis the state, as well as overall self-management by the popular classes in all areas of social, economic and cultural life. In other words, a transition must be made from state socialism to communitarian socialism. This does not mean eliminating the state's role but regulating it in such a way that processes of adjustment do not lead to the restoration of the liberal economy and bourgeois democracy. It will only be possible to overcome the limits of objective conditions by resorting to the opportunities and potential of subjective conditions, by acting on society [praxis]. ... Civil society [the organized masses] must take over the functions of the state and carry out a permanent campaign of education on the new values of solidarity and co-operation, as against the new values of competition and aggressiveness, in social relations. ... That is how we can oppose those who, on the basis of perestroika and the various processes of adjustment and stabilization [the polemic with Tirado is implicit], have raised the banner of scepticism, defeatism and demoralization. ... We must show that it is capitalism that is in crisis and that state socialism (authoritarian, developmentalist [*desarrollista*] and bureaucratic) is no longer able to confront that crisis.[26]

The debate over the transition to socialism – closed in the Soviet Union after the victory of Stalin and interrupted in Cuba following the departure of Che – is thus re-emerging and will continue to develop. Indeed, this text must be compared with the statements of left-wing Polish or Hungarian opponents. These are all the more interesting because these countries are at the forefront of the introduction of market reforms, and it is striking to see how they denounce their effects in similar terms. The reforms, they claim, are 'aimed at increasing the power of the bureaucracy over society ... modernizing the regime ... while intensifying exploitation and domination'.[26] As the authors of the Charter for a Left-Wing Hungarian Alternative have written, it is a case of 'saving the foundations of the old power structure through partial reforms. This process will preserve the domination of the rival elites, as well as dual exploitation by the state and private capital.'[27]

Such ideas contrast with those of the director of the Institute of the Economy of the World Socialist System at the Academy of Sciences of the Soviet Union, O. Bogomolov, who, referring to the Yugoslavian experience in a debate with the director of the Economic Institute of Zagreb, D. Vojnic, considered that negative effects (as in Hungary or China) were due 'to the inconsistency of reforms, the absence of political reforms, and ill-considered decentralization',[28] and that the market, monetary-market mechanisms, and the spirit of enterprise and competition could not be blamed.

Faced with the false choice between market reforms and liberalization, on the one hand, and centralized planning and bureaucracy, on the other, an alternative, third way must be found. For at the end of this century, the ideas of socialism are in danger of collapsing into a bureaucratic débâcle and an apology for mercantilism.

What are the premises for this third way? As the most lucid representatives of the opposition forces in the East point out, the bankruptcy of bureaucratic socialism cannot be fought with economic tools. While understanding that small market production will not be eliminated overnight, it remains the case that the construction of a real socialist society will be based on socio-political, indeed, ethical choices. As Nuñez rightly says, education, recourse to awareness and mobilization, and the self-organization of the masses are the tools for any economic development. A parallel can be drawn: just as the economic emancipation of women has not been enough to eradicate their oppression, likewise the abolition of private ownership is a necessary, but insufficient, condition for the construction of a socialist society.

The slogan of Deng Xiaoping – 'It does not matter whether a cat is black or white, as long as it catches mice' – is nonsense as far as building a socialist society is concerned. And that goes for the peasantry as well. As an old Chinese philosopher remarked:

> I am not saying that the economic dimension is not important, or that the peasants cannot be mobilized on the basis of their personal interests. What I am saying is that if that is the way you want to mobilize them, things will of course work for a while, but only until they stop working. ... We do not want to seduce the peasants through material interest. We want to rebuild their morale, to galvanize them for action. It is only on that basis that things will work.[29]

That is especially the case when, in the final resort, economic decisions in agriculture are linked to the dynamics of finding a tolerable level of social differentiation within the peasantry, and one that is compatible with the interests of the urban masses.

How monetary incentives and their limits are set depends on how priority needs are set, and thus on truly democratic planning. Social incentives in terms of housing, transport and the organization of work can be more effective than monetary incentives. But this pre-eminence of revolutionary consciousness and will cannot only emerge from either voluntarism or exemplarity, even in their truly egalitarian form as advocated by Che. First, it would mean removing the real disincentives to development represented by disorganization, and bureaucratic corruption and privileges; it would also mean understanding the social bases and the common political and ideological features of groups 'whose goal in itself is to govern society and live parasitically off it',[30] even though 'socialism can only be based on the principles of social justice and social equality'.[31] Secondly, it would mean 'political democracy, a state of law, the coherent achievement of all human rights, the right of each member of society to develop his or her personality, and the restructuring of industrial society so that it is compatible with the need to protect the environment'.[32] And finally, it means workers' decision-making power and self-government, for 'only power can check power'.[33]

Such goals are incompatible with surrogacy, the power of leaders and any elitist approach that maintains the division between leaders and the led: 'We cannot depend on the power of any single leader', proclaimed the students of Tiananmen Square. Will this watchword be taken up by Cuban students and workers?

November 1989

Notes

1. Robert Graham, in the *Financial Times*, 17 February 1989.
2. The 1990 elections, held with a pistol at the country's head, were part of this plan.
3. *Le Monde*, 17 November 1989.
4. Statement of the Central Committee of the Communist Party of Cuba, 'For peoples, the problem appears as follows: either capitulating to imperialism or resisting and struggling', Paris, JCR pamphlet, 1967.
5. Tim Coone, in the *Financial Times*, 17 February 1989.
6. *New York Review*, 15 June 1989.
7. Ibid.
8. *El País*, 1 April 1989.
9. Their ephemeral nature was demonstrated by the recent condemnations of Cuba by the same commission. See the postscript.
10. Ernest Mandel, 'Towards a General Theory of the Transition from Capitalism to Socialism', report to the Managua symposium, mimeo, October 1988.
11. Ralph Miliband, 'Communism and Democracy', in *New Left Review*, no. 177, September/October 1989.
12. 'Declaration of the Rights of Exploited and Working People', 1918.
13. Carlos M. Vilas, *Transición desde el subdesarrollo*, Caracas, Editorial Nueva Sociedad, 1989.
14. Fidel Castro, speech at the Third Congress of Economists of Latin America, November 1987.
15. Ernest Mandel, in *Quatrième Internationale*, September 1987.
16. Marie-Agnès Crosnier, in *Courrier des pays de l'Est*, Documentation française, March 1987.

17. Report on the restructuring and politics of party cadres before the CPSU Central Committee, 27 January 1987, in *Izvestia*, 28 January 1987.

18. What Boris Kagarlitsky, leader of the Moscow Popular Front, calls 'market Stalinism' (*New Left Review*, no. 177, September/October 1989).

19. ANN, 3 May 1989.

20. Valeri Nikolayenko, in *Barricada*, 1 April 1989.

21. Movement for a Democratic and Self-Governing Socialism, 'Theses for a Left-Wing Alternative', Prague, quoted in *Inprecor*, no. 299.

22. Carlos M. Vilas, *Transición desde el subdesarrollo*.

23. *Barricada*, 31 March 1989.

24. *Barricada*, 1 April 1989.

25. Ibid.

26. J. Pinior, 'Reform oder Revolution?', in *Ost–West Gegeninformationen*, nos. 1–2, Graz (Austria), June 1989.

27. Charter for a Left-Wing Hungarian Alternative, in *Kritika*, March 1989, Budapest.

28. *Moscow News*, 21 May 1989.

29. Liang Shuming, in *Le Monde*, 30 May 1989.

30. J. Pinior, leader of the Polish Socialist Party–Democratic Revolution (PSP–DR).

31. Movement for a Democratic and Self-Governing Socialism, 'Theses for a Left-Wing Alternative', Prague, quoted in *Inprecor*, no. 299.

32. Appeal of Böhlen, quoted in *Inprecor*, no. 296, 30 October 1989.

33. Ralph Miliband, 'Communism and Democracy', in *New Left Review*, no. 177, September/October 1989.

Postscript

The pace of history has quickened since October 1989, the date of the French manuscript of this book. The world panorama as drawn up in the post-war period belongs to the past. Commemorating in their own way the bicentenary of the French Revolution, the peoples of Eastern Europe have risen up against the bureaucratic dictatorships exercised against them in the name of the supposed higher interests of the proletariat. A historic stage – that of Stalinist degeneration and the distortion of socialism – is coming to an end. The conclusion of this book was without doubt over-optimistic: the uprising of the peoples of Eastern Europe, while releasing energy and breaking the bureaucratic yoke, is not, for the time being, taking the path of a renewed and democratic socialism. The attraction of economic liberalism and Western parliamentarism, as well as the re-emergence of nationalism and, in some instances, xenophobia, bear witness to the ravages of Stalinism. The latter is identified with communism by the people who have but an ideal vision of capitalism – that of a consumer society in its optimum, wealthiest form, be it German or Swedish – and who cannot see that such a society relates to a small minority of the planet; that 'there's many a slip twixt cup and lip'; and that the possibility of enjoying similar gains is just not on the agenda, while instead they are in danger of suffering the effects of social tensions generated by economic difficulties. Only experience will be able to change the illusions clouding popular awareness in the East. It will be hard for democratic socialism to find a space between the liberal racketeering and fundamentalist nationalism which are developing on the compost of rotting Stalinist bureaucracy.

Unlike those of Eastern Europe, the peoples of the Third World know that actually existing capitalism also means poverty for hundreds of millions of men and women in the dominated countries which contribute to the prosperity of a small minority. For them, the US–Soviet agreements and the crisis in Eastern Europe are full of dangers. What they saw – despite all the risks – as their strategic rearguard, no longer exists. The Soviet Union is on the defensive, threatened by the reawakening of its nationalities, faced with drastic economic choices, and paralysed by political contradictions. In order to shake the monopoly of the CPSU, Gorbachev has relied on the state apparatus. Following the election of Yeltsin and the proclamation of Russia, the principal republic, as a sovereign state, the President's domination of all the Russias has been all the more weakened as control of the apparatus of the Russian party and of the other republics threatens to slip from his grasp: what power will he have left tomorrow when the other republics also demand their independence?

The effects of this situation have been quickly felt in Latin America and the Central American isthmus. The Malta summit was hardly over when the Pentagon unleashed the invasion of Panama. But with attention being held by events in Romania, this did not lead to mass protests. Such relative impunity was helped by media campaigns, as we can see now that the real number of victims in the two countries is known: around 100 dead in Timisoara, and 4,000 in Panama. There can be no doubt that the US invasion was facilitated by the débâcle of the dictatorships in Eastern Europe and socialism's lack of credibility, thus violating the sovereignty of the Panamanian people in the name of the struggle against drug trafficking. And having been the faithfull ally and subordinate of George Bush when he was in charge of the CIA, Noriega was merely one stooge among many in such activity.

The stemming of the FMLN's revolutionary offensive in El Salvador in November 1989 was also the result of this new international situation. A bothersome 'regional conflict', this fly in the ointment could only get in the way of Soviet–US rapprochement: deprived of its rear bases following the Nicaraguan elections, the FMLN is now on the defensive, although it is only thanks to US aid that the extreme right is holding its own in the field.

Finally, the electoral defeat of the Sandinistas in February 1990 has checked the spread of revolution in Central America, dealing a very serious blow to Cuba. The victory of the Sandinistas in July 1979 had ended Cuba's twenty-year-old isolation; in Maurice Bishop Fidel Castro had found an ally; sooner or later, victory had seemed inevitable in El Salvador. Today, the outlook is entirely different and events in Nicaragua have been a terrible trauma for the now isolated island. The concept of the 'besieged fortress' is once again a reality. Is not Castro the last of the dinosaurs, as US leaders would have it? As former Assistant Secretary of State for Inter-American Affairs Elliot Abrams revealed in the wake of

Violeta Chamorro's victory in Nicaragua: 'First Manuel [Noriega], today Daniel [Ortega], the next will be Fidel [Castro]'.[1] For Abrams 'Cuba is on the list. ... Castro is more isolated than ever ... we must see how we should act'.[2] For others, it is a question of waiting and seeing and, above all, of doing nothing and 'leaving [Cuba] alone'[3]. Moreover, a recent amendment to a law adopted by the US Senate – the 'Law of the Nascent Democracies of 1990' which will have extra-territorial application – is aimed at banning transactions between US companies and Cuba and sanctioning ships that have come via the island (by denying them access to US ports). According to an EEC commission, such a measure could, even in time of war, be considered an infringement of international law on neutral shipping; in time of peace, then, it is *a fortiori* totally unacceptable. The same amendment also envisages halting aid to countries which import sugar from Cuba.

The victim of a strengthened economic blockade and isolated in the region, the Cuban Revolution is truly threatened, and Fidel Castro is not exaggerating when he claims that the country is going through the most difficult period of its history. It is true that such difficulties are partly shared by other Third World countries which are also the victims of the unfavourable economic climate of the 1980s, suffering the effects of the dramatic fall in raw material prices and the absence of loans. As the Lomé IV Convention highlighted: 'There has been no development in the economies of the ACP countries. Quite the opposite. This affects all sectors of economic life. Poverty has increased and impoverishment is spreading ... hospitals and schools are closing because there is no money to pay for doctors, nurses and teachers, factories are at a standstill because of the lack of spare parts, raw materials and fuel.'[4] According to Unicef, the developing countries are currently paying the industrialized countries $178,000 million a year in debt service, that is, three times more than the aid they receive.

As the US writer Saul Landau has pointed out, this situation confirms that 'the capitalist countries in general have no valid model or alternative with which to guide the countries of the Third World in their transition from colonial status to real independence'.[5]

In drawing up its prospects for economic development, however, Cuba had relied – wrongly – on unfailing support from the 'socialist camp'. Today, the Castro leadership is paying dearly for its blinkered analysis of the socio-economic reality of such countries where the absence of political democracy is also cruelly felt. Indeed, the banning of any criticism or debate regarding the countries of Eastern Europe – presenting an apologistic picture of reality there – has had a double effect. On the one hand, it has not prepared the Cuban people for the current situation, the danger being that the level of their demoralization will be as high as their past illusions; and that the very idea of socialism will be discredited. On the other hand, the unconditional support given to the bureaucratic dictatorships has deeply isolated the Cuban Revolution in the eyes of the popular masses in the East. Today, the latter are certainly not prepared to show their solidarity with a country that, through the voice of Fidel Castro, did not dissociate itself from the intervention in Czechoslovakia, supported the Jaruzelski coup in Poland, and never protested against the repression they had all suffered. The limits of a one-way internationalism are thus being revealed. The profound injustice now being committed against the Cuban Revolution is facilitated by the stances taken in the past. The Castro leadership's professions of Marxist-Leninist faith echo in the desert; they are ridiculed because such 'ideological principles' are making a very late appearance given all the violations of those very principles in the past.

When questioned, Cuban officials now reply: 'We did not know.'[6] It is to be hoped that they are now drawing conclusions from such ignorance.

For the economic vulnerability of Cuba is becoming dramatically clear. The fear that the country may be the victim of a drastic reduction in oil deliveries is not just theoretical: between 1988 and 1989 oil deliveries fell from 13 million tonnes to 12 million tonnes. According to Fidel Castro, the country 'must be prepared for the worst ... if we do not receive the annual 12 million tonnes of [Soviet] oil, we must know what to do if there are only ten, or eight, or six, or five, or four'.[7]

The rationing of bread from February 1990 because of the non-delivery of wheat flour is just as worrying. While it is true that real problems did play a part in such difficulties (strikes in the Ukraine delayed wheat flour deliveries and ethnic conflicts in Bakou at the end of 1989 disrupted the departure of oil tankers) the fact remains that the campaign underway in the Soviet press to discredit the Cuban Revolution cannot encourage trade. On the contrary. It is significant that the journal *Argumenty i Fakty*[8] has revealed the (hitherto secret) cost of aid for the first time, basing itself hypocritically on 'Western estimates'! According to the journal, 'the volume of Soviet aid to Cuba is apparently 5,000 million roubles a year'. For his part, George Bush has been quick to take up these figures to make possible US aid to the Soviet Union conditional on a halt in Soviet aid to Cuba 'as it is difficult for Americans to understand why the $5 billion that go each year to Cuba cannot be used to help the Soviet population. There's Cuba, isolated, all alone, furiously swimming against the tide of freedom and democracy: if you want to save five billion, it's a good way to start.'[9] The fact that a halt in aid to Cuba is one of the essential conditions for the granting of US aid requested by Gorbachev could not have been more clearly expressed.

Not to be outdone, *Izvestia* also made public – something which had not been done before – the sum total of the Cuban debt: 15,000 million roubles. Such a revelation was similar to the criticisms that have appeared in *Moscow News* (which has not hesitated in praising the economic success of Pinochet's Chile)[10] and the sarcastic comments of Soviet television on Fidel Castro's 'ideological principles'. The discontent of dissidents is mentioned favourably, and it is known – for the Cuban chancery made an official protest – that a CPSU official for Latin America has made contact with Cuban exiles in Miami, no doubt to explore the possibility of 'national reconciliation'.

In such a context it is not surprising that Bulgaria and Hungary voted in favour of a Polish- and Czech-sponsored resolution at the UN condemning Cuba for human rights violations. (Following Vietnam and North Korea, Cuba also repatriated its students on training courses in Budapest in June 1990.) Such votes have been interpreted by the Cuban leadership as a bargaining chip with which to 'pay for' US financial aid. Although these countries only represent 15 per cent of Cuba's annual trade with Eastern Europe, the impact of a break would not be negligible, especially if one adds the inevitable effects of the GDR's integration into the EEC following its annexation by the German Federal Republic. The GDR was the second most important buyer of Cuban sugar in Comecon: unified Germany has suspended the economic agreements made between the former GDR and Cuba. According to Jürgen Warnke, Germany's Minister for Development, this measure is justified by the country's economic situation.[11]

Even if the Soviet Union is not going to make up for the shortcomings of its former Comecon partners and a substantial reduction of aid can be anticipated, several Soviet officials have confirmed that any sudden suspension of agreements is highly improbable. It is possible that the Soviet government will alter trade according to fluctuations in its domestic and international policies, as well as to the development of its relations with Havana, particularly when the benefits of economic trade are not unilateral. Cuba provides about a third of the sugar consumed in the Soviet Union; and 40 per cent of its citrus fruit production and more than half its annual nickel production also go there.[12] It should be remembered that Cuba is the fourth largest nickel producer in the world and that, along with the Soviet Union, it rejoined the International Nickel Council in June 1990.[13] Buying these goods on the world market would be very costly in terms of foreign exchange and Soviet agriculture is not in a position to produce the 4 million tonnes of sugar provided by Cuba.

At the twentieth session of the Soviet–Cuban Inter-Governmental Commission held in Havana in April 1990, Leonid Abalkin, the Soviet Deputy Prime Minister in charge of the introduction of economic reforms, stressed that the Soviet Union also benefits from its relations with Cuba. 'We need sugar, and Cuba needs oil', he declared.[14] But from now on there is every sign that trade will be planned on a one- to two- rather than five-yearly basis and will be subject to unforeseen changes, depending on socio-political developments in the Soviet Union and the interests of the now autonomously managed Soviet enterprises. According to Abalkin, such enterprises will, for the time being, benefit from fiscal advantages if they trade with Cuba.[15] But the protocol signed in April 1990 is only valid for a year. Under its terms the Soviet Union will continue to deliver fuels, foodstuffs, raw materials and capital goods to Cuba. For its part, Cuba must continue exporting sugar, minerals, citrus fruits and, for the first time, medicines and high-tech equipment, thus taking advantage of its recent specialization. Indeed, Cuba's achievements in public health – in some areas higher than in the Soviet Union – may lead to trade in this field. Cuban stomatologists are helping with medical assistance in the Soviet Union, particularly in mining regions; around 10,000 children in the areas affected by the Chernobyl disaster have been taken in by Cuban medical centres; many Soviet soldiers wounded in Afghanistan have received care in a Cuban advanced orthopaedic centre.

During his visit, however, Abalkin did not fail to emphasize that he did not know what would happen to relations between the two countries in 1991. And while he stated that differences between the two governments were not a tragedy, the Cuban economy is at the mercy of any upheaval in the Soviet Union, all the more so because Comecon is in the process of breaking up, with the different countries formerly making up the body now set on different paths, at least in the short term. According to the working group set up in Sofia in January 1990, prices within Comecon should be set at the level of world prices and bilateral payments should be made in convertible currency and no longer in transferable roubles. That, at least, is the reform proposed by Comecon's permanent financial commission which should gradually come into force from 1991 onwards. Comecon could then 'act as a "decompression valve" to facilitate, at least for the more exposed export sectors, a less costly insertion into the international trade circuit'.[16] The idea of turning the 'false market' of Comecon into a 'true market', of doing away with bulk-bartering and defining trade in terms of value with payment in hard currency, has unforeseeable consequences for Cuba. The latter still invokes the CMEA statutes, one of the aims of which was to 'raise the level of industrialization of the least industrially developed countries'.[17]

But whatever the agreements reached, it is the very dynamic of Soviet politics that is the most worrying for the Castro leadership, and on this point US and Soviet officials coincide. For Andrei Kortunov, foreign affairs adviser to the Supreme Soviet, 'German reunification is much more important for the Soviet Union than anything that may happen in Cuba, geographically, historically or militarily'; it is therefore desirable to revise upwards the price of oil sold, and revise downwards the price of sugar bought. In debates in the Soviet Parliament on the 1991 budget,[18] Kortunov did not miss the opportunity to justify his position on the grounds of Castro's alleged support for the conservatives in the Soviet Union.

Cuba has clearly become a stake in negotiations between the two 'superpowers' as well as between the different Soviet factions, and in this scenario the Soviet army is playing its own game. The military hierarchy – or at least a part of it – is not pro-Gorbachev. In a very fierce speech at the Congress of Russian Communists in June 1990, General Makachov, the commander of a military region, accused the reformers – and by implication Gorbachev, who was compared to King Lear – of wrecking the country's defence. Stating his belief that the idea that no one would attack the Soviet Union could only be shared by 'half-wits', he declared: '68 per cent of the Soviet army's troops are stationed on the territory of the Russian Federation. The army's party delegation here represents more than 800,000 communists. We're not going to surrender ideologically.'[19] It is therefore hardly surprising that Cuba has enjoyed significant military aid, including in particular the delivery in 1990 of MiG 29s. The Cuban army enjoys a special prestige with well placed Soviet military men who know that their aid, unlike other armies in the Middle East, is not granted in vain. Moreover, the balance of forces within the CPSU still enables the military hierarchy to enjoy a relative autonomy: it is significant that visits by Soviet military chiefs often concluded with the issuing of joint Soviet–Cuban communiqués. When Mikhail A. Moisseev, Chief of Staff of the Soviet armed forces, visited Havana in October 1990 he stressed 'the solid ties which have existed, do exist and will continue to exist between our peoples and our armed forces', and reaffirmed that collaboration and mutual aid between the two countries was as important as ever,' 'and concerned all economic, social and military matters.'[20]

And indeed *Pravda* has reiterated – in a short, unsigned article on 4 November 1990 – the need to base economic relations 'on efficiency and mutual benefits', for any disequilibrium in these relations 'would aggravate the situation in both countries'.

But the Cuban government can have no illusions about the fragility of this support, and is now preparing for every eventuality. Even before the restrictions of summer 1990, the mobilization prepared in case of 'peace-time emergencies' (notably a fall in oil deliveries) showed that for Castro the revolution was now threatened as much by political developments in Moscow as by Washington's vindictiveness.

In August 1990 the Cuban authorities announced that oil deliveries had dropped by two million tonnes since the start of the year. Grave enough in itself, this fall coincided with the Gulf crisis, the rise in oil prices, and the likelihood of having to pay hard currency for Soviet oil from 1991. The Castroite leadership thus faces an extremely serious situation, as the scope of the measures introduced by the government shows. Energy-saving measures have been introduced across the board: in the state sector petrol consumption has been cut by 50 per cent. The Punta Gorda nickel refinery which in normal times supplies 35 per cent of national output, was provisionally shut down in September 1990 because of fuel shortages, which had the (perhaps intended) effect of halting nickel deliveries to the USSR, which normally takes almost the entire output of the plant, around 15,000 tonnes of nickel per year. The construction of the nuclear power station, of an oil refinery at Cienfuegos, and of several thermo-electric factories, has been suspended, and the Cuban government is unable to say when it might recommence.[21]

Domestic electrical goods are to be strictly reserved for the social services: fridges will not be available in 1991 (this in a tropical country where temperatures often reach 30°C), and nor will air-conditioners, which use a lot of energy. Televisions, washing-machines, radios, record-players and tape-recorders will all be rationed, as will irons, coffee-makers and pressure-cookers.

Other goods will also be rationed, including clothes, shoes and furniture. In terms of food, the ration books already covered thirty-five basic products (rice, fats, meat, milk, etc.) to which will be added twenty-eight additional products formerly obtainable on the parallel market or on free sale (tinned fish and meat, mayonnaise, spices, cakes, cheese, conserved fruits, etc.).[22]

These facts alone should suffice to indicate the depth of the crisis. But we must also take into account the effects of energy shortages on irrigation, on the refrigeration of agricultural produce, and on transport: some 400,000 draught animals are being brought in to replace tractor-power. In this context the recent purchase of a factory in China to manufacture hundreds of thousands of bicycles is one of the less dramatic responses.

Shortage of hard currency, already serious before the present crisis, is now critical. The Cuban government has recently sold in Europe (through Sotheby's) several major items from the country's artistic heritage, including important paintings and a manuscript by Federico García Lorca.[23] Jeane Kirkpatrick can cynically rejoice: Cuba, she says, faces a 'special period of hardship when the revolution will be tested as never before'.[24]

The pledges recently made to the exiles in Miami by various Soviet envoys concerning changes in stopovers on certain Aeroflot flights which will in future go via Miami rather than Havana, can only raise the hopes of the US government and the most reactionary elements of the Cuban exile community. Moscow's emissaries have even held meetings with the Cuban–American Foundation, the co-instigator with the CIA of all the plotting and aggression against the island.

> No one knows today what will be the basis of our trade with the USSR next year, no one knows what they will pay for our sugar and other products, or what we will have to pay for the products they send us. A mere three months from the end of the year, no one knows how much oil we will receive. [At world market prices,] if the price of oil per barrel stays at $40, we will have to produce around 18 million tonnes of sugar to cover our needs.
>
> Fidel Castro, 28 September 1990

The price per tonne for Cuban sugar paid by the USSR has been on average equivalent to the production costs per tonne in the USSR, and sometimes even lower, while the price Cuba paid for oil was higher than Soviet production costs.

However, two months after Castro's alarmist speech, the Soviet Union was to confirm that it would preserve its privileged trading agreements with Cuba for an annual total of 4.2 million tonnes of raw sugar, to be paid for in roubles. By the end of the first seven months of 1990 Cuba had already exported 3.43 million tonnes of sugar to the USSR, as against 3.73 million for January to July 1989. The predicted harvest for 1990–91 of 7.5 million tonnes (compared with 8 million in 1989–90), as a result of drought and fuel shortages in factories, should nevertheless allow Havana to meet its commitments to Moscow.[25] As already indicated, a complete break thus seems ruled out in the short term, and yet the Castroite leadership is still evoking the possibility of moving to a subsistence economy. So is Castro's slogan 'Save the motherland, save the revolution, save socialism' (the order may be significant) really over-dramatic?

Certainly no one can deny the extreme gravity of the current crisis nor the critical turning-point which the Cuban Revolution now faces in this, the thirty-second year of its existence. While written before the tremendous upheavals in the Eastern bloc, this book has already explored the key elements of the situation. In terms of the general economic perspective, Andrew Zimbalist has summed these up as follows: 'low sugar prices, plummeting petroleum prices (Cuba's re-export of Soviet petroleum provided roughly 40 per cent of its hard currency earnings during 1983–85), devastation from Hurricane Kate, several consecutive years of intensifying drought, drastic dollar devaluation, the tightening of the US embargo and growing protectionism in Western markets, all combine to reduce Cuba's hard currency earnings by $337.1 million or 27.1 per cent.'[26] Yet these facts, dramatic though they are, should not be used to dodge the need for a more directly political balance-sheet. Given this context, how are we to evaluate the political–economic options facing the Castroite leadership, its institutional choices, and its conception of socialism?

The objective constraints and subjective choices must be analysed, and this must also be done comparatively, in relation to other countries, other economies in the Third World, whose situations, while not identical, may be similar. It is still premature to follow this route, for the Cuban Revolution – along with the Russian and the Chinese – represents one of the greatest social transformations of the twentieth century and one of the richest political experiences. But it is not too early to re-emphasize the two questions already discussed. The doubts that we have raised about economic policy and the direction of the rectification process now seem to be confirmed. So too are the evaluations of the consequences of the absence of political democracy.

While the Cuban government can still count on this support, it is nevertheless preparing itself for every eventuality: the mobilizations organized in anticipation of 'peacetime emergencies' (particularly in case of oil supplies being cancelled) show that, for Fidel Castro, the revolution is today as much threatened by political developments in Moscow as it is by the spiteful attitude of Washington.

For if the Cuban Revolution is indeed threatened, it can only really be endangered by a combined deterioration in the internal situation and external intervention. The radicalism of Cuban nationalism is not directed against the Soviet Union, but against its big neighbour, *el norte revuelto y brutal* [the disordered and brutal North], as José Martí used to say. That is why direct military intervention is doomed to failure if revolutionary mobilization prevails. That is where the shoe may pinch if the party leadership does not take radical measures: economic measures, in so far as they are within its power, and, above all, political measures. This conclusion, already presented in the French edition of this book, has since been confirmed. In Cuba itself the preparation of the Fourth PCC Congress is bearing witness to the leadership's concerns in this regard; yet a critical evaluation of the rectification process begun in 1986 still seems a long way off.

Market Mechanisms or the Law of the Market?

Four years after the suppression of the free farmers' markets, it is now possible to take stock of the situation in agriculture. According to Max

Azicri,[27] the political fallout of this measure should not have affected the government. State markets should have been able to guarantee supplies of basic foodstuffs at an acceptable level, even though the consumer could no longer take advantage of the private markets and the state markets at the same time. This view is clearly over-optimistic. On his return from making a film in Cuba, Saul Landau made a more negative assessment: 'There's no compensation for the shutting down of the private agricultural market, and food is harder to get now. Everybody understands that the minute the state takes over certain enterprises, it bureaucratizes them, whether they are little barber shops and restaurants or the distribution of commodities and foodstuffs.'[28] In fact since the suppression of the free farmers' markets in 1986, consumers have had access to two kinds of state market: the ration-book market and the parallel market where goods are sold at 'market price', which does nothing to prevent either queues in both systems – for supply is still insufficient, especially of goods most in demand – or widespread use of the black market.[29] According to Media Benjamin – who contradicts claims by Eugenio Balari from the Cuban Institute of International Demand – government officials have announced significant rises in the production of vegetables, rice and pork following the authorization of the first free markets. Benjamin claims to have noted the same trend.[30] The inequalities created by the free markets justified their suppression – but why should inequalities resulting from the black market be any better?

According to various observers the contradictions produced by the free markets could have been limited by proper social controls: 'I think they just failed to institute proper controls. If they had set ceilings on prices, or if the sellers had been licensed, regulated and taxed, the markets might have worked. As it is, they threw out the baby with the bathwater.'[31]

Although small-scale market production now only represents 8 per cent of land (with 92 per cent of cultivable land grouped in state farms and co-operatives), Cuban authors recognize that 'the farmers who are not members of production co-operatives are still selling more to the state than members of co-operatives, even though they have less personnel and fewer hectares'.[32] In other words, this confirmed that the productivity of the small private farmers was greater than that of state farms or co-operatives (although the co-ops are infinitely more efficient than the state farms), in spite of their very important role in fruit and vegetable production. Under rectification, the process of grouping private farms into co-operatives has speeded up. The fact that agricultural labourers work an average four- or five-hour day has led the party leadership to stress the need to increase the efficiency of the state sector.[33]

In such circumstances, it is legitimate to enquire as to the reasons for the fall in production of bananas, tubers, vegetables and coffee. It could be due to the increase in land devoted to sugar production at the expense of food production. According to Fidel Castro, such a choice may be challenged, given the international situation for the country is not self-sufficient in food. But it must also be asked whether the elimination of the free markets has not led the small farmers, in the absence of incentives, to reduce their production. If the state reduces the prices paid for private production, are not the farmers going to react by selling their surplus on the black market? And if repression prevents them from doing this, are they not going to reduce their production?[34] Experience shows that depreciating the interest of the agricultural producer for the land leads to a dead-end. The suppression of the free markets has probably affected the motivation of the private farmers, just as the social guarantees afforded to co-operative farmers seem, paradoxically, to have had the same result. Should one conclude, as Mesa-Lago does,[35] that only monetary interest and the extension of the private sector can increase agricultural productivity? Or should mechanisms that would leave the initiative with small farmers, within the framework of autonomous and democratically run co-operatives, be considered?

Serious breakdowns in the distribution system are a further problem. As the Cuban sociologist Juan Valdès has underlined, 'inefficiency in the state sector is at present one of the most destabilizing factors'.[36] Losses and bad organization in the state bodies responsible for the collection of fruit and vegetables are common knowledge, and the marketing of produce is disastrous. In such circumstances, it is necessary to take stock of the measures adopted in 1986; if the prohibition of private activity then decreed has led to growing difficulties for the population as a whole then these measures must be reconsidered. Socialization is meaningless unless it can bring real and equitable progress for the people, who are already suffering quite enough in this difficult conjuncture. Behind this problem, what is at issue is the whole dynamic of the rectification process.

Indeed, four years on, the initial aims of the rectification process, far from being clarified are actually running adrift. In the film he made in Cuba, *The Uncompromising Revolution*, Saul Landau clearly shows that in reality the rectification process is not an alternative, and that Fidel Castro is merely once more emphasizing the need to do things seriously and efficiently, while not attacking the roots of the problem.

Indeed, four years later the initial aims of the rectification process have not only not been clarified, but are running adrift. According to José Luis Rodríguez, deputy director of the *Centro de Investigaciones de la Economía Mundial* [Centre for Research on the World Economy], criticism of the SDPE should focus on the fact that 'it gave priority to "positive" material incentives – bonuses – without any balance in terms of control and penalties – fines. The latter are crucial to dealing with the non-achievement of the plan, in order to adequately assess the use of management controls and incentives.[37] Such an interpretation, tending to hold workers responsible for the problems faced by the Cuban economy, would have grave consequences if it were followed through.

No real overall scheme, plan or guideline has been designed. The questioning of the SDPE, of the economic policy followed between 1976 and 1986, as well as the attacks on capitalist mechanisms, have not led on to a truly alternative direction; and in retrospect, questions can be asked about the reasons for the sacking of the JUCEPLAN officials.

Once again, as Zimbalist and Brundenius point out,[38] 'non-ideological viewpoints, eclecticism and pragmatism have prevailed regarding development policy'. They are not invoked as such, however. Official pronouncements since 1986 have been increasingly at odds with policy followed, in two areas at least: the rationalization and reorganization of the workforce and wages, and the development of tourism.[39] The contrast between words and deeds can only fuel the cynicism of workers who will inevitably feel its effects, especially in a difficult economic situation. Per capita gross domestic product, which had grown 0.1 per cent in 1986, fell by 4.4 per cent in 1987 and the financial situation of the country has seriously affected imports paid for in hard currency. Worst affected by such restrictions has been the production of consumer goods. And the numerical growth of the workforce (82,900 extra workers before the return of troops from Angola) is creating further tensions.

The perfecting of the system of economic management under the rectification process, as summed up by Silvia Domenech, professor of economic policy at the PCC High School, implies the necessary centralization of investment, the adequate use of material incentives and monetary/market relations. Emphasis is placed mainly on the need for rigid discipline, both at the workplace and financial level. 'Production costs must be controlled, wastages eliminated and quality improved'; the role of central planning is reaffirmed, but equally the need 'to eliminate the tutelage of administrative bodies' and to give 'real economic autonomy to grassroots economic units ... although one must guard against entrepreneurs caring more for the interests of their own enterprises than those of the country'. As to wage policies, 'order, organization and discipline must be introduced';[40] and work attitudes must be corrected by combating indiscipline and carelessness. According to one Western observer, 50 million working hours were lost in 1988 through absenteeism.[41] Having denounced excessive wage and incentive payments, it would seem that there is now a return in non-sugar agriculture to a system of payment linked to productive performance.[42] Who are the guarantors for these measures? '... [In] the final instance, the party and the socialist state.'[43]

The importance assumed by joint ventures in the development of tourism (70 per cent of planned new buildings are to be carried out as mixed enterprises with Western firms[44]) is not intended to clarify the precise nature and aim of rectification in the eyes of the masses. It is now not just a question of developing such mixed enterprises, including in industry, but Fidel Castro has even expressed pleasure that there will be competition in the future between hotels run by foreign and Cuban managers. As to the party's presence in the hotels, its mission will not be to tell the manager what to do, but to 'support the management's efforts whether the manager is Cuban or Spanish', and to be the 'guardian of efficiency and discipline, striving for the best work, with the trade union concerned also having to make the same efforts, along with the party and youth'.[45] The recourse to foreign capital and the development of mixed enterprises is today taking on great importance, as Julio García Olivera, President of the Cuban Chamber of Commerce, has emphasized.[46]

At a time when the more the Cuban economy is strangled, the more Washington steps up its anti-Castro crusade and embargo,[47] joint ventures represent a final hope. Yet it would be not merely paradoxical but dangerous to boost capitalist enterprises whose foreign capital may be as much as 50 per cent, and whose managers have the right to hire and fire – something which is strictly forbidden in the rest of the country – while at the same time stopping the development of private activity in agriculture, services and small businesses, despite the soaring incompetence and bureaucratic inefficiency in these areas.

Some extension of market mechanisms would probably make daily life easier for the Cuban masses. Keeping check on taxi-drivers by compelling them to return to base after each fare hardly contributes to solving the terrible crisis of urban transport; on the other hand, allowing plumbers, carpenters and locksmiths to be self-employed would do much to improve the dramatically worsening state of flats and houses. Where the state cannot take proper responsibility for these activities, other solutions must be found. But one question remains: is it possible to do without private shopkeepers in the retail sector? In cities like Havana, where waste and misappropriation in the state retail system are notorious, the difficulties must be resolved.[48]

Once again, there is no room for illusions: the application of market mechanisms will always favour fiddling and corruption, but apart from the fact that these things already exist, social control by producers and consumers can limit the effects. This will also mean that major economic decisions bearing on key investments for the country's future, along with the main social services, must not be regulated by the law of the market. In farming, in a country like Cuba where an agricultural labour force existed before the seizure of power, it would be absurd to advocate a return to small-scale private property and the parcelling out of land: co-operatives have been a success and their extension should be encouraged.[49]

The contradictions created by the limited spread of market relations and privatization are undeniable. The frustration and anger felt by certain layers of the population over private wealth (something on which we have constantly insisted in this book) were not invented by Fidel Castro; a widespread egalitarian consciousness is one of the gains of the revolution. But these contradictions can only be – partially – overcome if the whole of society takes control of its own development. The idea that social control and the sovereignty of producers and consumers is the key problem of transitional economies is now central to debates on socialism. To the spurious 'market socialism' should we not oppose the socialization of the market? This is the position taken by Diane Elson in her polemics with Alec Nove and Ernest Mandel. For her, 'the price mechanism is an indispensable instrument of co-ordination for a socialist economy, but ... it must be socialized if it is to work for rather than against socialism.' And she argues that 'the social relations between buyers and sellers must be changed so that they are *not* antagonistic; the price formation process must be a public process, not one controlled by enterprises ...'[50]

The law of the market, a generalized return to private property, in other words, the restoration of capitalism, are certainly not a solution for Cuba. Anyone who needs convincing need only consider the situation in those other Caribbean countries where private property is king and there are no blockades or economic restrictions. But the stranglehold of bureaucracy is similarly disastrous. It will defeat the revolution.

Without question, the Cuban leadership is being forced into concessions and its room for manoeuvre is extremely tight. And tourism, in spite of its detrimental effects on the spirit of the people, may possibly provide the foreign exchange so crucial to the development of Cuba, suffering, as the country is, unprecedented isolation. But as well as being contradictory, Castro's words are a repetition of well-worn formulae and can only devalue the process of rectification that had raised hopes for a struggle against bureaucracy and a deepening of democratic rights.

Carmelo Mesa-Lago's view that this is a case of a 'counter-reform'[51] is not confirmed. As was highlighted in an essay which won the 1990 *Centro de Estudios sobre América* (CEA – Centre for American Studies) prize in Havana, 'a return to further experimentation involving decentralizing, market-linked features seems inevitable'.[52] This verdict is shared by G. Timossi who foresees 'a different agenda for change'.[53] The fact that the debate over such major economic decisions has begun can only be positive; relations between the plan and the market are at the heart of several analyses influenced by developments in Eastern European countries and debate in this area is far from over.

According to Juan Valdès, 'the toughest debates leading up to the Fourth Congress all concern the economic plan. The economic system has to be de-ideologized and decentralized. In the name of socialism we nationalized ice-cream vendors. Now these same ice-cream vendors are encouraging people to question socialism itself.' A different view is expressed by Luis Suarez: 'the social cost which would result from the abolition of rationing and the introduction of a free market, eliminating free social consumption and subsidized individual consumption, would marginalize 2.5 million people; the ending of full employment would marginalize a million workers. The ration book assures egalitarian distribution and to get rid of it would have a destabilizing effect. ... We may not have resolved the contradiction between efficiency and equality but nor has the free market system. It's one of the challenges we face. But one thing is clear: the right to work and guaranteed provision of basic social needs is a democratic achievement of the Cuban Revolution.' Dario Machado, head of the People's Opinion Unit, believes that 'the rule of the market hasn't solved problems of productivity in Mexico or Venezuela, countries with far more resources than Cuba.'[54]

But while there is a debate between 'specialists' on the Cuban economy, it has not for the time being reached the main parties concerned, in other words, the people who are to be encouraged to produce greater wealth. And Fidel Castro's approach cannot help matters. Rita Cauli, a contributor to the Nicaraguan magazine *Pensamiento Propio*, rightly wonders 'how the aspirations of a young and anti-authoritarian society can be channelled without escaping the control of the current leaders and without being channelled by an opposition movement that could involve a historical setback'.[55] This question, now being raised by friends of the revolution, should underlie debates at the Fourth PCC Congress which has been convoked in a manner that leads one to believe that it will perhaps be held in an atmosphere of more open debate.

The Urgent Need for Democratization

Published in March 1990 following the plenum of the Central Committee in February,[56] the call for the Fourth Congress provided an inkling that the methods, structure and policies of PCC cadres might be challenged. The functioning of popular power, of the National Assembly and mass organizations, as well as the approach to ideological and political work and cultural and information policies, were all criticized.[57] Internal democracy, respect for the different currents of thought within the revolution and acceptance of believers within the party are apparently on the agenda, as is the election, by secret ballot, of PCC leaders.

The call for the Congress stressed the need to 'reinforce further popular control over government activity so as to respond in a more convincing and efficient way' to the expectations of the people. Rank-and-file delegates elected by direct and secret suffrage should see their authority strengthened. For its part, the indirectly elected National Assembly, like other state bodies, should be subjected to much more systematic control. According to Gerardo Timossi, a CEA researcher in Havana, extending direct election to intermediate levels and strengthening the powers of the rank and file over National Assembly deputies could even possibly lead to constitutional changes.[58] This would not go amiss. Indeed, Timossi's assessment confirms, as was stressed in the first edition of this book, that the functioning of institutional mechanisms in Cuba is far from democratic. Rectification has brought to light the obstacles faced by the party rank and file in enforcing their own decisions and in correcting the errors of the different levels of leadership, and this is also true for the organs of people's power. The truth is that none of the mechanisms of accountability function and workers' decision-making power is reduced to its simplest expression. While the Cuban leadership is aware of this, and while international events should lead it to become increasingly acutely so, it is to be feared that the Fourth Congress will end up being limited to an attempt to restore the party's authority by a massive purge of bureaucratic and parasitic functionaries (50 per cent of the PCC's militants and officials lost their jobs in the struggle to thin out state and administrative bodies, along with political and mass organizations). It is not only a question of improving relations with the masses, but of fundamentally changing institutional mechanisms.

The lessons drawn from the defeat of the Sandinistas in Nicaragua are doing nothing but reinforcing Fidel Castro's resistance to any form of organized political pluralism. It is true that the Nicaraguan experience provides food for thought. Not only were the opposition parties funded by imperialism; more particularly, the FSLN was caught in the trap long since laid as part of the low-intensity war: after years of war organized from Washington and an economic blockade going as far as the mining of ports – leading to a situation where the standard of living of the masses had fallen – the vote for Violeta Chamorro appeared to be the only solution capable of ending the war and poverty with the benevolent aid of the United States. Certainly the mistakes made by the FSLN (concessions to the capitalist private sector, authoritarian measures taken against certain minorities at the start of the revolution, a verticalist relation to the people) contributed to the erosion of popular support for the Sandinistas. But the Sandinistas' political pluralism has rejuvenated the face of socialism, especially in Latin America.

Making all due allowances and taking into account the different situation, one can understand Fidel Castro's fears of a US-controlled election campaign backed up by TV Miami. Ortega's American-style presidential campaign certainly did not reassure him. But the Castroite leadership could surely do much to undermine the electoral demands of its opponents by organizing pluralist elections within the framework of its own institutions without foreign interference, having neither contras nor large-scale capitalism on its territory.

But the Cuban leader ought to draw another lesson: as the evaluations of the Sandinistas themselves show, the Front's first mistake was not to provide their own members with guarantees of a democratic debate (as demanded by sectors of the FSLN) under the pretext that this could not be allowed in view of the war and the crisis. This sanctioned a paradoxical situation in which the counter-revolution benefited more from political pluralism than the revolution's supporters. Such a debate might have avoided the emergence of what Henry Ruiz called 'a split between the leadership and the people'; and it might have reflected the need for an authentically popular democracy. For pluralism can, in a small country like Cuba, certainly take various forms. The expression of different political currents, and the right to organize can be regulated within a structure that does not allow interference, particularly financial, by foreign powers, and which respects the structure of the institutions of popular power, thus guaranteeing the national sovereignty of a small country that is under attack. Tran Bach Dang, an official of the Vietnamese Communist Party expresses the same concern, declaring: 'If the multiparty system is decreed, we will have, above all in the South, ten parties of the old regime financed from abroad.'[59] Saul Landau has argued that one cannot demand 'a revolutionary leadership in the Third World to adhere to US norms regarding civil liberties when it is attacked through force and violence by the US government'[60] and when the CIA supports subversion. Indeed, behind the word democracy hides a challenge to the revolution, aimed at re-establishing interests which have nothing to do with those of the people. But while Fidel Castro cannot be reproached for refusing to swap the legitimacy of the revolution for the legality of rigged elections, and while his demands for the lifting of the trade embargo and the return of the military base in Guantánamo are understandable, nevertheless one cannot endorse his general approach in which the single party/state party is the only guarantor of the revolution. After thirty-one years of revolution, the argument that publicizing Central Committee debates, the organization of open public forums on major economic issues and the holding of elections and presentation of candidates supported by distinct political organizations within the framework of the organs of people's power, could constitute a threat to the revolution has no credibility. It is significant that in her latest book[61] Marta Harnecker (whose influence in Cuba is far from negligible) questions for the first time 'the bureaucratic–centralist model of socialism' which she attributes to Stalin; for the first time she emphasizes Lenin's condemnation of Stalin and his advocacy of freedom of debate and the right to form tendencies: she recalls that Lenin was in a minority in his own party and had the courage not only to maintain his positions but to express them publicly. It is hard not to see in her allusions an indirect criticism of the Cuban party's current mode of operation.

As Frei Betto has written in *Teoria y Debate*,[62] the journal of the Brazilian Workers' Party, the fact that 'democracy is now at the centre of debates about socialism' is a point of view shared by most of the Latin American left. Moreover, Frei Betto himself takes great care to make it clear that such a democracy must be 'substantial' and not formal; and for the purposes of greater clarity, he refers to the writings of Marx on the Paris Commune and those of Lenin in *The State and Revolution*, advocating the self-government of producers and the right to the permanent recallability of those elected. Latin American communist parties are distancing themselves from the authoritarian, repressive and supposedly socialist models.[63] Cuban authors are beginning to challenge the 'symptom of unanimity' and to put forward the need for a 'culture of debate' in the struggle against bureaucratization. They assert that 'neither repression nor arbitrary command' are solutions and that 'a socialist-style democracy must be deepened', criticizing the Stalinist interpretation of Marxism.[64]

It must be said that, despite the hopes that had been raised by the changes introduced in the Penal Code (and described in this book), repression has not entirely stopped in 1990. Seven people accused of creating a Movement of Democratic Integration and claimed by *Granma*[65] to have attempted to 'promote a struggle of so-called civil disobedience through the creation of pyramidally structured and compartmentalized clandestine municipal cells have been judged by the Provincial Popular Tribunal of Havana for the crime of rebellion carried to the point of conspiracy, according to articles 98 and 99 of the Penal Code'. 'In any case,' *Granma* went on, 'it has been proved that some of the accused were in contact with the US Interests Section in Havana, as well as with presumed [*sic*] groups supposedly [*sic*] defending human rights ... printed anti-revolutionary propaganda material has been seized and it has been established that a press conference had been organized with foreign journalists ... the prosecutor at the trial has asked for ten to twelve years' imprisonment for the accused.' Assuming that the prosecution's case is correct, it bears witness to significant clandestine initiative and organizational ability. What if such initiatives spread? Even if they emanate from groups without influence, such initiatives have recently been spreading. Is it not to be feared that the terrible economic situation will foster dissent, desertions (the latest being that of a Cuban official in charge of negotiating Soviet aid, Ramón Gonzalez Viguera[66]), demoralization and division? In the present international context, are they best combated by repression? The historic experience of the Eastern bloc countries, as it has just unfolded, is conclusive and it is to be hoped that the Castro leadership will draw the right lessons. Otherwise, the Fourth Congress will be held for nothing; or rather it will be a dark omen for the Cuban Revolution which is so much in peril.

Thanks to the revolution, Cuba has left behind its neo-colonial status, and become an independent nation, in extremely unfavourable geopolitical conditions. This independence can only be preserved by challenging the bureaucratic model which is now devouring the revolution.

Paris, 20 November 1990

Notes

1. *La Jornada*, 21 March 1990, Mexico.
2. Ibid.
3. Tad Szulc in the *New York Review of Books*, 31 May 1990.
4. *Le Courier ACP*, EEC, March/April 1990.
5. Brenner, Philip (ed.), *The Cuba Reader*, Grove Press, New York 1989.
6. Lecture given by the Cuban Ambassador in France at La Maison de l'Amérique Latine, Paris, 15 May 1990.
7. Speeches on 4 and 7 March 1990.
8. *Argumenty i Fakty*, 17–23 March 1990.
9. Interview given on the eve of the summits of Nato and the Group of Seven most industrialized countries, *Le Monde*, 29 June 1990.
10. *Moscow News*, no. 12, 23–29 March 1990.
11. *El País*, 17 November 1990.
12. The *Guardian*, 11 May 1990; the *Financial Times*, 21 March 1990.
13. *Tribune de l'Expansion*, 21 June 1990.
14. *Granma*, 29 April 1990.
15. The *Guardian*, 11 May 1990.
16. J.D. Clavel, 'Les relations économiques Est–Ouest', Brussels, Bruylant, 1989.
17. Article 1, Aims, Principles and Statutes of the Council for Mutual Economic Assistance.
18. *Latin American Weekly Report*, 7 June 1990.
19. *Le Monde*, 28 June 1990.
20. *Granma*, 21 October 1990.
21. Report in *Granma*, 14 October 1990, of Fidel Castro's speech on the 30th anniversary of the CDR.
22. *Bohemia*, 5 October 1990.
23. *El País*, 17 October 1990.
24. *International Herald Tribune*, 6 November 1990.
25. *Marchés Tropicaux*, Paris, 2 November 1990.

26. Andrew Zimbalist, 'Perspectives on Cuban Development and Prospects for the 1990s', manuscript quoted in *NACLA Report on the Americas*, August 1990.
27. Max Azicri, 'Comparing Two Social Revolutions: The Dynamics of Change in Cuba and Nicaragua', in *Cuba after Thirty Years: Rectification and the Revolution*, Frank Cass, London 1990, p. 18.
28. The *Guardian*, 1 August 1990.
29. CNRS report, manuscript by Denise Douzant Rosenfeld, Paris, July 1990.
30. *NACLA Report on the Americas*, August 1990.
31. Professor Raul Hinojosa, quoted by M. Benjamin in *NACLA Report on the Americas*, August 1990.
32. See José A. Toledo, Dean of the Faculty of History and Philosophy of Havana, in *Cuba Socialista*, magazine of the PCC Central Committee, no. 38, 1989.
33. Pettersen Nodarse and Labrada Fernández, *Cuba Socialista*, no. 41, 1989.
34. See Mesa-Lago, in *Cuba after Thirty Years: Rectification and the Revolution*.
35. Ibid.
36. *Pensamiento Propio*, August 1990.
37. *Cuba Socialista*, no. 44, 1990.
38. Zimbalist and Brundenius, 'El desarrollo cuban en una perspectiva comparada', *Cuadernos de Nuestra América*, December 1989.
39. *Cuba Socialista*, no. 44, 1990.
40. *Cuba Socialista*, no. 41, 1989.
41. *Pensamiento Propio*, August 1990.
42. See 'Agricultura no canera: nuevo sistema de organización de trabajo y salarios', *Granma*, 20 March 1990.
43. Carlos García Valdès, *Cuba Socialista*, no. 38, 1989.
44. Casanova Montero and Monreal González, in *Cuba after Thirty Years: Rectification and the Revolution*.
45. Fidel Castro, speech at the inauguration of the hotels Paradiso and Sol Palmeras, Varadero, *Granma*, 27 May 1990.
46. *Granma*, 28 October 1990.
47. *Financial Times*, 1 August 1990.
48. See *CNRS Report*, Paris, July 1990.
49. The CPAs were started in 1975 but had their greatest success from 1980 onwards. See *CNRS Report*, Paris, July 1990.
50. Diane Elson, 'Market Socialism or Socialization of the Market?', *New Left Review*, no. 172, November–December 1988.
51. Mesa-Lago, in *Cuba after Thirty Years*.
52. Zimbalist and Brundenius, in *Cuadernos de Nuestra América*, December 1989.
53. *Pensamiento Propio*, May 1990.
54. *Pensamiento Pripio*, August 1990.
55. *Pensamiento Propio*, May 1990.
56. *Trabajadores*, 16 March 1990.
57. *Granma*, 17 February 1990.
58. *Pensamiento Propio*, May 1990.
59. *Le Monde*, 23 May 1990.
60. In *The Cuba Reader*, Grove Press, New York 1989.
61. Marta Harnecker, *Izquierda y crisis actual*, Ediciones TAE, Montevideo, 1990.
62. *Teoria y Debate*, May 1990.
63. See the statement of the Costa Rican, Honduran, Salvadorean and Argentinian Communist Parties in the magazine *Quetzal*, Italy, spring 1990.
64. See the articles by Fernando González Rey, Jorge Luis Acanda and Fernando Martínez Heredia in *Casa de las Américas* magazine, no. 178, January–February 1990.
65. *Granma*, 1 July 1990.
66. *Financial Times*, 1 August 1990.

Bibliography

Affaire, 1/1989, Fin de la filière cubaine, Havana, Editions José Martí, 1989.
Azicri, Max, *Cuba*, London, Pinter Publishers, 1988.
Azicri, Max (ed.), *Cuba after Thirty Years: Rectification and the Revolution*, London, Frank Cass, 1990.
Betto, Frei, *Fidel et la religion,* Paris, Le Cerf, 1986.
Bukharin, Nikolai, *Le Socialisme dans un seul pays,* Paris, 10/18, 1974.
Brenner, Philip, and others (eds.), *The Cuba Reader,* New York, Grove Press, 1989.
Brezinski, Horst, 'Cuba's economic ties with the Soviet Union and the CMEA in the mid-eighties', University of Paderborn (West Germany), August 1988, photocopy.
Brundenius, Claes, *Cuba, Crecimiento con Equidad*, Managua, Instituto de Investigaciones Económicas y sociales (INIES), 1984.
Castro, Fidel, *Rapport central au Ier Congrès du Parti communiste cubain* (1975), Paris, François Maspero, 1976.
Castro, Fidel, *Rapport central au IIe Congrès du Parti communiste cubain,* Havana, Editora Politica, 1981.
Castro, Fidel, *Rapport central au IIe Congrès du Parti communiste cubain,* Havana, Editora Politica, 1986.
Clerc, Jean-Pierre, *Fidel de Cuba (trente ans déjà),* Paris, Ramsay, 1988.
Conte Agüero, Luis, *Eduardo Chibás, el adalid de Cuba*, Mexico, Jus, 1955.
Debray, Régis, *Masques,* Paris, Gallimard, 1988.
Díaz, Jésus, *Los iniciales de la Tierra*, Madrid, Al Faguara, 1987.
Dumont, René, *Cuba, socialisme et développement,* Paris, Le Seuil, 1964.
Dumont, René, *Cuba est-il socialiste?*, Paris, Le Seuil, 1970.
Franqui, Carlos, *Journal de la révolution cubaine,* Paris, Le Seuil, 1976.
Franqui, Carlos, *Vie, aventures et désastres d'un certain Fidel Castro*, Paris, Pierre Belfond, 1989.
Frayde, Martha, *Ecoute Fidel*, Paris, Denoël, 1987.
Guerra Sánchez, Ramiro, *Azúcar y población en las Antillas*, Havana, 1961.
Guevara, Ernesto Che, *Ecrits d'un révolutionnaire,* Paris, La Brèche, 1987.

Guevara, Ernesto Che, *Obras revolucionarias*, Havana or François Maspero.

Gunder Frank, A., *Le Développement du sous-développement en Amérique latine*, Paris, Francois Maspero, 1970.

Harnecker, Marta, *Fidel Castro's Political Strategy (From Moncada to Victory)*, New York, Pathfinder Press, 1987.

Harnecker, Marta, *Le Rôle de l'avant-garde et les Défis de la lutte révolutionnaire actuelle*, 1989, awaiting publication.

Heredia, Martínez, *Desafios del socialismo cubano*, Havana, Centro de Estudios sobre América, 1988.

Hidalgo, Ariel, 'Cuba, l'Etat marxiste et la nouvelle classe', 1984, photocopy.

Horowitz, Irving Louis, *El comunismo cubano (1959–1979)*, Madrid, Editorial Playor, 1979.

Huberman, L., Sweezy, Paul, *Le Socialisme cubain*, Paris, Anthropos, 1969.

Julien, Claude, *La Révolution cubaine*, Paris, Julliard, 1961.

Karol, K.S., *Les Guérilleros au pouvoir*, Paris, Robert Laffont, 1970.

Leogrande, *Arms and Politics*, Pittsburgh, 1979.

Lew, Roland, *Bureaucraties chinoises*, Paris, L'Harmattan, 1987.

Liu Binyan, *Le Cauchemar des mandarins rouges*, Paris, Gallimard, 1989.

Löwy, Michael, *La Pensée de Che Guevara*, Paris, François Maspero, 1970.

Löwy, Michael, *Le Marxisme en Amérique latine*, Paris, François Maspero, 1980.

Malraux, André, *L'Anti-mémoires*, Gallimard, 1972.

Mandel, Ernest, 'En défense de la planification socialiste', *in Quatrième Internationale*, 1987.

Mandel, Ernest, 'Bureaucratie et production marchande; les bases théoriques de l'interprétation marxiste en URSS', *in Quatrième Internationale*, April 1987.

Mandel, Ernest, *Où va l'URSS de Gorbatchev*, Paris, La Brèche, 1989. (*Beyond Perestroika*, London, Verso 1989.)

Mandel, Ernest, *Traité d'économie marxiste*, Paris, Christian Bourgois, 1986.

Mandel, Ernest, 'La NEP en république populaire de Chine', in *Inprecor*, no. 234, 1987.

Matthews, Herbert, *Fidel Castro*, Paris, Le Seuil, 1970.

Mencia, Mario, *La prisión fecunda*, Havana, Editora Politica, 1980.

Mesa-Lago, Carmelo, *La economía en Cuba socialista (una evaluación de dos décadas)*, Madrid, Editorial Playor, 1983.

Miná, Gianni, *Un encuentro con Fidel*, Havana, 1987.

Miná, Gianni, *Habla Fidel*, Editions Mondadori, 1988.

Miller, Warren, *90 Miles from Home*, USA, 1960.

Nove, Alec, *The Economics of Feasible Socialism*, London, Allen and Unwin, 1985.

Nuñez, Orlando, *Quand l'Amérique s'embrasera*, Paris, La Bréche, 1989.

Preobrajensky, Eugène, *La Nouvelle Economique*, Paris, EDI, 1976.

Recarte, Alberto, *Cuba, Economía y Poder*, Alianza Editorial, Madrid, 1980.

Salama, Pierre, *La Dollarisation*, Paris, Ed. La Découverte, 1989.

Sweezy, Paul M. and Bettelheim, Charles, *Lettres sur quelques problèmes actuels du socialisme*, Paris, François Maspero, 1972.

Szulc, Tad, *Fidel*, New York, Morrow, 1986.

Tablada, Carlos, *El pensamiento económico de Ernesto Che Guevara*, prix Casa de las Américas, Havana, 1987.

Thomas, Hugh, Fauriol, Georges A., Weiss, Juan Carlos, *La revolución cubana 25 años después*, Madrid, Editorial Playor, 1985.

Trotsky, Leon, *Nos tâches politiques*, Paris, Belfond, 1970.

Trotsky, Leon, *La Rèvolution trahie*, Paris, Editions de Minuit, 1973.

Trotsky, Leon, *Leur morale et la nôtre*, Paris, Pauvert, 1977.

Trotsky, Leon, *La Révolution permanente*, Paris, Editions de Minuit, 1976.

Valls, Jorge, *Mon ennemi, mon frère*, Paris, Gallimard, 1989.

Vilas, Carlos M., *Transición desde el subdesarrollo*, Caracas, Editorial Nueva Sociedad, 1989.

Winocur, Marcos, *Las clases olvidadas en la revolución cubana*, Barcelona, Grijalbo, 1979.

Zeitlin, Maurice, *Revolutionary Politics and the Cuban Working Class*, Princeton New Jersey, 1967.

Zimbalist, Andrew (editor), Brundenius, Claes, Codina Jiménez, Alexis, Edquist Ekstein, Suzan, Feuer, Carl Henry, Turits, Richard, White, Gordon, *World Development*, vol. 15, no. 1, Pergamon Journals Ltd, 1987.